Crime, Police, and Race Relations

Crime, Police, and Race Relations

A STUDY IN BIRMINGHAM

JOHN R. LAMBERT

with the assistance of Robert F. Jenkinson
and a Foreword by Terence Morris

Published for the
Institute of Race Relations, London
OXFORD UNIVERSITY PRESS
LONDON   NEW YORK   TORONTO
1970

Oxford University Press, Ely House, London W. 1

GLASGOW   NEW YORK   TORONTO   MELBOURNE   WELLINGTON
CAPE TOWN   SALISBURY   IBADAN   NAIROBI   DAR ES SALAAM   LUSAKA   ADDIS ABABA
BOMBAY   CALCUTTA   MADRAS   KARACHI   LAHORE   DACCA
KUALA LUMPUR   SINGAPORE   HONG KONG   TOKYO

SBN 19 218188 2

Printed in Great Britain at
THE PITMAN PRESS, BATH

Foreword

Crime in advanced industrial societies is essentially a problem of urbanism, and the Midlands are no exception to this rule. The state of criminal statistics, however, is such that one can make only the most general statements about crime on a precise and comparative basis, and for this reason Mr. Lambert's survey of part of the Birmingham Police area is particularly valuable in that he has been able to go into greater detail than is the case with crime statistics presented in their usual form.

This Birmingham survey, although limited in scope, sheds a good deal of light upon what goes on in a city outside the great metropolis of London, in a city which is and has been for the last decade undergoing major social change and urban renewal. It has been carefully conducted and painstakingly written up. It also provides a number of facts that are sorely needed if certain issues are to be resolved by reference to concrete evidence rather than opinion and prejudice.

Birmingham was born like almost all of our industrial cities in the harshness of the industrial revolution, when cities were literally consumers of men. Humanity counted less than the needs of the machine, and if the sanitary improvements reduced the mortality of the labour force, the slums remained. Remained, that is, until the bombing of the Second World War made the post-war programme of urban renewal a reality as well as a necessity. In ten years or so, the heart of Birmingham has been recreated, new housing provided, and a vast network of modern roads has changed the old layout of the centre. But, as in every city that has embarked upon a programme of urban renewal, the changes that were originally intended to improve the urban environment for those who had suffered from the disadvantages of the old have been accompanied by changes in population. The West Midlands have become a major centre of settlement for immigrants from the Commonwealth, most of them non-white and many of them non-English-speaking.

Birmingham has, for the first time in its history, a significant coloured population. Immigration at the same time as urban renewal is not unique to Birmingham; it has happened in many other British cities, and, one might add, in many American cities too. But, unlike many other British cities, Birmingham has, on the other hand, had immigrants for a long time; for more than a century the Irish have settled there on a geographical axis that runs from London to Liverpool.

The problems of Birmingham are then shared by a large number of other cities throughout the industrial world. These problems are to be seen at their most intractable within the United States where attempts to remedy the ravages of nineteenth-century *laissez-faire* have been threatened or even overtaken by new population movements. In that country in the last three years the problems of the city have taken an ugly turn. Not only has crime increased within its boundaries, but more serious problems of public disorder. That these have been exacerbated by problems of poverty, housing, and employment is all too clear.

In Birmingham during the period 1961–6, there was a net migration rate of some 7 per cent, while in the areas identified by Lambert as containing high rates of criminal residence the migration figure has been over 20 per cent. But whereas in most American cities the migrants tend to exchange rural unemployment for urban unemployment, migrants have come to Birmingham for work. This is not a new phenomenon, and as the demand for labour has continued, so a supply has been forthcoming. Contrary to what some partisan theorists maintain, immigration is stimulated by a desire to find a job, not a place in the queue at the Social Security office. Birmingham's first immigrants came from across the Irish Sea, and it remains true today, as it did in the last century, that the largest group of migrants comes from Ireland. The Irish have assimilated in a curious way; they have settled and multiplied to the third and fourth generations, but in a very large number of cases have maintained their links with kin in the homeland. The more recently arrived migrants may, in the long run, be less able to preserve such contacts.

Those of every migrant group who arrive in search of work are to be found among the least affluent, and it is natural for them to gravitate either to the areas where housing is cheapest or, if it is not cheap, to those areas which have become by the subtle

interaction of individual prejudice and the operations of the
market, the unofficially designated ghettos. Again, this is not new,
and was a process analysed and documented more than forty
years ago by Robert Park and his colleagues in Chicago.

In the current climate of uninformed and popular thinking
it is often implicitly suggested that immigrants have created the
problems that face cities like Birmingham. True, there is pressure
on schools and on housing, and on certain sectors of the labour
market and the social services. But these services were inadequate
before. The immigrants did not bring the slums brick by brick
in their fibre suitcases or their cheap airline bags; they have been
there for a century, the legacy of the industrial revolution now
passed on by an affluent society to its currently disprivileged.

Not least of the problems of the city is that of crime and
juvenile delinquency, and it is to this question that Mr. Lambert
has turned his attention. He suggests that migrants into Birmingham as a group are rather more prone to crime than the over-all
population, particularly among the older age groups, but among
the younger offenders, the Birmingham-born predominate. This
suggests that in part the current crime problem is the work of
those who have lived for a long time in the criminal subculture
of the old-established slums. Another part of the problem is
related to areas where a large number of young male migrants
congregate in hostels and lodgings where thefts are comparatively
common as well as trivial.

Lambert's argument here is that among such migrants are
the Irish, whose proportional involvement in crime appears to
rise with age, suggesting that the passage of time sifts out 'a less
capable minority who fall into petty theft and criminality'. It is
not possible to plot this precisely, because of the difficulties of
making adjustments for age and sex as between the migrants and
the native-born population, but it is clear that among offenders
of all age groups the Irish are over-represented. On the same
basis, the rate of involvement in crime for West Indian and Asian
migrants is extremely low, considering that these groups tend to
live in areas where over-all crime rates are comparatively high.

In his study area Lambert found that 20 per cent of those
proceeded against for indictable offences and almost 50 per cent
in those proceeded against for non-indictable offences were born
of Ireland. The great majority of those arrested for such offences

were in the drunkenness category. His argument is that the tight-knit social controls of Church and family have less effect in the new setting, although the effect is differential. But if the Irish are over-represented among the urban poor, it is to be expected that they will be over-represented among the ranks of petty offenders.

Lambert found that the West Indians, in contrast, were remarkably free from involvement in crime and that they 'seek success within the general framework of values and rise above the delinquent and criminal standards prevalent in the areas in which they live'. If these legitimate aspirations are frustrated, then there is the danger that 'the crime and disorder which surrounds them will contaminate their life style and lead, in years to come, to a crime rate which matches that in their neighbourhoods'. Among the West Indians and Asians he notes three special factors as present when they are involved in infringements: domestic relations and landlord and tenant disputes, the use of cannabis, and the conditions of family life for migrants living in particularly stressful conditions.

The police have over the years built up a special set of relationships with what used to be termed the 'criminal classes'. Relations with immigrants, and in this context 'immigrant' means 'coloured immigrant', are of a different nature. Lambert writes of the sensitivity which is an essential element of good police work. There are real problems of language and problems of idiomatic expression, there are problems stemming from anticipatory attitudes on either side, and there is the problem of 'excitability' on the part of some immigrants. The Asians when brushing with the police expect them to be corrupt or corruptible, while the police are suspicious of them. With the West Indians the problems of language may be underestimated, but the police have expectations of 'excitability' while the immigrant has expectations of violence. Brown and black faces represent a new feature of the scene, while the Irish brogue does not. As Lambert points out, the crucial role of the police in race relations will most certainly alter as the cycle of assimilation moves on towards the second generation. Among American studies it has been shown that it is the children of the foreign born, rather than the foreign born themselves who are more heavily involved in law infringements. The lack of respect between police and coloured migrants which Lambert identifies will, if anything, increase if the second generation suffers both from the consequences of second-class citizenship and the self-perception of it. In this the recruitment of non-white policemen will not provide a complete answer; the Negro cop in the slums of Chicago or Hunters Point is no better loved than his white colleague. In South Africa the coloured policeman is loathed in the African township.

Already, since Lambert's study was completed, we have seen the signs of conscious rejection by the host community. Demands for total repatriation rather than restriction of the immigration of dependants have been matched by requests by local authorities for government control over the settlement patterns of new arrivals. 'Our town has had enough; its schools are bursting, its maternity wards full,' etc., etc., however unrealistic a basis for social policy, cannot fail to etch into the minds of the young a sense of rejection and alienation. And again, from what we already know of the cities of the United States that are in travail, alienation is the last sentiment that our society can afford to foster. If, by default, we allow race relations to deteriorate, it is a truism to say that we shall reap a bitter harvest indeed. But rejecting the rejectors is a natural response, and the reapers in the field will not be the politicians and the local councillors, the writers of letters to local newspapers, and the authors of racialist broadsheets, but the agents of order out there on the streets. It will not be of their sowing, but it will be the police who will bear the brunt of what may come.

TERENCE MORRIS

1 August 1968   London School of Economics
                                        and Political Science

Contents

List of Maps

Preface and Acknowledgements

This book reports on some research conducted in a sector of Birmingham during 1966 and 1967. Thus three years have elapsed between the first draft of this report being written and publication. To the author the delay, although unavoidable, is distressing. The temptation to rewrite large sections, to bring data up-to-date, to comment on observable changes has been overwhelming but has had to be resisted. During that period the mood of race relations in the city has not improved. Following the dreadful rhetoric of Mr. Enoch Powell, racist talk appears to be now legitimate and more common than before, discrimination continues, squalid unsatisfactory housing appears to be the lot the coloured citizen must share with his white neighbour. Certain action is under way, an improved Race Relations Act is in force, an Urban Programme has been launched, a refurbished Community Relations Commission is in existence, more is written and read on the subject, a House of Commons Select Committee has heard in a number of towns and cities the confused, conflicting, optimistic and pessimistic, paradoxical and changing story of race relations in Britain. All such influences would bring changes in emphasis and matter to the pages that follow. Already there is some evidence that in Birmingham there are more coloured youngsters being brought before the court than when this research was conducted.[1] Not far away, in Wolverhampton, there has been reported an outcrop of gang delinquency among coloured youth there.[2] Such evidence is not contrary to that reported here, rather it stresses the fluidity of the situation and the need for our interpretations and understanding to be flexible,

[1] 'Magistrates of Juvenile Courts in Birmingham . . . claimed that the number of coloured children appearing before them has risen by 25 times in the last three years. The magistrates accused the city authorities of a "lamentable failure" to cope with the problems immigrant children face.' (*Birmingham Post*, 5 December 1968.)

[2] Evidence of Chief Constable of West Midlands Constabulary to the Select Committee on Race Relations and Immigration, *Minutes of Evidence 58*, XI–XIII, para. 1541 *et seq.* (London, H.M.S.O., 1969).

and our social responses by police, courts, judges, schools, probation officers, and the like, to be sensitive and adaptable to change.

Three broad questions shaped the research. First, is there more
crime in immigrant areas of a city than in other areas and how much
of the crime is attributable to immigrants, white or coloured?

Secondly, what, if any, are the new problems faced by a
Police Force in carrying out its task under conditions of fairly
large-scale immigration of citizens from Asian countries and from
the West Indies whereby the society or community being policed
is now multiracial in character?

Thirdly, what evidence is there that the children of immigrant
parents are, or are likely to be in the future, more or less delinquent
than their non-immigrant peers?

Each of these questions raises significant issues for a society
in which relations between black and white sections of the population are of increasing concern to politicians, city authorities, and
citizens in general.

Host societies the world over tend to blame immigrants, often
a conveniently visible group of outsiders, for causing or contributing to a number of 'problems'; common among those problems
is crime. A reputation for criminality, with the ideas of violence
and viciousness it brings to mind, can be part of an invidious
stereotype of the immigrant held by the non-immigrant population. The racialists, in their pamphlets and papers, frequently
employ lurid stories of crime, sometimes backed by grim statistics,
to justify their arguments and to arouse fear and hate towards the
minority newcomers. But an expectation of high crime rates
among immigrants is part of a conventional wisdom adhered to
uncritically by people who might be expected to know better, or
at least be concerned with evidence rather than opinion.[1]

---

[1] When opening some new law courts, the Lord Chief Justice gave six reasons why
court business was going to increase, the third of which was reported to be that immigrants were coming into the country in 'hosts'. 'I am not saying they are any worse
than others, but until they settle down, they will add to the volume of crime.' (*Guardian*,
9 September 1967.)

Occasionally statistics are used uncritically to back up the point. Mr. Norman
Pannell, in *Immigration: What is the Answer?* (London, Routledge, 1965), pp. 28–9,
cites figures culled from a major criminological work which was at pains to accompany
its cautious attribution of some of the increase in violent crime to Irish and Commonwealth immigrants with many qualifications about the particular nature and content
of such crime while stressing its over-all infrequency. These considerations, essential to
making any sense of the statistics, Mr. Pannell chose to omit.

Other countries which have experienced large-scale immigration have paid considerable attention to the issue of crime rates among immigrants. In Australia there was in the immediate post-war years a concern about rising crime rates and the part recent migrants played in its cause. An official inquiry showed that the native population had about twice the rate of the immigrants; and furthermore, a far higher proportion of the newcomers were in the age group 15 to 35 in which the vast majority of offenders occur.[1] The conventional wisdom in this case was shown to be highly inaccurate and misleading.

The major source of data, however, is the United States. Modern criminology owes much to a whole series of studies pioneered by Clifford Shaw and Henry McKay in Chicago in the first decades of this century. As a result of their work explanations of crime and delinquency shifted in focus from the narrowly psychological and biological—the criminal being seen as some kind of genetically weak throw-back to a primitive past—to the sociological. Studying areas of crime and delinquency over a period of three decades, Shaw and McKay showed that certain areas maintained very high rates although the ethnic make-up of the population changed almost completely in the intervening period.[2] 'Crime and the Foreign Born' was the subject of a major inquiry carried out by a United States National Commission on Law Observance and Enforcement which reported in 1931. A painstaking analysis of four and three-quarter million crimes committed in the decade 1920–30 suggested that the foreign born committed proportionately fewer crimes than the native-born population.[3] These findings were the subject of considerable re-working and analysis by other authorities whose statistical exegeses

[1] Commonwealth Immigration Advisory Council, *Third Report of the Committee Established to Investigate the Conduct of Migrants* (Canberra, Commonwealth Government Printer, 1957), cited in E. Sutherland and D. Cressey, *Principles of Criminology*, 6th edn. (Philadelphia, Lippincott, 1960), p. 144.

[2] Clifford R. Shaw and Henry D. McKay, *Delinquency Areas* (Chicago, University of Chicago Press, 1929), *Juvenile Delinquency in Urban Areas* (Chicago, University of Chicago Press, 1942). Interesting excerpts from these works can be found in Wolfgang, Savitz, and Johnson (eds.), *The Sociology of Crime and Delinquency* (New York and London, Wiley, 1962), and in Burgess and Bogue (eds.), *Urban Sociology* (Chicago, University of Chicago Press, 1967).

[3] National Commission on Law Observance and Enforcement, Report No. 10, *Crime and the Foreign Born* (Washington, D.C., U.S. Government Printing Office, 1931), Section XIV.

2

do little but suggest that more than statistics are needed to explain wide variations in rates and types of crime for different groups in the population.[1] These studies did, however, contribute to a much deeper understanding of the social context in which crime occurs. Theories of what happens when cultures are in conflict in a single milieu developed, and the emphasis shifted from the immigrant to his children and to the Negro who was in many respects an immigrant to the northern industrial city from the rural South. The somewhat crude statistics of the earlier era lost their significance.[2]

What was observed to be happening was that successive waves of immigrants to the great cities found only the poorest areas of cities as their first homes. The parent generation, frequently a cohesive group with close kin relations, set about the task of making a foothold from which to attain success in the new society. Their children were more exposed to the host society at its worst. As the immigrant group was assimilated into American society, the initially low rates of crime and delinquency adjusted to equal whatever rate was pertinent for the type and status of the area where assimilation occurred.[3] Lack of success—as individual or group—meant a longer period in the slum areas of the city, and a higher rate of delinquency among the second generation. More immobile than the immigrants, trapped in the poorest areas by prejudice and discrimination, were the Negroes whose rates for crime and delinquency persisted at a high level. Yet even among the Negro population—as refutation to the racist quick to jump to conclusions based on statistics—there were areas and groups as crime-free as the 'best' white

[1] See, for instance, D. R. Taft, 'Does Immigration Increase Crime?', *Social Forces* (1933), and 'Nationality and Crime', *American Sociological Review* (Vol. 3, 1936); C. C. van Vechten, 'The Criminality of the Foreign Born', *Journal of Criminal Law and Criminology* (Vol. 32, 1941–2).

[2] For the general discussion, see Sutherland and Cressey, op. cit. In addition, see Thorsten Sellin, *Culture Conflict and Crime* (New York, Social Science Research Council, 1938) for a classic statement of the central sociological issue. Also, Guy B. Johnson, 'The Negro and Crime', in Wolfgang et al. (eds.), op. cit., pp. 145–56. Two works have surveyed the historical and statistical linkage of crime with racial characteristics: W. Bonger, *Race and Crime* (New York, 1943), and Wolfgang, 'Race and Crime', in Klare (ed.), *Changing Concepts of Crime and its Treatment* (London, Pergamon Press, 1966).

[3] See H. Ross, 'Crime and the Native Born Sons of European Immigrants', *Journal of Criminal Law and Criminology* (Vol. 28, 1937).

areas; variations were as marked between the white as between the black areas.[1]

Attention shifted to the conditions where crime occurs and in which delinquent families live. It was suggested how sub-communities within society organize to cope with the inequalities and distress that society imposes in promising equality of rewards while denying equality of opportunity. For some, crime can become a way of life; for others, a gang can afford a kind of compensation that yet risks a whole process of official sanctioning whereby opprobrium is heaped on the unfortunate; still others, temporarily or permanently retreat into the twilight area of the addict or the hustler.[2]

This summary glance at the American experience and its criminological explorations of the effects of immigration and race, discrimination and segregation on crime rates, is intended to do no more than point to a wider purpose in the present research rather than to gather supposedly reassuring or alarming statistics about the current rate of crime among immigrants. More important than comparative rates is the context in which crime occurs. A milieu of poverty and disorganization, hostility among the host society towards the immigrants, the presence of discriminatory behaviour and processes, limited or unsatisfactory job opportunities, and an insensitivity towards the needs of the rising generation of immigrant youth are sure signs of a future shift in crime rates. The danger of such is, of course, that with time the host society may fail to recognize in such a process its own failure and lack of justice, and be inclined to view the immigrant and his family as failures or inadequates worthy only of punitive action or attitude. The gathering of evidence about this complex issue is thus of great importance.

[1] A survey in Philadelphia found that locally-born Negro juveniles had an appreciably higher rate of delinquency than migrant Negro juveniles; see L. Savitz, 'Delinquency and Migration', in Wolfgang et al., op. cit., pp. 199–205. A complex statistical analysis of delinquency rates in Baltimore showed that areas of racial homogeneity (black or white) share the lowest rates, while the highest rates occurred in areas of marked racial heterogeneity. The 'best' Negro areas were as free from crime as the 'best' white areas. See B. Lander, *Toward an Understanding of Juvenile Delinquency* (New York, Columbia University Press, 1954), summarized in Wolfgang et al., op. cit., pp. 184–90.

[2] Amidst a vast literature from America about the relation between subcultures and motivation and persistence in criminal behaviour, see R. A. Cloward and L. Ohlin, *Delinquency and Opportunity* (Illinois, Free Press of Glencoe, 1960).

There is some limited evidence about comparative rates among immigrants in this country. A. E. Bottoms has recently surveyed some English criminological studies that have in passing shed some light on immigrant involvement in crime. He presents the reader with a thorough context of American studies and theorization which show the pitfalls of a simplistic approach to the subject, and concludes:

Crime among the Irish appears to be relatively high in most offence groups even after allowance has been made for age. Qualifications need to be made, however, in respect of many social factors. Crime among Commonwealth immigrants tends to be generally low, except in crimes of violence where, however, domestic disputes play an important part in adding to the statistical total of violence. Similar qualifications of the data need to be made as in the case of the Irish.[1]

In Birmingham it was possible to explore in some detail crime in an area where approximately 7 per cent of the population was Irish and 7 per cent of the population was from Asia or the West Indies. It broadly confirms the above suggestions, while able to explore in some depth some of the many social factors to which Bottoms refers.

A major problem facing a criminological researcher is what sense and value to attach to the criminal statistics. In the first chapters an attempt is made to describe a profile of crime in one police division. It is stressed there that to understand crime and criminal statistics there is a need to study the administrative procedures whereby some of the criminal behaviour that occurs becomes processed into statistics of crime. Not all criminal behaviour is observed or reported, let alone prosecuted. The processes of selection are not random. Some kinds of crime only partially apparent in the published statistics are never reported to the police and are only discovered by planned police action. How the police plan, what resources are allocated to different tasks, are issues decided by the police themselves. Thus the statistics to a marked degree reflect as much about how the police choose to organize as about the actual behaviour of wrongdoers. The process of observation, detection, and arrest by the police

[1] A. E. Bottoms, 'Delinquency Among Immigrants', *Race* (Vol. VIII, No. 4, 1967), pp. 359–83.

plays an important part in explaining what kind and age of offenders are brought before the court. It has been suggested how in America this process may discriminate against the Negro offender and distort the statistics:

The administration of justice itself is from beginning to end so much a part of the whole system of Negro–White social relations that it must be viewed as a process which discriminates against Negroes and thus biases the statistics of crime.[1]

The discretion that is afforded the police to decide whether or not to prosecute, and the discretion enjoyed by Police Forces to respond differentially to different kinds of crime and disorder, places them in an extraordinarily crucial role in any society where equality and justice are still remote from large numbers of the population. For the police inevitably as symbols of authority in society are seen as upholders not only of the law and order of society's aspiration but also of the lawlessness and injustice of society in action. Thus the patrolman and his Force in American cities are increasingly being cast as scapegoats for decades of misrule and discrimination in the slum areas where black Americans must make their homes. The hostility between black and white in America is nowhere more vivid than in relations between black residents of ghettos and the most frequently seen representative of white society—the cop. In America, of course, the history of lawlessness and disorder within Police Forces deepens the hostility. Grievances about police brutality and inefficiency were pervasive in the cities where riots occurred in recent summers; many riots were precipitated by inept or unwarranted police actions.[2] To draw parallels from America to Britain without acknowledging differences in tradition, history, organization, and social relations would be foolish; yet there is sufficient in the American literature to point to ways in which the police as an ever present agency in action among communities of all kinds will suffer the effects of discrimination and segregation as surely as the population at whom discrimination is aimed: for the policeman's task is to work on the streets of society even if that

[1] Guy B. Johnson, in Wolfgang et al., op. cit., p. 153.
[2] See the National Advisory Commission on Civil Disorders, *Report* (New York, Bantam Books, 1968), Ch. 2; and S. Lieberson and A. R. Silverman, 'The Precipitants and Underlying Conditions of Race Riots', *American Sociological Review* (Vol. 30, 1965).

xxii PREFACE AND ACKNOWLEDGEMENTS

society is intent on making ghettos of some of them. There is considerable scope for the police to add to or lessen their difficulties. A 'business as usual' policy may add to the level of discrimination felt by minority groups by approving or seeming to approve certain attitudes and behaviours. Careful planning, on the other hand, and determined action, may convince minorities that they can expect respectful and just policing and that deviations from high standards of conduct will be forbidden within the police service, however common or acceptable such standards may be to white society at large.

America is learning that to structure the necessary relations between Police Forces and black communities requires firstly action within Police Forces. It is many years since William Kephart in a pioneering study showed how attitudes within Police Forces and relations between black and white officer affect the quality and style of urban law enforcement in marked ways.[1] Other studies have shown how the racial bias of policemen can inhibit progress towards the desired level of police-community relations.[2] But even if significant numbers of black patrolmen and officers are employed, the policeman carries a stigma of the past and symbolizes a present that perpetuates distrust:

A Negro cannot allow himself to take the policeman at face value because his experiences with policemen as a group have led him to believe that they are his enemies . . . a policeman must recognize that he bears a stigma simply for being a policeman in the same way that the Negro bears a stigma simply for being a Negro.[3]

The situation in Britain about relations between police and coloured immigrants contains elements which invite both pessimism and optimism. In some areas, Police Forces have been swift

[1] W. Kephart, *Racial Factors and Urban Law Enforcement* (Philadelphia, University of Pennsylvania Press, 1957.)

[2] See, for instance, Jerome H. Skolnick, *Justice Without Trial: Law Enforcement in Democratic Society* (New York and London, Wiley, 1966), pp. 80–6; I. Piliavin and S. Briar, 'Police Encounters with Juveniles', *American Journal of Sociology* (Vol. LXX, 1964); The President's Commission on Law Enforcement and the Administration of Justice, Field Survey IV, *The Police and the Community*, 2 vols. (Washington, D.C., U.S. Government Printing Office, 1967).

[3] O. Luster, Paper read at a Conference on Law Enforcement and Racial and Cultural Tensions, Berkeley 1964 (California, Regents of the University of California, 1966).

to move to establish good relations and develop the many opportunities for service and constructive support that police can effect in a community. At other levels, there has been a silence or intransigence or insensitivity; or an unwelcome defensiveness that may hinder many needed reforms. The research reported here attempts to explore some of the problems and opportunities that exist for the police to avoid deepening hostility and become a constructive force in relations between the races.

Prejudice, discrimination, and other unhelpful responses from the receiving society are only some of the stresses that immigrants and their families face. For immigrants from India and Pakistan with a distinctive culture, language, religion, dress, and so on, it might be supposed that the clash of cultures would set up great stresses. On the other hand, that very distinctiveness, the maintenance of close kin relationships and firm family ties, enhances the cohesiveness of communities in the new society and protects the immigrant from possibly demoralizing effects of migration. Immigrants from distant lands tend to be among the most capable, energetic, and adaptable of their nation. To break ties, to risk the unknown, to raise or borrow the money for the fare, often to obtain a promise of employment: such things suggest a number of strengths likely to be found in any immigrant population. This is not to say that there will not be any problems of adjustment: to move from a rural to an urban society, to experience the British climate, and to confront the curiosities of the British character, may be bewildering. It is to be supposed that the West Indian immigrant with aspirations shaped by a loyal conception of Britain as the mother country, without a ready-made community or colony structure with whom to relate, may be quicker to be disappointed if aspirations are not satisfied and will be more sensitive to, and more affected by, discriminatory and prejudiced tendencies in the host community.

These kinds of differences will lead to a distinctive and varying kind of family life among immigrant communities. Studies of immigrant groups in America show frequently high rates of delinquency among the second generation of children of immigrant parents.[1] Such findings point to the need to examine how family structure is coping with the stresses imposed by immigra-

[1] H. Ross, loc. cit.; A. L. Wood, 'Minority Group Criminality and Cultural Integration', *Journal of Criminal Law and Criminology* (Vol. 37, 1946).

tion.[1] Clearly, economic opportunity and housing standard will be of vital importance, as well as the age of the immigrant group and the pattern of migration itself—whether it is of young unmarried males or of whole families.[2]

Delinquency is found over-represented in specific age groups, in particular areas, and at a particular socio-economic level. Much delinquency in Britain is mild, sporadic, unplanned, and, though committed in groups, not really 'gang delinquency' of the American pattern. David Downes, in his study of delinquency in the East End of London, suggests that much delinquency is a likely response to boredom and frustration specifically in a context of leisure rather than in the more sustained and purposeful criminality of the American delinquent.[3] This leisure response which involves mild delinquency is related to traditional working-class values which sustain a boy against the relative lack of success he will gain from school or from work. Such mild delinquency explains why so many first offenders among delinquents never reappear in court; family and group norms provide a check

[1] See W. I. Thomas and F. Znaniecki, *The Polish Peasant in Europe and America* (New York, 1920), Vol. II, *Social Disorganization*; E. Franklin Frazier, *The Negro Family in the United States* (Chicago and London, University of Chicago Press, 1966); also D. P. Moynihan, *The Negro Family: the case for national action* (Washington, D.C., U.S. Dept. of Labor, 1965).

Some research, conducted in Israel, of a 15-year period and designed to test the culture conflict theory found rates of delinquency highest in urban areas of marked cultural diversification. Rates of delinquency were found to be higher for the second generation than for an immigrant generation or the older established groups. Rates of delinquency were found to be higher where the cultural gap between the immigrants and receiving community and the barriers against the upper vertical mobility of the immigrants were greatest. The agricultural area's rates were lowest, and for immigrant groups who possessed a high level of cohesion there were negligible. These findings largely confirm the suggestions of the American literature and show how factors of family cohesion and urbanization and delinquency are closely interrelated. Immigrants were found to be younger than non-immigrants and they also committed milder offences. The authors noted how in achieving integration the structure of the family may have to undergo change and that integrative processes can be destructive if they injure or shatter the social and economic status of the head of the family. 'This and other effects of the process of integration may weaken the cohesion of the family unit and thus hamper the family control over the young.' F. S. Shoham *et al.*, 'Immigration, Ethnicity and Ecology as Related to Juvenile Delinquency in Israel', *British Journal of Criminology* (Vol. 6, No. 4, October 1966).

[2] The 1961 Census figures reveal that 90 per cent of Pakistanis, 63 per cent of Indians, 59 per cent of West Indians, and 56 per cent of the Irish were males.

[3] David Downes, *The Delinquent Solution* (London, Routledge, 1966). A most useful and thorough survey of the state of research and inquiry into delinquency is D. J. West's *The Young Offender* (Harmondsworth, Penguin Books, 1967).

on too great risks being taken. If the family is unable to provide the check and guide the child to an understanding of the rules of the game of living in society, offences and court appearances may be repeated and a child increasingly defined as a deviant, an outsider to be trapped in a life of crime.

The family is thus a prime source of socialization through which delinquency is avoided or nurtured. Immigrant families, with further problems of understanding and orientation towards the social values of the host society, may be insufficient or only partially effective as a means of socializing; or the strengths and adaptability of the immigrant family and the high aspirations for success may mean that families are ultra-efficient socializers; or too great an emphasis on success requiring too great a conformity from the children may itself provoke hostile delinquent reactions; or parental quest for economic success may lead to their ignoring a child's other needs; or close governance of young children within a colony may make problems when he is a teen-ager and wants to move outside the colony and seek success in the host society's terms, only to find himself lacking in awareness of the norms and values of that society. These are just a few of the possibilities. To begin to explore just such issues is the task undertaken in the last section of this book.

The purpose of research in race relations in this country has been well stated:

The condition of England question for our generation is whether our society is able to deal with the problem which has been dramatised through the process of immigration, namely that of the whole range of social inequalities and injustices which even the Welfare State legislation of the post-war years has not succeeded in eliminating. In exactly the same way, the chief challenge facing President Lyndon Johnson's Great Society is to find some way of closing the running sore of the American Negro's bitterness and alienation in the face of his continued failure to enter that society on equal terms. In the field of race relations, research stands or falls by the extent to which it can contribute towards the solution of questions like these.[1]

The research approach adopted here has been deliberately descriptive. It raises more questions than it answers. Crime is to be explained in terms of a system of social relations and process

[1] Nicholas Deakin, 'The Necessity for Research into Race Relations', in *Immigration: Medical and Social Aspects* (London, Churchill for C.I.B.A., 1966).

whereby certain groups, differentially positioned to social goals and rewards, are in a higher risk category than others to become defined as criminal or delinquent. The same system produces a structure of relations between groups such that competition and conflict, expressed or latent, invite behaviour that is prejudiced or discriminatory. The emphasis on social relations and process requires that dynamic elements are stressed in any situation studied. Such is not always possible in social research, and it will be apparent to readers that the data on which this book is based are by now ancient history. Yet an attempt has been made to stress the continuing and long-term implications of those data and to show, in studying one broad class of behaviour and one aspect of the administration of justice, how they are inextricably linked with other behaviours and other aspects of administration. Injustice and inequality, whether in housing or job opportunity, in education or youth employment, in fact in relation to a whole spectrum of citizen rights, are implied in any explanation of crime and delinquency and in any explanation of the current state of race relations. The solution to problems of inequality depends first of all on an awareness of their existence. This book is a contribution to that awareness.

Research of the kind reported here would be impossible without the co-operation and interest of a large number of persons and organizations and a preparedness on their part to spend time and energy in active assistance to the researcher. I was particularly fortunate in Birmingham to have been met with a spirit of friendly co-operation which made the task so much the easier.

I am particularly grateful to the Chief Constable of Birmingham for permitting the research to be undertaken on his 'territory'. Many members of his H.Q. staff spent a considerable amount of time furnishing advice and data of an essential kind and making possible the study in depth of one division. To Chief Superintendent J. A. Babb I have a particular indebtedness of enabling me to carry out the research on 'F' division. The continuous interested co-operation shown by Mr. Babb and by his Deputy Superintendent, Mr. K. Johnson, added greatly to the research and enabled unanticipated avenues to be explored. Through their good offices I was able to spend time with many officers of all ranks, whose frankness and friendliness made the research task an enriching experience.

For six months I had the pleasure of being a regular visitor to the offices of the Birmingham Probation Service. I am grateful to Birmingham's Principal Probation Officer, Mr. A. Worthy, for allowing this and to his deputy, Mr. A. M. Robbins, for taking a continuing interest in the project and introducing me to members of his staff. I am deeply appreciative of the generosity of those individual officers I met with on a regular basis for allowing me to draw on their considerable knowledge and insight.

At Birmingham's office of the Children's Department, I was fortunate to meet with Mr. F. A. Noble who suggested the direction the study might take, and his assistant, Mrs. M. Jones, who made easier a difficult task of data collection. I am grateful to Mr. J. B. Chaplin, the City's Senior Children's Officer, for allowing the research to be done.

To Mr. J. Burns, the Principal, and to the Managers of Kingswood Approved and Classifying Schools, I am grateful for allowing the survey of Approved School boys to be made; and to Mr. A. Collison, the Warden of the Classifying School, and to Mr. R. Clarke, for their advice and assistance in collecting the data.

In Birmingham a home was found for the research at the Centre for Urban and Regional Studies, Birmingham University, by the Centre's Director, Mr. J. B. Cullingworth, who made it possible for me to be an associate of the Centre for nine months and to benefit not only from his personal advice and encouragement but also to draw upon the Centre's considerable resources of data. In addition, the move to Birmingham allowed me to benefit from the full-time assistance of Mr. Robert Jenkinson of the Centre's Research Staff. To Mr. Jenkinson fell the major portion of the crime data collection and analysis, the preparation of the demographic data, and the writing of a first draft of the first part of the book. His influence extends throughout the book, however, for our association allowed endless discussion and debate about the many issues. My debt to his interest and conscientiousness throughout the several months he was associated with the research is gratefully recorded.

From its inception the project was fortunate in finding as consultant adviser Dr. Terence Morris, Reader in Sociology (Criminology) at the London School of Economics. I was grateful for the benefit of Dr. Morris's many prescriptions for improving the research at every stage.

While conducting this research I was employed by the Institute of Race Relations as Research Officer. I can imagine no researcher finding more ideal employers than the Director of the Institute's 'Survey of Race Relations in Britain', Mr. Jim Rose, and Assistant-Director, Mr. Nicholas Deakin. They nursed the project from the start and were exemplary parents in their balanced provision of assurance, encouragement, and admonition to what looked at times like a delinquent study.

Having listed so many helpers and advisers, the familiar proviso that none are responsible for the outcome but myself is especially necessary. A study like this by its nature must be a blend of fact, opinion, anticipation, and idiosyncratic interpretation with the attendant hazards of excess and aberration: for these I alone am responsible.

J. R. LAMBERT
Centre for Urban and Regional Studies
Birmingham University

Part I: Crime

CHAPTER 1

Crime in the City

1. *What* is *Crime?*

Under a large banner headline, CRIME WAR SUCCESS, the *Birmingham Evening Mail* of 22 July 1967, gave commendable prominence to the local Chief Constable's half-yearly report on the state of crime in Birmingham: 'He said that [in the first six months of 1967] the overall total of city crime dropped from 19,055 cases at the same time last year to 18,638 cases.'

On the previous day the *Birmingham Post* had published part one of a revealing series under the title 'Crime in the Second City', following a special investigation into the extent of crime in the city. Three long articles appeared in successive days concerned with prostitution, drugs and the pedlars, and the protection racket.

It is curious but significant that the crime referred to by the Chief Constable in the *Mail* had nothing in common with the crime of the *Post*'s revealing series. Neither offences relating to prostitution nor those concerned with drug traffic, let alone those from the shady world of protection, are in the category of reported indictable crime, the subject of the official criminal statistics, the Chief Constable's reports, and the familiar clear-up rate. This illustrates very clearly the need to know what is meant when reference is made to crime and crime rates. No doubt the *Post*'s 'crime' is nearer to the public stereotype of crime, and in some ways, perhaps, it is comforting to believe in crime as something which happens in a shady underworld where evil people plot and exploit among clubs and brothels and other dens of vice. Comforting, because, thus defined, it is remote and abnormal, something that can be left to the police to deal with, something committed by evil abnormal people who are very different from you or me or our neighbours.

The 'crime' reported in the *Mail* via the Chief Constable is a reminder of the mundane reality that the bulk of crime is not matter for a headline in a Sunday newspaper, but small thefts from cars and gas meters, shops and houses. This is not, of course, meant to imply that there is no significance to be attached to crime statistics from various sources, nor that there is no serious indictable crime, no prostitution, drug, or protection problem. What is required is definitional precision whenever crime is discussed, particularly if figures and statistics are to be used.

The data collected for this survey include data from both the broad categories of 'crime': indictable and non-indictable offences. This distinction, originally conceived to differentiate kinds of judicial proceedings appropriate for various classes of offence, is no longer very useful, although by and large it does separate incidents which are reported to the police by a member of the public who has experienced a personal wrong from those incidents where the police initiate action against persons whose offence and wrong are not against any particular person, but actually affect, or are thought to affect, the general well-being of society. Thus, the important distinction is in terms of the nature of police work involved. In passing, it may seem odd that the usual measure of police efficiency, the clear-up rate, applies only to indictable offences reported to the police and includes nothing of categories where the police themselves take steps to control, prevent, or prosecute non-indictable disorder events.

Yet within the two broad categories of crime and disorder there are problems of interpretation of the statistics. It is impossible to measure how much crime goes unreported and how much disorder goes unnoticed: this mystery proportion, the so-called 'dark figure', and its probable variations for each offence category inhibit the use of crime figures as measures or indicators of human behaviour. Even after report or notice, a large number of possible 'treatments' are available which will determine how the event will finally be recorded and processed as a statistic. Such administrative variations prevent any meaningful comparisons between areas and over time, even if the unlikely assumption is made that the dark figure is of constant proportions in each area and does not change with time.

Yet despite the dark figure problem and the wide variation in rates of crime that exists from place to place,[1] the pattern of crime throughout the country is fairly uniform if broad categories of events are considered. This is shown in Table 1 where the type of crime and the over-all rate for two conurbations are compared with those for all conurbations and the rest of England and Wales. Rates of crime are very much higher in conurbations than elsewhere; between conurbations there is some variation. Over-all,

TABLE 1: DISTRIBUTION OF INDICTABLE CRIME IN CONURBATIONS,* 1962

	West Midlands	West Yorkshire	All conurbations	Rest of England and Wales
Personal violence	1·6	2·0	1·6	2·1
Sexual assault	2·2	2·1	1·4	2·9
Robbery	0·2	0·2	0·4	0·2
Breaking offences	22·9	32·3	22·6	20·4
Thefts	71·0	61·1	71·7	71·2
Other	2·1	2·3	2·3	3·2
	100%	100%	100%	100%
Total indictable crime	50,491	40,871	414,951	481,473
Rate per 10,000 population	206	225	244	163

* The six conurbational areas according to the Registrar's General classification.
Source: F. H. McClintock, N. Howard Avison, and G. N. G. Rose, *The State of Crime in England and Wales* (London, Heinemann, 1968), Ch. 5. I am greatly indebted to the authors for permission to study the chapter prior to publication and to use these data.

more than 90 per cent of all indictable crimes are offences against property. There is a tendency for there to be proportionately rather more violent and sexual crime outside the conurbations; over-all, these crimes are very few. Due to differences in recording techniques employed by Police Forces, variations within broad categories of offence are likely to be the result of administrative practices rather than indicative of differences in criminal behaviour, and comparisons of detailed categories are likely to be misleading

[1] Thus for housebreaks, burglaries, and thefts from dwelling-houses (Standard List Offences 28, 29, and 40), in 1961, the rate in Birmingham per 10,000 of population was twenty-eight, in Manchester it was forty-two, in Bristol it was eleven, and in Bradford thirty-two. Over-all for England and Wales it was eighteen.

rather than revealing.[1] Even more variation is to be expected in the pattern of non-indictable offences, for they lack even a modicum of constant reportability that may attach to indictable crimes. Figures for non-indictable arrests show the police responding to particular problems at particular times and places in ways which reflect different and changing needs of different and changing communities.[2]

The data analysed for this research include both reported crimes and non-indictable 'disorder' offences. By collecting data from week to week during a four-month period in one particular sector of the city which was almost entirely in one police division, it was possible to be confident of at least procedural uniformity. The research objectives precluded any attempt at assessing changes in crime patterns over a period of time. The analysis offered is in terms of several categories of event distinguished by the procedure whereby they were recorded. This close attention to procedural detail was valuable and essential for understanding the nature of the work of the Police Force; working in one particular area, it was possible to pay particular attention to the situations in which crime arose so as to assess the nature of crime in immigrant areas and compare it with crime in non-immigrant areas. This approach, it was thought, would permit a more precise description of the nationalities of offenders in the various offence categories.

During the four months of data collection 2,046 indictable

[1] For 1961, housebreaks and burglaries (Standard List 28 and 29) in England and Wales were recorded more often than 'larceny dwelling-house' (Standard List 40); the proportion was 68:32. In Birmingham the proportion was 65:35; in Manchester 75:25; in Bristol 58:42; in Bradford 88:12. It seems unlikely that such variations indicate an actual greater propensity for criminals in northern cities to break and enter than their Midland counterparts; more probably it indicates that some Police Forces have stricter definitions of what constitutes a breaking offence. It was noted in accompanying police officers on visits to scenes of crime that 'mild' breaking offences were not infrequently recorded as larcenies, mainly to assist the local C.I.D. in keeping up a good 'success' rate in clearing up 'breaking' offences, for which there was considerable interdivisional competition.

[2] In 1961, for example, 3,600 arrests were made in Birmingham for offences against Intoxicating Liquor Laws (mainly for offences of drunkenness). In Liverpool the figure was 8,680; in Nottingham 226; and in Bradford 1,294. In the same year, 890 arrests were made in Birmingham for offences against Police Regulations (mainly disorderly acts); in Liverpool the number was 998; in Nottingham 76; in Bradford 320. For living on immoral earnings and brothel-keeping, 46 arrests were made in Birmingham in 1961; 65 in Liverpool; 12 in Nottingham; and 25 in Bradford. Similar fluctuations could be shown to occur from year to year from city to city.

crimes were reported; ninety-six of these, mostly thefts of cycles or motor vehicles, whose recovery subsequent to their being reported missing allowed the supposition that they had never in fact been stolen (a crime), only borrowed (taken and driven away without the owner's permission—a non-indictable offence), were eventually categorized as 'no crime'; furthermore, forty-nine of the crimes were recorded when an offender, prosecuted for an offence, asked that others for which no previous complaint could be traced be 'taken into consideration'. The majority of these were thefts from parked cars whose owners did not notice or did not bother to report the fact of theft. Five hundred and three persons were arrested, summonsed, or cautioned for their part in some of these offences; and collectively they admitted responsibility for 192 other offences which they asked to be taken into consideration.

During the same period there were 528 events involving the arrest of 616 persons for non-indictable offences. Most of these were arrests for drunkenness, but the number also included arrests of prostitutes, drug pedlars, persons caught taking and driving away motor vehicles, and certain other offences.

Another category of events has also been included, known as 'minor incidents', to which the police were summoned, often by the 999 emergency system, but at which they found no crime committed or any need for an arrest or charge. These incidents were mainly family disputes or disputes between members of households, often between landlord and tenant. These incidents have been included in a 'crime' survey for two reasons: in the first place, they take up a great deal of police time and reflect a particularly difficult and interesting aspect of the work of the Police Force; and secondly, because of the relationship between crimes of violence and disputes of the kind which make up the majority of 'minor incidents'. These points are dwelt on at greater length in the text of the section that follows. Here it is to be noted that minor incidents, to the extent that some involved a degree of violence between the disputing parties, may have involved actual breaches of the law. But these were not complaints about crime where the complainant sought legal action by the police, nor were the police inclined to treat them as crime complaints, although frequently they could advise an injured party of his or her legal remedy for the 'wrong' by application to the magistrates'

court for a summons under civil procedure. Thus, 'minor incidents' provide some indication of how the dark figure is reached
in relation to violent crime through complainants being unwilling
witnesses and through the police exercising a discretion in procedure.[1] In some instances, described hereafter, minor incidents
did 'blow up' into actual cases of violence followed by arrest,
court appearance, and imprisonment. Thus it has been thought
interesting to include the 'minor incidents' along with the other
law-breaking incidents in the crime survey.

In addition, it was possible to make a survey of 500 motoring
offences prosecuted in a similar four-month period.

These raw data are analysed first, briefly, in relation to the
pattern of crime in the division for a whole year and that pattern
in relation to the city's over-all crime pattern. Thereafter follows
a fuller descriptive analysis of the events for their context, by
location, and in relation to the persons responsible. This leads to
a summarizing chapter on crime in immigrant areas and on the
nationalities of offenders.

What is required first is a description and explanation of the
area of the city which generated the general incidents and events
analysed hereafter.

2. *The Area Studied*

At the outset it seemed advisable to locate the study in one police
division, both to be confident of procedural uniformity in the way
crime is recorded and processed, and also for technical reasons of
research feasibility.[2] Birmingham City Police Force is organized
in six divisions. 'A' division covers the city centre; the other five
cover sectors of the city from the centre to the boundary. (See
Map 1.) Birmingham lies off centre from the West Midland
conurbation area: its boundaries to the south, east, and north are
towards progressively more suburban and rural areas; to the west
it merges into the old industrial and somewhat decaying residential areas of Smethwick, Oldbury, and West Bromwich. The
immigrant population is not evenly dispersed throughout the city
but is clustered in characteristic areas of the inner ring within a

[1] An analogous situation exists in America which has been the subject of some
study and comment, see pp. 161-2.
[2] It was planned that the sole researcher could spend up to six months collecting
data and information for the study.

Map 1. Police organization in Birmingham: divisional and ward boundaries.

Source: Drawn from an enlargement of a City of Birmingham map published by the Geographers Co. Ltd.

mile or a mile and a half of the city centre, except to the west where the kind of housing is uniformly poorer and less suburban.

The 1961 Census revealed substantial numbers of West Indian immigrants in the wards of Rotton Park, Soho, and Sandwell to the west; in Handsworth and Aston to the north; in Saltley and Small Heath to the east; and in Deritend and Sparkbrook to the south. Asian immigrants were clustered in Soho, Aston, Saltley, Deritend, and Sparkbrook. The Irish were found to be somewhat more widely dispersed but with particularly large groups in Rotton Park and Soho, Aston and Gravelly Hill (in the north-east), in Small Heath, and in Deritend, Moseley, Sparkbrook, and Sparkhill.

From the 1961 Census estimates were made of the immigrant populations resident within each of the six police divisions. These estimates are given in Table 2. They suggested a choice of either

TABLE 2: ESTIMATES OF POPULATIONS BY BIRTH-
PLACE IN THE SIX POLICE DIVISIONS OF
BIRMINGHAM, 1961

Division	Estimated total population	Estimated Irish population	% of Irish population	Estimated coloured population	%	Total immigrants as a % of divisional population
A (centre)	20,000	2,000	3	400	1·5	11
B (SW.)	175,000	7,000	11	2,000	7	5
C (west)	220,000	14,000	23	9,500	35	11
D (north)	235,000	11,000	18	5,000	18	7
E (east)	220,000	11,000	18	4,000	14·5	7
F (SE.)	230,000	16,000	26	6,500	24	10
Total	1,100,000	61,000	100	27,400	100	—

Source: Figures from 1961 Census material in Birmingham Abstract of Statistics 9 (Birmingham City Statistics, 1964).

'C' or 'F' divisions in which to conduct this survey. Although 'F' division was less of an immigrant area than 'C' division, it was finally chosen for three reasons. In the first place, the immigrant areas in the north are larger, both in area size and numbers, than those in the south, which are geographically fairly well defined: the divisional boundary to the north slices through the area in which immigrants live and to do justice to the area as a geographical unit the study would have had to concentrate on

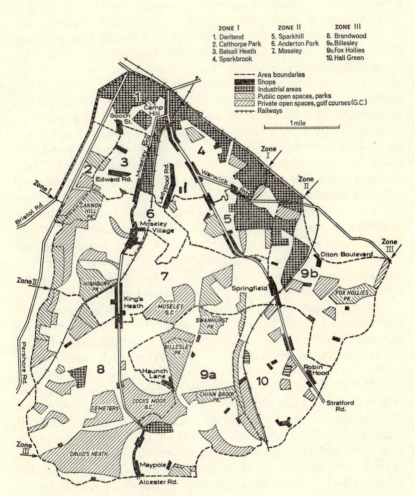

Map 2. The division studied, showing the eleven areas and three zones.

two divisions. Furthermore the 'C' division boundary merges into the indistinguishable area of Oldbury and Smethwick. These geographical reasons were important for it was intended to utilize census data to distinguish areas of immigrant residence from non-immigrant areas, and the discontinuity of natural boundaries and divisional boundaries in the north and west would have added to the difficulties. 'F' division, on the other hand, enjoyed somewhat natural boundaries, ranging from suburban to near-rural conditions beyond the city boundary, and providing compact and easily defined adjacent areas with high and low proportions of immigrants. In addition to these geographical and technical reasons, 'F' division included within its boundaries Sparkbrook, which had been the subject of a major study of housing and race relations whose insights into the nature of community life in a multiracial zone were of great interest and value to the researcher.[1]

The decision to work within the confines of one division was not strictly adhered to: geographically part of the 'F' division area included in the adjoining 'B' division is an area of intrinsic interest to a criminological researcher and for a study of race relations. This was a small, fairly well defined area of three or four streets centred on Varna Road, notorious as the city's vice area and frequented by cheap house-based prostitutes.

The division can be imagined as a triangular segment of the city with its base on the boundary between Kings Norton to the west and Acocks Green in the east and its apex at the Bull Ring in the city centre (see Map 2). It is an area which runs from the city centre, through the old and decaying areas of Sparkbrook and Balsall Heath, out to the new council or owner-occupied estates in Brandwood, Billesley, Hall Green, and Fox Hollies near the boundary. Its western boundary is formed by the Bristol Road, Cannon Hill Park, and the River Rea by Pershore Road. Its eastern boundary is formed by the railway line from Moor Green Station, through the ward of Sparkbrook to Tyseley, and then follows Olton Boulevard to the city boundary at Acocks Green. The divisional area includes the administrative wards of Brandwood, Billesley, Hall Green, and most of Fox Hollies; all of Moseley and Sparkhill and a small sector of Acocks Green; and all of Deritend and Sparkbrook west of the railway line.

[1] John Rex and Robert Moore, *Race, Community, and Conflict: A Study of Sparkbrook* (London, Oxford University Press, for Institute of Race Relations, 1967).

For purposes of convenience to assist in the description of the area and an analysis of its crime, it was found helpful to consider the division as being formed of three concentric zones at approximately one and a half miles, three miles, and five miles from the Bull Ring; and within the three zones to distinguish eleven areas which seemed to be distinctive geographical, housing type, or broadly 'cultural' districts. These were unequal in area size and population but provided a convenient frame for the analysis and comparisons. The actual boundaries of zones and areas were drawn to coincide with the nearest and most appropriate enumeration district boundary used for the 1966 Sample Census.[1]

ZONE I

Zone 1, the innermost zone, has its southern boundary formed by Edgbaston Road at Pershore Road, Brighton Road, Durham Road across Stratford Road to Warwick Road, incorporating the small housing and industrial estate of Greet.

Area 1. Deritend is a low-lying industrial area separated from the city centre rebuilding of the Bull Ring Centre by the markets and a maze of small streets of small industrial and commercial premises. None of the industry in Deritend is large scale, and much is part of the long-established Birmingham metal-working trades. A few old terraced houses remain among the factories, but the local authority has cleared the slums immediately to the south of the factories and is replacing them with tall flats and high-density housing. Much of the area is a clearance site. There are two central cinemas on the Bristol Road standing with the remaining churches, isolated among the parked cars and debris. Small cafés and restaurants front on to the streets near the market. A few night-clubs are sited among the industrial premises. The old shops in Gooch Street and Camp Hill allow their paint to peel as they await imminent demolition.

Most of the population of 12,000 live in council flats or council-owned housing awaiting demolition. There are a few coloured families here and rather more Irish, but the overwhelming majority (88 per cent) are native-born residents.

---

[1] The following pages should be read in conjunction with the map of the area (Map 2). Rather fuller demographic data for the area are provided below, pp. 91–113.

Area 2. Calthorpe Park has no industry, no offices, and very few shops. Some of its large old houses, on the Bristol Road, hide their 'respectable' multi-occupation among large old trees. But others round Varna Road have deteriorated considerably with over-use and misuse. The area is notorious as Birmingham's brothel district. The local authority has built flats between Bristol Road and Pershore Road, and its plans to demolish Varna Road have been moved forward.

Many of the population of 8,000 live in furnished lettings, accounting for 42 per cent of all households.[1] There are about equal numbers and proportions in owner occupation or in council-owned property (about 20 per cent each), and the remainder are in unfurnished rooms or flats (about 16 per cent). This is an area where many immigrants have to live: 14 per cent of the population are of Irish origin; 26 per cent are coloured immigrants.

Area 3. Balsall Heath is also scheduled for much redevelopment. But the houses to be demolished are small and unfit through inadequacy of amenities rather than misuse. Shops bordering the area along Moseley Road have the same semi-derelict air as Camp Hill. But the small shops in Balsall Heath Road and Edward Road are a bustle of activity, which is taken over in the evenings by the cafés and pubs. Many cafés and several shops are run by Asian immigrants: Lahore Stores in Mary Street, the Anarkali and the Maqu in Edward Road. There are three cinemas catering for Asian audiences. The houses to the south of Edward Road are larger, and do not come within the redevelopment programme. Four of these streets have multi-occupied three-storey houses, with many immigrant residents; but a substantial proportion of the two-storey houses are also owner-occupied by immigrants.

Forty per cent of the households, in a population of 15,000, are in council-owned property—much of it 'patched' housing in the redevelopment area; 20 per cent of the households are in owner occupation; 23 per cent are in unfurnished, and 13 per cent in furnished, lettings. This is another area with large numbers

[1] The Census defines a household as 'any group of persons, whether related or not, who live together and benefit from a common housekeeping; or any person living alone who is responsible for providing his or her own meals'. Thus it is the basic accommodation unit of the Census.

of immigrants: 10 per cent are Irish and 18 per cent coloured immigrants.

Area 4. Sparkbrook is composed of parts of the wards of Sparkbrook and Sparkhill. It covers the area studied by Rex and Moore.[1] The diversity they describe extends to the whole area. The western side of Stratford Road is small terraced housing, which, though similar to much of Balsall Heath, is not included in the city's present programme of comprehensive redevelopment. This housing is served by a long row of busy small shops along the Ladypool Road. The lodging-houses to the east of Stratford Road, which were Rex and Moore's main concern as immigrant residences, are complemented by lodging-houses on either side of Stratford Road further south which were until recently an Irish stronghold. The respectable terraces built by the Barber Trust extend to the east of the lodging-houses. The Stratford Road runs through the area and its shops, pubs, cinemas, and clubs make it a hive of activity and business throughout the day and evening.

This is a large area (nearly 40,000 population) with a great diversity of housing types but distinguished from Areas 1 to 3, which are geographically and 'culturally' distinct. Sparkbrook has 34 per cent of its households in unfurnished lettings, 13 per cent in furnished lettings, 31 per cent in owner occupation, and 19 per cent is council-owned. The 1966 Census recorded 10 per cent of the population as Irish and 15 per cent as coloured immigrants.

Within the narrow confines of Zone I live over a third of all the division's population, over a half of the Irish, and two-thirds of the coloured immigrants. To indicate the extent that the zone is one of overcrowding and multi-occupation, 64 per cent of the households were without exclusive use of hot water, bath, or w.c. (over-all figure for the division is 30 per cent) and 14 per cent of households were living at more than one and a half persons per room, the standard overcrowding measure (over-all divisional figure 7 per cent). This is also the area where 64 per cent of all the recorded crime events that constituted the survey occurred.

[1] Op. cit.

ZONE II

The southern boundary of Zone II approximates to the outer ring road which runs from Stirchley, through Kings Heath, to Hall Green, then the zone boundary veers north-westwards along Reddings Lane to Tyseley. Within this zone there are three areas.

Area 5. Sparkhill is a settled area of small semi-detached and terraced houses interspersed with some larger houses in 'respectable' multi-occupation. There is plenty of open space around Sparkhill Park and Reddings Lane Recreation Ground and surrounding the quarries and brickworks near the Warwick Road. Roads are wider, there are more trees; the shops at the southern end of the Stratford Road, past the swimming-baths, stand back from the road.

Owner occupation accounts for 54 per cent of all households in the area, while 33 per cent are in unfurnished tenancies with minimal amounts of council housing and furnished lettings. Eleven per cent of the enumerated population of 18,000 are Irish, 5 per cent are coloured immigrants.

Area 6. Anderton Park is a small wedge of the zone between Moseley Road to the west, Yardley Wood Road to the east, Brighton Road to the north, and Wake Green Road to the south. Its name derives from one of the residential roads in the area and is also the name of a recently formed residents' association whose letters frequent the pages of the Press, and whose most prominent member is a Conservative councillor well known in Birmingham for a hard separatist line on matters affecting race relations. In recent years kerb-side prostitutes have been active in the area.

The streets in the area are of large three-storey terraces interspersed with large detached houses built to a grand Victorian scale, now providing much scope for multi-occupation. This is reflected in the fact that 42 per cent of enumerated households were in furnished lettings, 25 per cent in unfurnished; 28 per cent were in owner occupation and 3 per cent in council-owned. Eleven per cent of the enumerated population of nearly 7,500 were Irish, 16 per cent were coloured immigrants.

Area 7. Moseley contains the whole of the electoral ward of Moseley excluding Anderton Park. Its two focal points are Moseley

Village and Kings Heath High Street. Ample open space— Cannon Hill and Highbury Parks, Moseley Golf Course, and playing-fields—wide tree-lined streets, large houses old and new, make this what estate agents refer to as a 'sought-after residential area'. In Kings Heath there are some older terraced houses near the main shopping centre, and one or two patches of prefabricated houses line the south-eastern boundary. Although there is con- siderable multi-occupation, particularly in the area between Wake Green Road and Kings Heath, this is the area where that means students, nurses, and young people acquiring professional training, rather than the working men and families, who are forced into the overcrowded and poorly-amenitied houses of Anderton Park.

Sixteen per cent of the households are in furnished lettings, 21 per cent in unfurnished, 30 per cent are in owner occupation, and 11 per cent in council-owned. Seven per cent of the enumer- ated population of over 25,000 are Irish, 3 per cent are coloured immigrants.

Rather less than a quarter of the division's population live in Zone II. Within this number are slightly more than a quarter of the division's Irish and about 20 per cent of the division's coloured population, mainly clustered into the small and distinct area of Anderton Park. In Zone II 21 per cent of the events which constituted the crime survey occurred.

ZONE III

The outer suburbs of the division constitute Zone III—uniformly small modern houses which can be seen as arranged in four areas.

Area 8. Brandwood is mixed modern suburbia. Owner-occupied houses near Kings Heath were built shortly before 1914, but the rest were built piecemeal in small developments up to the present day. Some of the most modern were built by self-build groups. There are pre-war local authority estates of about 800 houses around Pineapple Road and Allens Croft Road, and post-war low-rise housing further south. On the southern boundary, on one of the last remaining large vacant sites in the city, the local authority is currently building a complex of houses, maisonettes, and high blocks of flats known as Druids Heath. There are parks and recreation grounds near local authority estates, and ample open space towards the south, with room for a golf course, a greyhound track, and a large city cemetery. Clusters of shops meet purely local needs.

The extent to which Brandwood is a mixed suburban area is indicated by 53 per cent of the enumerated households being in owner occupation and 34 per cent in council-owned. Ninety-six per cent of the population of 30,000 is native born.

Areas 9a and 9b.[1] Billesley and Fox Hollies are large pre-war local authority estates, with about 5,000 houses each. All have gardens; trees line the geometrical street patterns at regular intervals; and parks divide the main sections of housing. There are a few modern industrial sites: at Warstock Road in Billesley and Lucas's and other electrical manufacturers in the north of Fox Hollies. Post-war local authority building is evident on two small sites where there are blocks of flats. Individual paintwork and additional paraphernalia betray occasional houses sold by the local authority to resident tenants.

Sixty-five per cent of households are council tenancies, 26 per cent are in owner occupation, and 9 per cent of the population of 55,000 is native born.

Area 10. Hall Green, which divides Billesley and Fox Hollies, is an area of small modern semi-detached houses. It is served by local shopping centres at the Stratford Road and at Springfield. Public open space is limited, but private tennis courts and sports grounds are dotted over the area.

Eighty-four per cent of the households are in owner occupation; and 10 per cent in unfurnished lettings indicates the presence of one or two small blocks of flats and a few privately-rented small houses. Ninety-seven per cent of the population is native born.

In Zone III live more than 100,000 of the division's 225,000 residents. The 1966 Census enumerated nearly 3,000 Irish born (20 per cent of the division's Irish) and 620 coloured immigrants (less than 5 per cent of their number in the division). Fifteen per cent of the division's crime events occurred in Zone III.

3. *A Profile of the Division's Crime*

In the four months during which data were collected there were

---

[1] For some calculations, utilized in Chapter 4, it was not possible to separate these two areas although they are geographically distinct, hence the designation 9a and 9b.

reported and recorded 2,046 indictable crimes. Table 3 compares the legal categories of these crimes with the 1966 divisional and city figures. 'A' division, which covers the central area of the city and shows an abnormal distribution of crime in relation to the other residential divisions, is treated separately. Also provided is an indication of comparative rates of crime.

TABLE 3: PERCENTAGE DISTRIBUTION OF INDICTABLE CRIME IN BIRMINGHAM 1966, COMPARED WITH THAT COMPRISING THE PROFILE

Crime category	Birmingham	'A' division	Rest of Birmingham	'F' division	Crime profile
Personal violence	1·6	0·9	1·7	1·2	0·9
Sexual assault	1·4	0·7	1·5	1·1	0·6
Robbery	0·3	0·5	0·2	0·3	0·3
Breaking offences	20·0	8·0	23·0	14·0	15·0
Thefts	73·0	83·0	70·0	78·0	82·0
Other	4·0	7·0	3·0	4·0	0·5
	(100)	(100)	(100)	(100)	(100)
Total indictable crime	36,887	6,287	30,600	5,682	2,046
Population	1,085,500	20,000	1,065,500	226,560	—
Rate per 10,000 population	340	3,144	287	251	—

Source: Divisional data provided by Birmingham City Police.

Table 3 shows how the use of rates of crime per 10,000 of population can mask great differences in rates between areas. The low rate for 'breaking' offences in the division studied is probably due to the system of recording such crimes rather than an actual difference in the types of crime committed. The some- what low incidence of violent and sex crimes among those making up the crime profile may be attributed to the fact that the four months of data collection were all winter months and the seasonal variations of these crimes is such that they tend to occur more often in the summer. The somewhat high proportion of theft offences in the profile data probably includes some which should properly be recorded as 'other'. By and large it can be seen that the crime events analysed are not atypical of a normal divisional crime load.

The clear-up rate is the result of a complex of procedures to be described later (see pp. 42–4). Table 4 compares clear-up rates for the city, the division, and the profile.

TABLE 4: PERCENTAGE OF INDICTABLE CRIMES 'CLEARED UP' IN THE CITY AND IN THE DIVISION DURING 1966, COMPARED WITH THAT FOR THE PROFILE

	Birmingham	'A' division	Birmingham	'F' division	Profile
Personal violence	69	57	71	82	70
Sexual assault	59	59	59	57	45
Robbery	64	91	52	39	43
Breaking offences	40	40	40	67	47
Thefts	28	39	25	26	25
All indictable crime	33	42	32	35	30

The high clear-up rate for thefts in the central 'A' division is due to the large number of shop-lifting offences which occur there and which by their nature command a 100 per cent clear-up rate. The abnormally high rate of clear-up for breaking offences for 'F' division was probably a freak for the year: it will be noted that the profile clear-up rate is nearer the normal for breaking offences. The over-all low rate of clear-up for the crime profile must be understood in relation to the short period during which data were collected.

It was not possible to obtain divisional figures for non-indictable offences but the Chief Constable's 1966 Report indicated the number of prosecutions for the main categories included among those so dealt with in the crime profile. These figures are provided in Table 5.

The high proportion of arrests of prostitutes is explicable in terms of the divisional area studied including the main 'vice' area in the city. The low rate of offences of taking and driving away is more difficult to explain, although this may be very much a schoolboy offence favoured in the long hot summer holidays. It

TABLE 5: CITY AND PROFILE PATTERNS OF NON-INDICTABLE OFFENDERS

Category	City 1966 %	Profile %
Found drunk	25	24
Drunk and disorderly	35	40
Disorderly behaviour	8	5
Malicious damage	6	2
Soliciting	3	11
Possessing drugs	1·2	1·5
Taking and driving away	16	8
Driving under the influence	5	7
	(100)	(100)
Total numbers	6,751	584

Source: Annual Report of the Chief Constable of the City of Birmingham (1966), from Table 3, pp. 90–1.

must be remembered that arrests for all these kinds of offences show marked fluctuations from area to area, and from year to year, reflecting how they are the result of police-initiated action in response to observed incidents and not the result of citizen complaints, as is the case, by and large, of reported indictable crime.

The data comprising the crime profile belong to six broad categories.[1]

1. Reported crime which at the end of the study period remained uncleared.
2. Reported crime subsequently cleared up either by the arrest of a suspect, or by an inquiry leading to a person being summonsed or cautioned.
3. Reported crimes subsequently 'cleared' by an offender, caught for another offence, asking for them to be taken into consideration.
4. Reported crimes subsequently found to be such as to be treated as 'no crime'.
5. Events leading to the arrest of a person or persons for non-indictable offences.
6. Minor incidents to which the police were called but from which no criminal or non-indictable offence arose.

[1] Motoring offences are dealt with separately, see p. 85–90.

The over-all distribution of these six categories between the three zones of the division is given in Table 6.

TABLE 6: RECORDED EVENTS CONSTITUTING THE PROFILE OF THE DIVISION'S CRIME OCCURRING BETWEEN 1 NOVEMBER 1966 AND 28 FEBRUARY 1967

	Zone I		Zone II		Zone III		Divisional total	
	No.	%	No.	%	No.	%	No.	%
1. Uncleared crime	834	42	288	44	252	55	1,374	44
2. Crimes cleared	211	10	74	12	50	11	335	11
3. Crimes T.I.C.	129	6	54	8	58	13	241	8
4. 'No crime'	50	2	25	4	21	5	96	3
5. Non-indictable incidents	411	20	91	14	26	4	528	17
6. Minor incidents	378	19	122	19	60	13	560	18
Total events	2,013	100	654	100	467	100	3,134	100
Zonal distribution	64		21		15		100%	

The analysis which follows in Chapter 2 distinguishes five broad categories of offence type by the kind of police work involved. As was suggested earlier, police statistics derive from several distinct procedures and situations, and precision in discussion of crime can only occur with explicit reference to those procedures. The five categories are:

(a) PROPERTY OFFENCES

These constitute over 95 per cent of all reported indictable crime. The majority are reported to the police by a complainant who finds that his car, house, or shop, has been subject to a theft. A number—particularly those concerning industrial premises—are notified by automatic alarm systems. Some come to police notice through a member of the public reporting some suspicious circumstance. More result from the observations of patrolling police officers on foot or in a car after seeing persons behaving suspiciously or investigating some incident which catches their attention. Shop-lifting offences reported by shop personnel following their catching a person stealing also fall in this category. The routine procedure following a crime complaint is for a uniformed officer to visit the complainant, take brief particulars, and fill in a crime report which is then passed to the local C.I.D. office for their attention. The uniformed officer makes an initial classification of the reported offence—whether it was a simple larceny, a house-breaking offence, and so on—and this is the source of the data presented here. Subsequent inquiries, of course, may have resulted in a different classification but the majority can be assumed to have been finally recorded as they were initially classified.

(b) PERSONAL DISPUTES AND VIOLENCE

Violent crime is a relatively infrequent occurrence; much of it arises from domestic disputes and street fights or arguments. The police are called to many disputes either by one of the disputants, or by a passer-by. Some disputes may involve actual violence but in such circumstances that a prosecution is thought inappropriate; in other cases a minor charge may be made; very occasionally incidents involve serious woundings which merit a major charge under the terms of the 1861 Offences Against the Person Act. The procedure at such serious events is for the C.I.D. to be brought in at the earliest possible time to conduct the inquiries in which eye-witness statements may play a vital part in determining the just outcome. The procedure following a minor incident is for the brief details and the names and addresses of the persons concerned to be entered by the police officer concerned in a special book for this purpose at the local police station. It has been thought useful to treat the fairly substantial numbers of these minor incidents in relation to the small number of actual violent crimes that occurred in the period. Also in this section are included the small number of sexual offences (mostly minor assaults) and the small number of reported robberies.

(c) STREET DISORDERS

The largest component of this category is that concerning events of drunkenness with or without disorderly behaviour. A small number of incidents involving malicious damage to property (often shop windows) and disorderly conduct not related to drunkenness are also included. These are all non-indictable offences in relation to which the police have a power of arrest. Whereas the majority of property offences and offences of violence come to police notice through an injured party lodging a complaint, although some incidents of disorder are brought to police notice by passers-by or annoyed local residents, most are the result of routine observations and patrols by police officers. They are thus the result of police-initiated action and not of a citizen complainant. There is accordingly no clear-up for this category, although not every reported or observed incident will lead to an arrest. The police exercise a discretionary judgement in whether to arrest or not: in fact, arrest is often a last resort only exercised when persuasion to 'go along quietly' fails.

(d) VICE

The two main categories in this section relate to prostitution and drug trafficking. Again this is an area where citizen complainants infrequently initiate police action. Action derives from the work of specially appointed police officers organized to plumb the depths of this sector of 'the underworld'. This in Birmingham is work entrusted to a divisionally based plainclothes section of the uniformed branch of the police. In other cities it is an adjunct to the duties of the plainclothes C.I.D. branch of the police. Again there is considerable opportunity for the police to exercise their discretion both organizationally (how many men to spare to the tasks) and individually (how the men interpret their tasks in this sometimes extraordinarily complex situation). Again there is no clear-up rate and, as noted, offences arising from this category are not part of the normally published *Criminal Statistics*.

(e) MOTORING OFFENCES

As a separate exercise to the crime profile data collection, a survey was made of 500 motoring offences occurring in an approximate four-month period. The jurisdiction in relation to motoring offences places a great burden on police organization in such a way as to allow individual officers considerable discretion in whether to report motoring offenders for prosecution.

The purpose of the analysis which follows is twofold. In the first place, by paying attention to the extent and variety of crime, by looking at areas of occurrence, at the content of crime events, and at the offenders responsible, it is hoped to present some precise information about both the characteristics of crime in immigrant areas and the characteristics of offenders. Secondly, by considering the relation between crime and the police procedures of which they are the result, as well as giving a more precise interpretation of crime, it is possible to study the work of policemen, the operations of the Police Force and to assess what kind of role the Police Force can be expected to play in terms of race relations.

CHAPTER 2

Elements of the Crime Wave

1. *Property Offences*

During the four months of data collection there were recorded some 2,000 offences involving the theft of property. The nature of the offences testified to the aptness of a recent pamphlet advising on crime prevention which suggested 'all police experience shows that the great majority of thefts are committed by people who are quick to seize opportunities offered by neglect or carelessness'. Some 800 of the thefts did not involve the thieves entering premises where they had no right to be, but were thefts from vehicles or of vehicles, thefts from telephone kiosks, thefts from the person of wallets, purses, or handbags, or offences of shop-lifting. These kinds of thefts, called here minor thefts, occurred as in Table 7.

TABLE 7: MINOR THEFTS* IN THE THREE ZONES

Nature of theft	Zone I		Zone II		Zone III		Divisional total	
	No.	%	No.	%	No.	%	No.	%
Cycle	42	10	27	14	55	32	124	15
Motor cycle	10	2	1	1	7	4	18	2
Other vehicle	58	13	12	6	13	8	83	10
Theft from vehicle taken	19	4	12	6	7	4	38	5
Theft from parked vehicle	200	46	86	46	59	34	345	43
Theft from phone kiosk	22	5	6	3	5	3	33	4
Theft from the person	31	7	6	3	4	2	41	5
Shop-lifting	15	3	14	7	3	2	32	4
Other	41	9	26	14	19	11	86	11
Total	438	100	190	100	172	100	800	100
Zonal distribution (%)	55		24		21		100%	

* Most of these would appear in the official records as 'Other simple and minor larcenies', within Section 2 of the 1916 Larceny Act.

From this it will be seen that 43 per cent are thefts from parked cars, usually of car radios, or portable radios left in cars, or of accessories or other small items. The majority of these occurred in the innermost zone of the division where there are large car parks or where cars are parked in the streets while the owners are at business, shopping, or spending the evening at the cinema or other places of entertainment. In 5 per cent of the cases, cars that had been taken and driven away, when subsequently recovered, were found minus some property. The figures for car thefts require some explanation: following a report of a car missing, 48 hours lapse before it is recorded as a theft, for, in the overwhelming majority of cases, 'stolen' vehicles are recovered in that time, often only a few miles from the place of theft. Of the eighty-three vehicles recorded here as stolen, forty were subsequently recovered after more than 48 hours and the final entry in the records will be one of 'no crime'. In the majority of cases, it would seem, such borrowings do not involve thefts of property from the vehicles. With cycle thefts the position is slightly different: thefts are recorded immediately and are entered as crimes, although a number are subsequently found and thus become 'no crimes'. In the survey period, thirty-one cycles were so recovered. If these were omitted, the preponderance of thefts *from* parked vehicles among minor thefts would be magnified. Thefts from telephone kiosks were frequently in the nature of vandalism— removing the handsets or mechanisms which have souvenir value rather than money value. Shop-lifting offences are somewhat different from others in this category: the relatively high number in Zone II is due to one store in Kings Heath High Street having a blitz week during the study period when extra vigilance was extended to shoppers and those apprehended handed over to the police. For these offences the police are only notified if and when a person is caught: policies from shop to shop from week to week vary considerably and of course such reports bear little relation to the actual number of such thefts occurring. The 'other' category of minor thefts includes a variety of incidents—some 'false pretence' or 'tricking' offences whereby housewives were swindled into parting with cash or goods.

It will be noted that even if thefts from parked cars are excluded, over half of all minor thefts occur in Zone I. The pattern of offences within each zone is fairly even, except for thefts of cycles which tend to occur in Zone III more often than elsewhere.

Rather more of the property offences are thefts from houses or other premises. Table 8 distinguishes thefts from gas meters in houses, other house thefts, offences of breaking and entering houses or shops, thefts from shops or other premises, thefts from cloak-rooms inside other premises of various sorts, breaking offences in industrial premises, and other kinds of situation: collectively they are here referred to as major thefts.

TABLE 8: MAJOR THEFTS* IN THE THREE ZONES

Nature of theft	Zone I		Zone II		Zone III		'F' division	
	No.	%	No.	%	No.	%	No.	%
1. Meters	156	21	32	13	27	13	215	18
2. House thefts	180	24	87	35	41	21	308	26
3. House or shop breaks	112	15	41	17	50	24	203	17
4. Shop, factory, office thefts	103	14	24	9	19	10	146	12
5. Cloak-room thefts from all kinds of premises†	68	9	27	11	27	13	122	10
6. Factory, etc., breaks	63	8	8	4	9	4	80	7
7. Enclosed yard thefts	10	1	1	0·4	4	2	15	1
8. Building site thefts	18	2	8	3	13	6	39	3
9. Other	46	6	18	7	11	5	75	6
Total	756	100	246	100	201	100	1203	100
Zonal Distribution (%)	63		20		17		100%	

* Categories 1, 2, 4, 5, 8 would appear in the official records as 'Other simple and minor larcenies', within Section 2 of the 1916 Act. Some in categories 1 and 2 would appear as 'Larceny dwelling house' within Section 13. Categories 3 and 6 would appear as breaking offences (Section 26) or 'breaking with intent' (Section 27). Initial recording did not distinguish burglary offences which have to occur between certain hours of the night-time and are included here in the general category of breaking offences. The 'other' category includes a number of 'snowdropping' offences of thefts of clothes off clothes lines, some thefts from premises not included in the various categories, and some offences of thefts by employees of their employer's property (Section 7, 1916 Larceny Act).

† Includes warehouses, schools, clubs, cinemas.

Again it must be noted that there will be differences in reportability of offences in these categories, although it might be supposed that most thefts from houses and shops would be reported, especially if the theft involves a forced entry. Clearly not every theft from a cloak-room is reported, and some firms will only report a selection of thefts from offices and factories depending on their attitude to pilfering; much stuff must disappear from building sites unnoticed; and so on. Yet it is interesting that despite the preponderance of such offences in Zone I, the distribution of *kinds* of offences is similar in each zone with a tendency for more meters to be 'done' in Zone I (where anyway there will be more meters) and proportionately rather more breaking offences occurring in Zone III.

To allow rather more precision in locating the situations where major thefts occurred it was possible to classify the premises involved in a slightly different way. Five classes of non-residential premises and six classes of residential property were identified. This classification attempted to distinguish not just tenure types in housing, but also a style of housing. Thus, blocks of non-council flats, hostels, hotels, and so on, formed one group, modern privately-owned houses another, council-built houses or flats another. Terraced houses were divided into two groups: well-maintained houses with bay windows and small front gardens (Terraced II) were distinguished from those which open straight on to the street and show their age in a state of disrepair. Terraced houses were differentiated from a multi-occupiable category, for which the criteria were a building date before 1916, more than two storeys, and evidence of multi-occupation in the same street. Table 9 sets out the situations of the nine categories of major thefts.

Among non-residential situations, which over-all account for just less than half of all major thefts, it will be seen that shop-breaking offences are recorded as occurring about as often as thefts from shops; offices attract more cloak-room thefts than 'breakers', while factory premises suffer rather more from breaking offences than from thefts of objects from cloak-rooms or working areas. Hardly surprisingly the majority of cloak-room thefts reported are from places of entertainment or from schools.

Among residential situations it will be noted that more than half of all meter thefts occur in the poor terraced housing associated with the central areas of Zone I; half of all thefts from houses are reported in multi-occupied premises and housebreaking offences are equally distributed among the four small house categories with multi-occupied houses accounting for 18 per cent of all such offences. Over-all, it will be noted that houses in the multi-occupied group comprise the largest single category of situations subject to major thefts.

TABLE 9: MAJOR THEFTS BY THE SITUATION WHERE THEY OCCURRED GIVING THE PROPORTIONS OF EACH CATEGORY OF OFFENCE IN THE VARIOUS SITUATIONS

	1 Meters		2 House thefts		3 House or shop breaks		4 Shop, etc., thefts		5 Cloak-room thefts		6 Factory, etc., breaks		7 Enclosed yard thefts		8 Building site thefts		9 Other		All major thefts	
	No.	%	No.	%	No.	%	No.	%	No.	%	No.	%	No.	%	No.	%	No.	%	No.	%
Non-residential situation																				
Building site or yard									2	1·5			13	87	39	100	1	1·3	55	5·5
Factory or warehouse							27	18·5	24	20	45	55					20	26	117	10
Office							7	4·5	25	20	11	14					1	1·3	44	4
Shop					106	52	96	65	6	5							11	15	219	18
Café, club, cinema, etc.	1	0·5					16	11	57	47	24	30	1	6·5			9	12	108	9·5
Residential situation																				
Terraced I	117	55	93	30	14	7											4	5·5	228	18
Terraced II	12	5·5	13	4	11	5											1	1·3	37	3
Multi-occupiable	47	22	154	50	36	18											8	11	245	20
L.A. built	32	15	24	8	17	8											2	2·6	75	6
Modern private	6	2	16	5	17	8											3	4	42	4
Other residential			8	2·5	2	1			18	6·5							1	1·3	19	1
Unclassifiable																	14	17·7	14	1
All situations	215	100	308	100	203	100	146	100	122	100	80	100	15	100	39	100	75	100	1,203	100
Percentage distribution of major thefts	18		26		17		12		10		7		1		3		6		100	

It has been noted (Table 8) that 63 per cent of major thefts and 55 per cent of minor thefts (Table 7) occurred in Zone I, the portion of the division nearest the city centre. The descriptions of the kinds of crimes involved in these categories, and a consideration of the kinds of premises in which they occur, suggest how the over-all distribution of crime in the city is most uneven and subject to subtle variations due to the character of opportunities for thieving that exist in a locality. If a crime map is considered the extent of this variation is most marked (see Map 4). The purpose of describing eleven distinct areas within the division is to show something of the social context in which crime occurs (see also Chapter 3). The areas described earlier are unequal in size and population but, by adopting the customary unit of 10,000 of population on which to base a rate of crime event, something of this variation in crime occurrence can be expressed numerically.

Table 10 sets out the comparative rates of minor and major thefts in the eleven areas.

TABLE 10: RATES OF OCCURRENCE OF MINOR AND MAJOR THEFTS IN THE ELEVEN AREAS OF THE DIVISION EXPRESSED PER 10,000 OF POPULATION IN EACH AREA

	Area	Estimated population	Minor thefts	Rate	Major thefts	Rate
1.	Deritend	11,900	174	147	192	164
2.	Calthorpe Park	8,040	43	54	62	77
3.	Balsall Heath	15,000	89	61	175	118
4.	Sparkbrook	38,760	177	31	327	86
5.	Sparkhill	18,260	50	28	72	40
6.	Anderton Park	7,340	33	47	70	99
7.	Moseley	25,200	87	39	104	42
8.	Brandwood	30,810	56	19	76	25
9a. 9b.	Billesley Fox Hollies	57,200	77	14	97	18
10.	Hall Green	15,530	33	22	28	18

Table 10 shows clearly how much of the high rate of crime in Zone I is attributable to its innermost area, Deritend. Reference to the categories of crime and the situations in which crimes occur shows that the high rate is attributable to the large number of thefts of and from cars in this area and to the fact that in Deritend a quarter of all factory breaking offences and a third of all thefts from offices or other business premises occurred. Reference to Map 8 shows clusters of thefts from cars in Balsall Heath, Anderton Park, Moseley, and Hall Green associated with car parks, or streets in which cars park near to clubs or other centres of entertainment. Thefts from meters inflate Balsall Heath's rate of major thefts, while the three areas where multi-occupation is widespread—Calthorpe Park, Anderton Park, and Sparkbrook—show high rates due to the frequency of thefts from such houses.

For major thefts, distinguishing residential from non-residential premises highlights the relative security of households against theft in the various areas. Table 11 measures major thefts from residential premises as a rate per 1,000 households at risk in the area.

TABLE 11: MAJOR THEFTS FROM RESIDENTIAL
PREMISES PER 1,000 HOUSEHOLDS IN EACH OF THE
AREAS OF THE DIVISION

Area	No. of households	No. of major thefts	Rate per 1,000 households
1. Deritend	3,450	45	13
2. Calthorpe Park	1,900	54	38
3. Balsall Heath	5,400	119	22
4. Sparkbrook	12,200	177	15
5. Sparkhill	6,000	34	6
6. Anderton Park	2,600	54	21
7. Moseley	8,000	70	9
8. Brandwood	10,000	44	4
9a. Billesley 9b. Fox Hollies	17,300	48	2
10. Hall Green	4,700	7	1·5

Table 11 shows the relative security of Deritend, despite its over-all high crime rate, and the serenity of the outer suburbs which show no evidence of being attractive areas for property offences among the better class, more richly-stocked, owner-occupied housing. In contrast, Calthorpe Park and Anderton Park have high rates of thefts from houses although Sparkbrook appears relatively undisturbed.

Thus, property offences of various kinds are distributed in various situations. Such variety makes any assessment and analysis of the nature and value of goods stolen a mammoth task, beyond the scope of a single researcher. Obviously many thefts are of objects of little value on an exchange market. The Birmingham

Chief Constable's Report for 1966 revealed that during the year the value of property stolen exceeded £1 million, from nearly 35,000 property offences.[1] The data used in this research, being preliminary data, did not include any systematic reference to value or nature of goods stolen. Where estimates of value were possible (in 1,080 cases), 135 were of values of less than £1; 659 less than £10; 207 between £10–50; and seventy-nine more than £50. There was some indication of the nature of the goods stolen in about 1,500 cases, listed as follows:

Goods	No. of cases
Cash	500
Radios	124
Car tools or accessories	115
Electrical household appliances	126
Jewellery or watches	38
Groceries	104
Clothing	159
Wallets and handbags	89
Builders' equipment	82
Metal	45
Miscellaneous	122

Clearly the nature of the event, the nature and value of goods stolen affect the detectability of these offences. The vast majority of minor thefts are such that unless a person is caught in the act of his theft (like shop-lifters) detection is practically impossible. The possible exceptions are larcenies from the person and false pretence or 'larceny trick' offences where a snatcher or swindler is liable to be recognized should he try thefts again and again. The nature of the goods stolen in minor thefts is such as to be infrequently convertible into cash, although checks on dubious second-hand dealers may well bring to notice radios or other items stolen from cars, and so on. But it would seem probable that satisfaction for such thieves is more in the act of thieving than in the value any stolen goods realize.

Likewise, for many major thefts, the majority seemed to involve small sums, usually of money, obtained during a brief visit which might involve breaking a window or a lock to obtain entry. Once free of the scene, chances of getting caught must be minimal. Only where goods are marketable or require a 'fence'

---

[1] *Annual Report of the Chief Constable* ..., op. cit., p. 61.

for their conversion into money would there seem to be scope for detective work. An attempt was made to classify the major thefts and some of the minor thefts by the nature of the action involved and the kind of objects stolen. Of 1,267 examined, 758 (60 per cent) seemed to be the result of lucky-dip sneak thieves responding to an opportunity of an open door or an unattended parcel on a doorstep to effect a theft of easily concealable or unexceptional objects—cash, a watch, or a clock or cigarette lighter from a kitchen or back room left, perhaps momentarily, by an owner.

A further 272 (21 per cent) suggested that a somewhat more deliberate attempt at thieving was made involving a longer period inside the premises but involving odds and ends of valuables— frequently just cash—which were taken for their immediate rather than convertible value.

Some 190 (15 per cent) suggested, either from the value or nature of the goods stolen, a firm element of planning, the need for more than one person to operate, the need of a vehicle to transport bulky goods, and a suggestion that the thieves knew in advance what was waiting for them to steal.[1]

In addition there were eighteen (1·5 per cent) reported thefts from prostitutes' clients, often large sums were involved, often the report was in the form of a somewhat ambiguous letter from the complainant to the Chief Constable starting off, for example: 'While I was visiting a friend of mine in Varna Road recently. . . .' Twenty-nine (2·5 per cent) were of a variety of circumstances distinct from the above.

By this rough estimate only about 15 per cent of the property offences are such as to give a detective much optimism of actual detection. This is a necessary perspective for any discussion of clear-up rates, the work of the C.I.D., and indeed the idea of the war against crime. Unfortunately the published statistics at the moment make insufficient distinction between the mass of petty undetectable thefts and the serious major crimes. And this un-differentiated mass makes up the burdensome case loads of C.I.D. men.

---

[1] Among these was one theft from a warehouse in Zone II for which a woman was charged with receiving. This, it was revealed, was something in the nature of a holding charge against a well-organized gang of criminals who had been carrying out large-scale thefts of electrical household goods all over the Midlands. 'The biggest thing for years' was how one C.I.D. man described it.

Before considering the work of the C.I.D. in relation to property offences and the nature of the proceedings whereby a number of the 2,000 recorded offences were cleared up, it is useful to consider a number of aspects of police organization and operations in this field.

(a) PROPERTY OFFENCES AND THE UNIFORMED OFFICER

Routine patrols, of course, may occasionally bring suspicious incidents or persons to police notice. Some officers brought offences of theft and fraudulent use of vehicle excise licences to notice, and to court, through their patrolling observations. More often a patrol may be directed to, or observe, a youngster, perhaps, getting at a telephone kiosk with a screwdriver. Other incidents included in the survey data were somewhat more curious in nature:

Example 1. One enthusiastic officer during our period of study became keenly interested in cars by which were placed, as parking lights, the paraffin-lit red warning lights that building contractors place around street obstructions. If he felt that these were stolen (it was apparently possible to purchase these but such were distinctively marked) he would interview the car owner and submit a file: there were signs that such zeal was contagious and other officers in other stations started a similar activity. Perhaps dissuaded by senior officers, the practice died out; yet our crime figures include some dozen such cleared 'simple larcenies'. In each case the offender was cautioned.

The most frequent source of contact with crime for the patrolling officer or area-car man comes through his attending the scene of a crime complaint. A member of the public, who finds his house broken into or thieved from, will in the first instance be visited by a uniformed officer who will take brief first particulars. On his first assessment and description, which he makes by filling out a crime complaint form and by typing the information on a crime report, the C.I.D. branch will go to work. This contact with the public is important in two ways: first, the effect of a theft can be very distressing, particularly to the less young and to women, and the kind of reassurance that a policeman can bring will restore a sense of well-being and perhaps quell excessive fears; secondly, the skill that is exercised in carrying out the preliminary investigation may well be crucial in making detection likely. The two purposes are easily related, for nothing is probably more reassuring than an air of confident professionalism in conducting the investigation.

Although most crime inquiries start from a complaint, special kinds of crimes lead to special measures designed to effect the arrest of persons caught in the act. An arrest from one such an incident is revealing in a number of ways about the nature and content of police work.

Example 2. There had been a spate of thefts from cars parked in the vicinity of two night-clubs. Two men from the beat patrol had been detailed to keep watch—for this they were permitted to wear plain overcoats rather than uniform and to dispense with helmets. At about 12.45 a.m. they radioed to the station to say that they had stopped a man suspected of stealing property from cars—he had in his possession two overcoats, a portable record-player such as fits in a car, and a case of about twenty small 7-inch records. They brought him to the station, his belongings were turned from his pockets (among which was a suspicious-looking kitchen knife), and he was bundled into the small interview room and subjected to some pretty rough questioning, not only by the two men who had arrested him, but by the office sergeant, another police officer who happened to be in the station at the time, and by a C.I.D. officer who was called and came within five or six minutes of the man's arrival. Throughout the man stoutly maintained his innocence saying that the articles had been given to him by a friend with whom he had been drinking earlier in the evening. The pressure of questioning was kept up. He was also questioned about his home situation, for among his possessions were papers indicating that he was currently unemployed, owing to ill health, and under notice to quit from his council-owned property for arrears of rent. In the face of this unrelenting battery of accusation from a succession of different police officers (the duty inspector was not present at the time, nor, as far as I could ascertain, was he informed of the proceedings), the man, now reduced to tears, still refused to admit guilt in any crime. After several minutes, the two arresting officers and the C.I.D. man seemed to give up and left the suspect alone with the other police officer. Things got quieter; more phone inquiries were made both to see if there had been any report of a car theft from the adjoining division and also to see if there was anything recorded against the man at the central file index at Police Headquarters: neither calls revealed anything. After ten minutes or so, the police officer who had been left in quiet conversation with the man emerged to say that he was now ready to make a statement admitting the theft from a parked car. This was done by one of the arresting officers while the other officer and the C.I.D. man went to try to locate the car and its owner. The man had not been very precise about the location which was anyway a mile or so away in another division. About an hour after he came to the station, the man, having made his statement, was formally charged and put in the cells.

This episode is revealing for a number of reasons. It was clear that in the arrest of a suspect for crime the police felt they were fulfilling their primary task. 'This makes it all worthwhile', a sergeant remarked to me as the man was brought in. And clearly one can appreciate that for the arresting officers who had spent a succession of very cold nights watching cars without reward, the arrest was some solace, although the man had not been operating in the area they were keeping under surveillance nor was he exactly skilled or experienced in his business. (He must have walked a good mile along a busy main street before being stopped by the officers.) Certainly, making a good arrest—which seemed by definition one that helped to improve the clear-up rate—is still felt to constitute the main way in which a constable proves his worth and improves his prospects of promotion.

Yet it was difficult to perceive any marked procedural regularity attaching to the situation. No one officer seemed to be in control of ordering the process. No senior officer was present and it seemed the form that both sergeants present should leave the major part of the inquiries to the arresting officers (both of whom were young men and relatively inexperienced). The role of the C.I.D. man in this case was small, probably due to the clear-cut nature of the event and the inexperience of the suspect. Bigger fish would no doubt have been played with greater skill and circumspection.

More interesting, perhaps, is the way this minor but not for that reason atypical case illustrates the way in which the Judges'

Rules actually apply in an operational setting.[1] Few officers—
senior, uniformed, or C.I.D.—evinced much support for the Rules
even in their modified (1964) form. Few of the men indicated that
by training or experience they gained any deep understanding of
the purpose and aims of the Rules. It was frequently remarked
that often the police know the guilty men but have insufficient
evidence to prove it in court. With some bitterness, incidents were
cited where criminals (in the police view) had escaped conviction
through a knowledge of the system and their knowing how and
when to assert their rights. Findings of not guilty in court promote
further dismay or cynicism: understandable, perhaps, when it is
realized that court proceedings are only instituted if and when
the police feel there is sufficient evidence for a finding of guilt. A
'not guilty' finding is felt to indicate a police 'error', whereas the
police feel—and this view was expressed most forcibly to me by a
chief inspector—that if a man was not guilty he would not be in
court and a not guilty finding means that a man has escaped
justice rather than that the police have made a mistake. This
leads to the police putting a high premium on a plea of guilty and
an incontrovertible sworn statement admitting guilt. The fear of
the court (or the prosecuting solicitor who presents police cases)
finding insufficient evidence is very great.

Thus, in the incident described the most important product
was a statement admitting theft which became even more of a
necessity when it seemed that no complainant could be found to
identify the goods stolen. It was incomprehensible to the police
why a person so palpably guilty, one as good as caught in the act,
should persist in his unlikely tale of innocence. These considerations—where an overriding certainty on the part of the police
was apparent—were of more importance than any niceties of
procedure. Here was a customer who was by no one's estimation
an important criminal. He was inexperienced, unskilled, and quite
overwhelmed by the situation in which he found himself, and in
fact only began to behave reasonably when something of the chaos
and confusion surrounding his arrest had subsided.[2]

[1] For a full discussion of the Rules, their inception, and modification, see R. M.
Jackson, *Enforcing the Law* (London, Macmillan, 1967), pp. 58–78.

[2] It was not my impression that the confusion was planned as a 'softening-up'
procedure to make a 'voluntary' statement more probable. Nor did it seem that fear
of any police violence induced the man to confess although the atmosphere in the
early stages was one in which violence seemed more than a possibility.

One could not help wondering how things would have turned out if the man had kept his head and acted 'cool', which were certainly not aspects of police behaviour: no doubt the role of the C.I.D. would have taken on increasing importance. What the incident revealed were something of the tensions and pressures under which the police work and how elements in the situation seemed to control procedure rather than the personnel involved.

Arrests of criminals by uniformed officers accounted for just half of all arrests. Most frequently these were by crews of cars patrolling the area being directed to the scene of a suspected crime. Uniformed officers were also responsible for the apprehension of most of those subsequently dealt with, not by arrest, but by summons or caution (see also p. 43). In all such cases it would be normal for the uniformed officer to complete the initial inquiries and then hand the case over to the local C.I.D. man for him to complete the inquiry.

(b) PROPERTY OFFENCES AND THE C.I.D.

The clearing-up of crime, interrogation of suspects, interviewing of witnesses, and so on, are the function of a specialist detective branch of the police administered separately but in parallel to the uniformed branch. At each sub-divisional station there is a small staff of detective sergeants and detective constables under the direction of a detective inspector.[1] At divisional level in over-all supervision is a detective chief-inspector. At city level a comprehensive index of criminal records and a co-ordinating and administrative staff of no mean size are maintained. At city H.Q. the specialist city crime squad is also organized; and liaison is maintained and staff contributed to a regional crime squad. These latter two groups are fairly recent innovations aimed at controlling and detecting the more organized and often highly mobile criminal groups. The local C.I.D. men have tasks relating to everyday local crime but the various specialized branches reflect an increasing need for co-ordinated activities between areas, both for a special class of crime and for the exceptional major crime requiring massive police effort.

The case loads of the local C.I.D. men consist of the partially complete crime reports passed to them by the uniformed officers

---

[1] The C.I.D. account for about 10 per cent of all police personnel.

who make the preliminary visit to each crime complaint. In addition they conduct and continue inquiries in cases where the initial arrest may have been made by uniformed officers. They may also take over inquiries when shop-lifters come to police notice.

In addition, of course, they must maintain observations and use local informers to mark the comings and goings of criminals and stolen goods on their 'patch'. From these sorts of activities C.I.D. men make arrests following detective work: during the four-month period just over a hundred arrests were made by C.I.D. officers.

The C.I.D. has a tradition of skilled individuality and independence of means and approaches. As currently administered the contrast in methods, aims, and organization from those of the uniformed branch is most noticeable and because tremendous value throughout the Police Force attaches to work to do with crime (reported indictable crime) and criminals, and since this is the special sphere of the C.I.D., they are seen as and behave as something of an *élite* corps of 'real' policemen.

Thus, not surprisingly, relations between the uniformed branch and the C.I.D. seemed to vary from station to station. A frequently articulated concern was that neither branch should share 'special' information. Uniformed men believe (probably rightly) that a good arrest will further their reputations and are, therefore, disinclined to transmit information to the C.I.D. who are claimed to be quick to steal all the thunder. A reputation for long hours of hard-drinking and something of a group ritual of meeting each morning in court to exchange notes and gain hints of what the city grape-vine is bringing, instanced some cynicism, sometimes tinged with envy, among uniformed officers.

It was hard for an outside researcher to understand the reasons for so marked a dichotomy between the two branches. Clearly the specialized crime squads at city and regional levels, and the special tasks concerned with distinct major crimes—murder, large-scale robbery, frauds, and so on—require special skills and no necessarily localized interest. A dichotomy at a high level and even specialized entry at that level would seem to make sense. But at a local level C.I.D. work seemed to be more of a specialized administrative kind concerned with completing and clearing-up work initiated by the uniformed branch rather than any particularly demanding and truly detective work.

This is so, despite the intense pressure of a huge case load under which the C.I.D. works. But, as has been suggested, a great many of the cases are such that actual detection is well-nigh impossible and C.I.D. work can mean no more than a visit to the complainant, a filling-up of a *modus operandi*, and then filing the papers, in the hope that following an arrest of a person for some other crime it may eventually be cleared up. In other cases, the C.I.D. 'process' already detected criminals, and many of these cases passed through the court. Thus, in talking of the work of the C.I.D. there is a need to distinguish formal and actual case loads and to distinguish those pressures which are organizational and administrative from those deriving from the scale of actual *detective* work.

Some of these matters may become clearer if we consider what happened to the 2,000 recorded crimes described earlier. The most frequently articulated measure of police efficiency is that which expresses those crimes that are cleared up as a proportion of the total number of crimes recorded. This is sometimes referred to as the detection rate, or as the clear-up rate; the latter is to be preferred for, as has been indicated, the procedure whereby the proportion is reached is administrative rather than detective.

There are three major components of the clear-up rate: persons arrested; persons proceeded against by summons or by caution; and crimes cleared through a person being proceeded against in some other matter admitting an offence and asking that it be 'taken into consideration' by the court when a decision as to sentence is made.

In addition certain information about some recorded crime comes to light after the initial recording such that the file on that case can be closed and the crime expunged from the statistics of uncleared crime. Stolen motor-cars and cycles that are found and returned to their owners are treated in this way. Persons serving a prison sentence may admit a part in previous exploits, and absconders from penal institutions may commit minor offences which are never formally prosecuted although admitted. These may be finally recorded as 'no crime' and the figures adjusted accordingly.

Just over 200 crimes were cleared by the arrest of a suspect (or suspects). About half these arrests were effected by uniformed officers on the beat or on car patrol; the remainder were effected by C.I.D. men either as a result of inquiries or while investigating other matters.

Nearly a hundred crimes were cleared by inquiries leading either to a summons being made for an appearance in court or to a person being cautioned by a senior police officer. It is usual to treat juvenile offenders in these ways rather than by formal arrest. In addition, shop-lifters are dealt with by means of a summons; and also among those cautioned were those twelve persons who admitted using contractors' red warning lights as parking lamps (see p. 35).

Some of the 435 offenders arrested or summonsed, between them, asked for a total of 238 further offences to be 'taken into consideration'.

Ninety-three recorded crimes were written off as 'no crime': seventy-one were cases of vehicles or cycles taken but found and twenty-two were admissions by prisoners or abscondees.

This complex detective and administrative process which produces the published clear-up rate allows for considerable variations in the over-all rate for different categories and types of offence. Table 12 presents the extent of this variation for the 2,003 minor and major property offences.

The actual clear-up rate is calculated by adding the crimes cleared by arrest or summons to those cleared by using 'T.I.C.' (taken into consideration) and expressing this figure as a percentage of the total of finally recorded crime in each category. It can be seen that minor and major crimes obtain the same over-all clear-up rate of 29 per cent. The range of variation is very marked: from 2 per cent for cycle thefts to 48 per cent for house-and shop-breaking offences, and to 100 per cent for shop-lifting offences—which are only reported if detected by the shop staff. It is also apparent that the more serious crimes of house- or factory-breaking are more frequently cleared up than the more common sorts of thefts.

It is also notable that 39 per cent of minor thefts, 46 per cent of major thefts, and 44 per cent of all thefts that are cleared are done so through being among those taken into consideration. It is interesting that 66 per cent of the clear-up rate for four categories which account for almost 50 per cent of all recorded property offences—those involving thefts from cars, and thefts from private houses not involving breaking and entering—are due to crimes taken into consideration. It is surely curious that the only measure of police efficiency, and one that is widely publicized, is very dependent upon the whim of offenders declaring their interest in previous exploits in the probably groundless hope that they will receive better treatment in court. This dependence on getting offenders to confess to maintain a success rate has, I believe, important consequences for police administration and organization. These are explored in Chapter 5.

TABLE 12: DIFFERENTIAL CLEAR-UP RATES FOR THE VARIOUS CATEGORIES OF MAJOR AND MINOR THEFTS

Category	Total recorded	No. crime written off	Total actual crime	Cleared by arrest or summons	Cleared by 'T.I.C.'	Actual clear-up rate %
Cycle	124	31	93	1	1	2
Motor cycle	18	1	17	1	3	28·5
Other vehicle	83	39	44	3	2	11
Theft from vehicle taken	38	—	38	3	4	18
Theft from parked vehicle	345	4	341	33	43	21
Telephone kiosk	33	—	33	6	4	30
Theft from person	41	—	41	8	1	22
Shop-lifting	32	—	32	29	3	100
Other	86	—	86	42	20	72
All minor thefts	800	75	725	126	81	29
Meters	215	1	214	4	27	15
House thefts	308	6	302	29	59	29
House or shop breaks	203	4	199	53	42	48
Shop, etc., thefts	146	3	143	18	9	19
Cloak-room thefts	122	—	122	6	10	13
Factory, etc., breaks	80	—	80	31	5	45
Yard thefts	15	—	15	2	1	20
Site thefts	39	—	39	10	1	28·5
Other	75	4	71	28	3	43
All major thefts	1,203	18	1,185	181	157	29
All property offences	2,003	93	1,910	307	238	29

Not every arrest or summons or offender reveals further offences. Only seventy-four of the 435 offenders cleared the additional 238 T.I.C. offences. In thirty-three cases one additional offence was revealed; eighteen revealed up to five further offences; five up to ten further offences; six up to an additional fifteen; and in eight cases offenders asked for more than fifteen cases to be considered.[1]

[1] The 'cases' do not add up to seventy-four, because some cases involved more than one person.

The majority of events that led to an arrest or inquiries leading to a summons or caution involved persons who committed crimes alone. Table 13 sets out the number of persons dealt with for minor and other thefts.

TABLE 13: NUMBER OF PERSONS INVOLVED IN THE COMMISSION OF PROPERTY OFFENCES

Category	1 person	2 persons	3 persons	4 persons	Total
Minor	89	26	9	2	176
Major	117	53	8	3	259

The majority of offenders were also residents of the divisional area: some were resident in the immediate locality,[1] a few lived elsewhere or had no fixed address. This information is listed in Table 14.

TABLE 14: RESIDENCE OF THE 435 OFFENDERS AGAINST PROPERTY SHOWING PROPORTIONS RESIDENT IN OR NEAR THE DIVISION

Residence	Minor	Major	Total	%
On division	119	137	256	59
Immediate vicinity	37	66	103	23
Elsewhere	4	5	9	2
N.F.A.	16	51	67	16
Total	176	259	435	100

Table 15 sets out the ages for the offenders in each group and shows what proportion of the major age categories was of locally resident offenders, including those resident in the immediate vicinity of the division.

Table 15 shows that half of all property offences are committed by local residents under the age of 21. The proportion is somewhat higher for offences which involved entering premises, although it must be borne in mind that the minor thefts include thirty offences of shop-lifting and twelve thefts of red warning lights, all of which involved adults. It also suggests that younger

[1] Defined for these purposes as giving an address in one of the wards of the city which had a boundary with a ward in the divisional area or living in one of the boroughs immediately beyond the city boundary to the south of the division.

juveniles engage in petty thefts while post school leavers tend towards more ambitious offences. Some further comments on the age of offenders will occur later (see pp. 121–2).

TABLE 15: AGES OF THE OFFENDERS AGAINST PROPERTY SHOWING PROPORTIONS ENGAGED IN MINOR OR MAJOR THEFTS AND SHOWING WHAT PROPORTION OF EACH AGE GROUP WERE LOCAL RESIDENTS

Age	Minor thefts	%	Major thefts	%	Total	%	Proportion resident %
10–12	8		13		21	5	
13–14	20		19		39	9	
15–16	12		30		42	10	
Sub-total juvenile	40	22·5	62	24	102	24·5	97
17–20	33	19	72	28	105	24	85
21–30	56		82		138	31·5	
31–40	27		30		57	13	
40+	20		13		33	7·5	
Sub-total adults	103	58·5	125	48	228	52	75
Total	176	100	259	100	435	100	89

The nationality or birth-place of the offenders is shown in Table 16.

The interpretation of comparative rates will occur in a later chapter. Here it can be noted that the number of coloured immigrants involved in property offences is very small; the Irish offenders are associated with housebreaking offences to no small degree, constituting nearly a third of all offenders; and over half of all offenders are persons born in Birmingham.

(c) SUMMARY

1 Over 95 per cent of the indictable crimes included in the four-month survey of crime in one police division were offences against property: thefts from shops, houses, or cars, breaking offences, shop-lifting offences, etc. Eight hundred (40 per cent) were minor thefts which did not involve the offender in entering premises,

TABLE 16: BIRTH-PLACE OF PROPERTY OFFENDERS BY THE MAIN OFFENCE CATEGORIES

	Birmingham		England, Scotland, Wales		Ireland and N. Ireland		West Indies		Pakistan		Other		Total	
	No.	%	No.	%	No.	%	No.	%	No.	%	No.	%	No.	%
Category														
Thefts of cars, cycles, etc.	9	1	—		—		—		—		—		10	
Thefts from vehicles	36	14	6		—		—		—		—		56	
Shop-lifting offences	20	14	2		4		—		1		41			
Other	34	20	7		4		1		3		69			
All minor thefts	99	56	49	28	15	8·5	8	4·5	1	(1)	4	(2)	176	
Thefts from property	48	14	14		2		1		—		79			
Breaking offences	64	15	40		2		1		—		122			
Thefts from sites or yards	7	1	6		—		—		—		14			
Other	21	9	14		—		—		—		44			
All major thefts	140	54	39	15	74	27·5	4	1·5	2	(1)	—		259	
All property offences	239	55	88	20	89	20	12	3	3	(1)	4	(1)	435	
Estimated % of total population	86				6·7		4		2·3		1			

residential or otherwise, to effect a theft; 1,200 (60 per cent) were major thefts which did involve a theft from a house or shop or other premises.

2 The largest category of minor thefts was that of thefts of property from parked cars; these, numbering 345, accounted for over 40 per cent of minor thefts and nearly 20 per cent of all property offences. Among major thefts, 523 (43 per cent) were either thefts from gas or electric meters or thefts from houses which did not involve the person breaking in. This number is over 25 per cent of all property offences.

3 Major thefts were distributed almost equally among residential and non-residential property. More than a quarter of all major thefts occurred in shops, factories, or warehouses, and

breaking offences against these kinds of premises account for over 10 per cent of thefts. Eighty per cent of thefts from houses and nearly 80 per cent of thefts from meters occurred in two distinct kinds of housing: that associated with multi-occupation (old, three-storey Victorian residences) and old, decaying terraced housing in the inner areas of the city. Less than eighty, that is about 7 per cent, of other thefts, and less than 4 per cent of all property offences occurred in owner-occupied modern terraced or semi-detached or detached houses.

4 Fifty-five per cent of minor thefts, 63 per cent of major thefts, and 60 per cent of all property offences occurred in the innermost zone of the division, within one and a half miles of the city centre; about equal amounts occurred within the other two zones. The highest rate of crime occurrence in both categories was found in the area nearest the city centre (Deritend) where a large number of thefts from cars and from industrial or shop premises occurred. The second highest rate occurred in Balsall Heath, particularly because of major thefts due to a large number of meter thefts. Rates were also high in Calthorpe Park and Anderton Park, the latter being particularly interesting because its over-all rate was nearly twice that for the other areas in Zone II, and exceeded that of Sparkbrook (Zone I) in both categories and that of Calthorpe Park (Zone I) for the major category of property offence. Rates in the outer areas were about half those in Zone II and a third of those in Zone I. Considering the major thefts in residential premises alone, rates were highest in the areas associated with multi-occupation (Calthorpe Park and Anderton Park) and almost negligible for the outer suburban areas. Although within each zone the pattern of property offence is similar, there were marked local variations reflecting differences in opportunities for the different kinds of thefts.

5 The nature and variety of the offences render many of them insoluble unless the offender is caught in the act. Only 15 per cent, by virtue of the nature of the goods taken or the scale of the operation, reflected any sign of planning or organization. In 800 cases the value of goods stolen was estimated at less than £10. For some categories events are only recorded and reported if and when an offender has been detected either by a store detective or by a patrolling policeman. A great many thefts of cars are subsequently not recorded as thefts when the vehicle is

recovered. In the majority of cases vehicles are recovered within 48 hours and are never recorded as thefts; nearly half of those which are recorded as thefts are subsequently treated as 'no crime'.

6 For some categories the clearing-up of offences is very dependent upon persons caught for other offences who admit their part in previous exploits. Most offenders are arrested by, or the subject of inquiries initiated by, uniformed officers. C.I.D. men effected about 50 per cent of arrests following their inquiries or observations. Seventy-four out of these 307 arrests or inquiries led to a further 238 crimes being cleared up by being taken into consideration. Forty-five per cent of the over-all clear-up rate was attributable to this group of offenders.

7 The 301 arrests or inquiries involved a total of 435 persons. The great majority (82 per cent) were local residents either living in the division or in the immediate locality. This was particularly true of juveniles who accounted for nearly 25 per cent of all offenders. Young persons (17–20) accounted for 24 per cent of all offenders and 85 per cent were local youths. Juveniles tended to commit offences in company with others. More juveniles who were past school-leaving age were involved in major thefts: younger children tended to be involved in minor thefts.

8 Seventy-five per cent of the offenders were born in England, Wales, or Scotland; 20 per cent in Ireland or Northern Ireland; 3 per cent in the West Indies; and 3 (less than 1 per cent) in Pakistan. Those of Irish birth accounted for a third of all those arrested for breaking offences, 17 per cent of those arrested for thefts from houses and shops, but only 8·5 per cent of those arrested for minor thefts.

2. *Personal Disputes and Violence*

During the study period, the police reported 562 incidents to which they were called to assist members of the public in dispute but following which no charges of any kind were made by the police. The disputants were often advised that there were no grounds for police action; not infrequently they were advised that if they so wished they could institute a civil action through the courts to remedy the wrong complained about. There was a striking variety of such incidents which is indicated in Table 17. From this it can be seen that more than two-thirds of these incidents occurred in Zone I. Over-all, just over half of all such incidents involved members of the same family, tenants of a house, or immediate neighbours—the largest single category being that of family disputes. About equal numbers were disputes between landlords and tenants, or arguments in a café, pub, or some other public place.

TABLE 17: MINOR INCIDENTS IN THE THREE ZONES

Nature of incident	Zone I		Zone II		Zone III		Division	
	No.	%	No.	%	No.	%	No.	%
Landlord and tenant dispute	19	18	24	20	4	7	97	17
Dispute between tenants	19	5	7	6	1	2	27	5
Family dispute	142	37	47	39	38	63	227	40
Neighbours dispute	25	7	13	11	8	13	46	8
Dispute in pub or café	39	10	2	2	1	2	42	7
Dispute in other public place	44	12	9	7	4	7	57	10
Dispute between shopkeeper and customer	12	3	5	4	0	0	17	3
Dispute between employer and employee	3	0·8	3	2	1	2	7	1
Other	27	7	12	10	3	5	42	7
Total	380	100	122	100	60	100	562	100
Zonal distribution %	68		22		11		100	

Disputes are significant for they are sometimes precursors of more serious events.

Example 3. During November the police were called on more than six occasions to deal with a dispute between a landlord and tenant. The landlord—an elderly Pakistani—lived in the house with his son (aged 16) and brother. Early in November his son misguidedly told a West Indian acquaintance who had nowhere to go when evicted from rooms that she could move into a room in his father's house. She arrived, with four children, whereupon there started a succession of disputes between her and the owner. He claimed that she was engaged in prostitution and took exception to a succession of her male visitors who were coming to and fro in his house. He called the police. Unable to confirm his allegation about prostitution, they advised him that he should seek advice from a solicitor as to eviction. This, it seems, the man sought but with no satisfaction and embarked on what the woman claimed was a policy of intimidation to make her move. She complained to the police who advised her that it was not a matter for them and that she should seek redress through a civil action in the magistrates' court. The situation deteriorated: the landlord cut off supplies of water, gas, and electricity; notified the authorities that the woman's children were being ill-treated and neglected; and tried to bar visitors to his house. The climax of weeks of frequent police involvement was an ugly attack in which the landlord wounded the woman's boy-friend. He was arrested and charged under Section 18 of the Offences Against the Person Act, 1861 (and the most serious of wounding charges). The judge at assize court, although commenting on the provocation, and having a Social Enquiry Report from a probation officer testifying to the man's previous good character and excellent work record, during twenty years of residence, passed a sentence of eighteen months' imprisonment.

Example 4. On two occasions within a few weeks the police were called by the tenant of a part of a house complaining of his Pakistani landlord's actions in seeking to evict. The police advised him that this was a civil matter in which they could not help. Subsequently, as a result of Press publicity and representations being made by the local M.P., proceedings were instituted against the landlord under the Rent Act for harassment; he was fined. The Press commented that such a case showed the need for swifter action of a 'policing' type for by the time the case 'matured' the tenant, after a long struggle, had given up the fight and moved away and the proceedings were negative in so far as they brought him no satisfaction.

These are perhaps two extreme cases and exceptional in that they involve a racial element. Yet prima facie both reveal police inability to *prevent* crime. It can be argued that both instances were scarcely preventable for there were insufficient grounds for police action. This focuses on a major problem for the police in the crime prevention field. There are certain measures that can be used against suspects who might commit a larceny but none that are applicable in a potentially violent domestic situation. The police are seemingly forced to stand by and watch unless they are in a position to activate a series of (non-punitive) procedures to prevent dangerous situations worsening into crime.

Most landlord and tenant disputes are less serious and

threatening than these. A landlord may threaten a non-paying tenant with a vague threat of fetching the police; or an irate tenant may seek to get the police to restrain an over-inquisitive or over-importuning landlord. Where the police are just being used, a curt dismissal, no doubt, with the advice to take the matter to court is probably adequate; in other cases distress may be genuine and police reassurance a useful damper of angry tempers.

Example 5. At 11 p.m. on a Sunday night, the elderly caretaker of a lodging-house contacted the P.C. on patrol in the area and complained about one of his lodgers who, despite warnings, kept bringing a girl friend to spend the night in his room. He was told that it was not a police task to supervise the private lives of lodgers. At 11.45 p.m. the same caretaker, much worried and mildly bruised on his face, came to the station claiming that the same lodger had burst into his room and abused him for interfering. It seemed that the caretaker had spoken to the girl while the man was out and told her to leave the house. Again he was firmly but sympathetically told that it was not a matter for the police but that an officer would return with him and see that no further hurt was caused. This was done, and the officer returned saying that he had spoken to the offending lodger who was reasonable and compliant and the parties were at peace. But at about midnight the man was back again, worried about his wife who was upset by the episode and in need of a doctor—could the police call one for him? Once again the officer went with him to the house, reassured him and his wife, and helped the man make a telephone call to his doctor.

There are numerous similar instances where the police are involved to advise and reassure the weak and insecure. The police themselves have an ambivalent attitude to such work; it is thought to bear little relation to police work in terms of controlling crime, yet it is a public service that presumably someone must do and the police are the only locally based, 24 hour-a-day agency prepared to do it.

In conversation policemen remark that it is their lack of formal powers in such settings that makes their role so unsatisfactory. They will cite instances where, when summoned by a

distressed wife complaining about her drunken and violent
husband, her distress has turned to anger and abuse when the
police officer remonstrated with the husband and threatened an
arrest. At other times, the sight of a policeman may lower the
temperature of the occasion, allowing each party to have a say
and receive a few words of advice, which may restore calm without
resolving the frequently insoluble. The kinds of disputes in such
an area vary enormously: some, seemingly trivial, are the result
of a clear if complex pre-history; others, a depressingly routine
occurrence, related to drink and the (alleged) 'going with another
woman'.

At most such 'family-barneys' the police can adopt a socially
and morally superior position of detachment which is understood
by all the parties; and frequently the police can bring order to a
confused setting. Any success depends on the parties behaving
reasonably and, in response to an outside and authoritarian
presence, making some adjustment in behaviour. The occasional
incident involving a 'better class' family was the subject of
comment by policemen as being the worst of such family incidents
to attend, where police presence is an embarrassment and where
the blunt and homely advice given to a 'poor' family is far better
left unspoken. But such incidents were very few.

The nationality of the disputants was not always recorded
but it was possible through a scrutiny of the names and addresses
of those concerned, which were always recorded along with brief
particulars of the nature of the dispute, to establish the nationality
of the parties involved in most incidents.

It was possible to distinguish four major kinds of disputes:

1. Disputes between landlords and their tenants, which include
cases in lodging-houses and those where a landlord or agent
visited a tenant.
2. Disputes between tenants in the same house, or between
neighbours.
3. Disputes between members of the same family.
4. Disputes in public houses, cafés, and in other public places—
mostly minor brawls, 'punch-ups', noisy arguments where threats
were bandied about.

Table 18 sets out the nationalities involved in these four
categories and in a fifth, 'Other', category which included such

TABLE 18: MINOR INCIDENTS: NUMBERS AND PROPORTIONS OF THE MAJOR CATEGORIES BY THE NATIONALITY OF THE DISPUTANTS

Nationality	1 Landlord/tenant		2 Tenants/neighbours		3 Family		4 Pub/café		5 Other		Total		Distribution between nationalities
	No.	%	No.	%	No.	%	No.	%	No.	%	No.	%	
English	12	6	19	9	119	58	27	13	29	13	206	100	37
Irish	7	10	5	6	44	62	12	17	4	5	72	100	13
West Indian	6	11	11	23	29	51	7	12	1	2	54	100	10
Asian	11	37	3	10	6	20	8	26	2	6	30	100	5
Mixed Asian	40	48	14	17	6	5	13	16	11	14	84	100	14
Mixed West Indian	3	11	4	16	8	31	8	31	3	11	26	100	4
Other*	16	36	11	20	8	17	8	18	4	9	47	100	9
Not known	2	4	6	14	7	16	16	36	12	30	43	100	8
Total	97	—	73	—	227	—	99	—	66	—	562	—	100

* Includes 16 European, 19 English/Irish, 12 West Indian/Asian.

things as disputes in shops, at work, on buses, and in a variety of other situations. From this it appears that slightly more than a third of all such incidents involve the police with coloured persons; and in just over half of those the dispute was between persons of different races.

Within the five major kinds of disputes, there is a significant difference in the type of disputes involving English or Irish persons, coloured persons, or persons of different races. The major difference is the proportionately high number of mixed incidents that involved landlords and tenants and a corresponding low number that involved family or other disputes. To a less marked extent this also distinguished the Asian incidents from the native British and Irish cases. There was a marked similarity between the English, Irish, and West Indian patterns of these incidents although the Irish tend to more disputes in pubs and cafés, and proportionately more West Indians are involved in family disputes.

Table 17 indicates how most of these incidents occur in Zone I of the division. In Table 19 is set out the relative proportions of the five categories of incident in each of the eleven areas in the division, together with a comparative over-all rate for each expressed in relation to 10,000 of the resident population.

TABLE 19: MINOR INCIDENTS: RELATIVE PROPORTIONS OF FIVE CATEGORIES IN EACH OF THE ELEVEN AREAS WITH OVER-ALL NUMBERS EXPRESSED AS A RATE PER 10,000 OF POPULATION IN EACH AREA

		Incident category %					No.	Rate per 10,000 population	Rate order
		1	2	3	4	5			
1.	Deritend	3	4	48	32	13	100 63	53	3
2.	Calthorpe Park	36	8	33	18	4	100 57	70·8	1
3.	Balsall Heath	15	14	31	27	13	100 92	61·3	2
4.	Sparkbrook	19	15	37	17	12	100 167	43·2	5
5.	Sparkhill	17	16	35	13	19	100 45	25	6
6.	Anderton Park	27	11	43	8	11	100 37	50	4
7.	Moseley	15	24	38	8	15	100 39	15	7
8.	Brandwood	—	25	60	15	—	100 20	7	8
9a. 9b.	Billesley Fox Hollies	6	12	66	3	12	100 34	6	9
10.	Hall Green	33	—	50	—	16	100 6	4	10

The two areas with most disputes, Calthorpe Park and Balsall Heath, although they share a similar proportion of family disputes (Category 3), show contrasting proportions of landlord and tenant disputes (Category 1) with pub disputes (Category 4): a similar juxtaposition is observable between Deritend and Anderton Park. The latter is perhaps interesting in that it has a rate and distribution more like that of Zone I than Zone II. Both in Calthorpe Park and Anderton Park the comparatively high rate can be attributed to the number of landlord and tenant disputes occurring, most frequently between Asian landlords and their white or coloured tenants.

These figures indicate not inconsiderable contact between immigrants and the police in a wide variety of situations. The large number of disputes involving persons of different races and the varieties of kinds and areas of occurrence make any comparative rates between the different nationality groups quite meaningless. It is to be expected that strangers to the country and area will experience more difficulty and misunderstanding in their new surroundings than the established population: and consequently they can be expected to show greater reliance on formally established agencies of help and advice, whereas the resident population within the community may be expected to have informal means of solving their problems established through time and custom. What is interesting and important is the way the police are involved, not only by the established population but also by the newcomers—Irish, West Indian, and Asian—in this variety of dispute. Many are quite trivial, others are fairly straightforward, but some may be thought to indicate a serious misunderstanding or breakdown in a relationship or communication; all require of the police particularly sensitive handling, not least those where there is potential opportunity for racial conflict.

The real interest in these incidents lies in the fact that many included an element of violence, and violent crime not infrequently occurs in similar settings. F. H. McClintock[1] in his study of violent crime in the metropolis in the years 1950, 1957, and 1960 showed that about a third of all violent crime between 1950 and 1960 derived from attacks relating to family disputes, quarrels between neighbours or between persons working together; nearly 20 per cent derived from attacks in or around public houses,

[1] F. H. McClintock et al., *Crimes of Violence* (London, MacMillan, 1963).

cafés, and other places of entertainment; and nearly 30 per cent were attacks in thoroughfares and other public places.

Domestic violence was the largest single category in each of the three years studied and although over 60 per cent of domestic violence was shown to lead to charges of the least serious nature, about 7 per cent resulted in charges of murder or attempted murder, and over 25 per cent resulted in charges of the most serious wounding.

This London inquiry also found a seemingly high proportion of offenders who were Irish or Commonwealth immigrants. Between 1950 and 1960 the Irish proportion rose from 9·7 per cent to 12·2 per cent and the Commonwealth proportion rose from 6·2 per cent to 13 per cent. But most interesting and significant of all, it was shown that it is the two categories of attacks arising from domestic disputes and from fights in pubs and cafés that bring about this high rate for crimes of violence for the immigrant groups.[1]

In this way the 'minor' incidents can be seen to mirror the situation of violent crime considerably. It was noticeable that in many of the disputes there was evidence of actual violence, much of which may have technically been an offence against a person under the terms of the 1861 Act but which was thought by the officer concerned not to merit a charge. In this the police exercise their discretion not to prosecute every known offender. The prevalence of violence in some areas in personal relationships is quite marked and the police match this social toleration of violence by not treating some violence as crime: an area and its inhabitants gain a reputation for violence so that only extreme outbursts get court treatment when usually the sanctions applied are most severe (see Example 3, p. 49).

It was difficult to determine what factors had to be present before a charge was made. If the dispute is between husband and wife or between partners in a secure common-law relationship, the victim seldom wants her man taken to court, only restrained for the moment, for she knows that all will probably be forgiven by the morning. If the victim is vehement but the police uncertain, the police can say that an action for assault should be made by the complainant without police action—for in such cases of frayed tempers, mutual acrimony, and a paucity of witnesses the police

[1] McClintock *et al.*, op. cit., pp. 27–35. See also A. E. Bottoms, op. cit.

will be loath to bring charges. If, on the other hand, a repetition seems likely or if other members of the family are endangered, the police may be inclined to arrest even if subsequent proceedings are delayed and the charge mild in character. The nature of the wound and how it is inflicted are likely to be most important in determining the process.

On one occasion there was an instance of admitted violence which the police dealt with by caution, but this was an instance where a woman struck her husband in a fight which occurred late one Saturday evening when the husband came home in an aggressive mood after a drinking-bout. The woman immediately contacted the police and confessed her 'crime'. This was to all intents and purposes a minor occurrence with the crucial distinction that the assailant, not an assaulted complainant, called the police.

Frequently the police can advise the injured party to institute his or her own proceedings by summonsing the assailant.

Example 6. At about midnight, one Saturday, a young Irishwoman called the police having been assaulted by the man with whom she had been living for five years. The circumstances were that the man had left her a fortnight previously but returned on the night in question and accused her, when she returned from an evening out, of associating with other men. He punched her in the face and beat her quite severely. He left before the police arrived and they advised her that there was little they could do but that she could summons him privately for assault. She followed the advice and obtained a summons for hearing about three weeks later. On the day of the hearing, the court received a letter in which the woman apologized for not coming to court and for wasting the court's time, but she and her man were now reconciled, had talked over the incident, and she now saw that she was somewhat to blame for what had happened. She hoped the court would be able to consider the matter closed.

Example 7. A call came on a Friday afternoon, just before 5 p.m., about a fight at a local factory between an Indian and a Pakistani worker, as a result of which one man was sent to hospital. The police attended and interviewed the foreman and other workers and got a picture of insult and provocation which led to one man hurling some pieces of scrap metal at the other. A record of the incident was recorded in the minor occurrence book. Subsequently at hospital it was found that the wounds were serious. The assailant was arrested on the following day and appeared in court on a major charge. After a week's remand for the police to explore the case further (with a special view to establishing whether the man was liable for deportation) the case was heard at assizes. It was revealed that a year previously, in not dissimilar circumstances (in the face of hostility and provocation by a workmate), the man had wounded himself. For a time he had received psychiatric treatment. The assize judge, who did not have the benefit of a probation officer's Social Enquiry Report in this case, acknowledging the provocation the man had suffered, passed a sentence of eighteen months imprisonment and recommended deportation.

It can be seen that the incidents described here as minor are of no little importance if a relation with crimes of violence is accepted; between minor incidents and crimes of violence the line is faint and uncertain; in the cases reported some were of actual violence; others were latently violent situations where police involvement by reducing tempers may have prevented crime; and some led inexorably, like that in Example 3, to an eventual violent outburst and court appearance.

By considering these minor incidents and the nature of police discretion, some light may be thrown on the dark figure and explain the considerable variations from city to city that exist in the pattern of violent crime that emerges from the criminal statistics.[1]

The great value of McClintock's London study is the way it challenges the stereotype of the violent criminal and focuses on the infrequency of such crimes, how frequently the violence is

---

[1] For example, in 1961 in Birmingham, indictable violent crime accounted for 57 per cent of all such crime and the rate per 10,000 of population was 0·67; for Bradford, the over-all rate was 1·83 but 18 per cent was indictable; while for Hull the rate was 1·05 but 78 per cent was indictable crime. Clearly these variations are due both to area differences in the nature of crime and to differences in police interpretation of how such crime should be treated. The distinction between indictable and non-indictable for these offences is probably most important as it may markedly affect the kind of sanctions the courts apply to violent offenders.

slight, and how frequently it arises in situations in particular slum-like areas and conditions, between persons who were known to one another. This should have important consequences in terms of treatment and prevention. So long as judges at assizes treat even first offenders with severe sentences of imprisonment for violent offences, it is probably as well for the police to exercise some discretion in whom and when to prosecute. The wisdom of treating with such severity persons more frequently acting out of desperation than premeditation is questionable. And whether the police practice of matching the level of toleration of violence in interpersonal disputes that exists in certain areas (even when there are warning signs that a major crime is in prospect) accords with any principle of prevention is dubious. Clearly *prevention* in this sphere is as problematical and complex as the circumstances of violence themselves, but it is an easy evasion of justice to say of persons in an area, 'they all fight there', or of persons of a kind, 'all coloureds fight each other—but its only among themselves'. Recognition of the conditions which promote violence, a consideration of the nature of violence, and an awareness of how the police administer the law in this sphere are a necessary perspective for a study of violent crime.

The legal categories of violent crime most usually distinguish those where a serious wounding (involving an actual break in the skin) was committed with intent to occasion grievous bodily harm (Section 18, Offences Against the Person Act, 1861); those where actual bodily harm of a serious nature occurred but without intent (Section 20); and non-felonious woundings of a mild nature (Section 47). Assaults on police officers can either be dealt with under a section of the Police Act (this is usual for mild cases or aggravated obstructions) or, if serious, under the 1861 Act. Possessing an offensive weapon is usually a charge under the Prevention of Crime Act. Robbery is a special category which involves elements of theft and violence. For convenience, in the discussion which follows, the small number of sexual offences which occurred, some of which involved an element of assault and violence, are considered with violent crimes and robberies.

During the four-month study period twenty-eight wounding offences, three offences of possessing an offensive weapon, and seven offences of robbery were recorded; in addition, there were eight instances of indecent assault and three cases of unlawful sexual intercourse. There was also one unsubstantiated allegation of rape.

Considering the woundings and possessing-weapons offences as a group and following McClintock's classification of such crimes,[1] the distribution was as shown in Table 20.

TABLE 20: CRIMES OF VIOLENCE OCCURRING DURING THE PERIOD OF DATA COLLECTION CLASSIFIED BY THE SITUATION IN WHICH VIOLENCE OCCURRED

Category	Cleared	Number uncleared	Total
Attacks in order to perpetrate a sexual offence	I	I	2
Attacks on police officers, or offences of possessing offensive weapons	6	—	6
Attacks relating to family disputes, quarrels between neighbours, or between persons working together	5	—	5
Attacks in or around public houses, etc., or other places of entertainment	I	2	3
Attacks in other public places	7	2	9
Other attacks	2	4	6
Total	22	9	31

Twenty of these offences occurred in Zone I, seven in Zone II, and four in Zone III.

The assaults with a sexual intent consisted of one in the Varna Road vice area, probably a drunken accost by a would-be client of a prostitute on a nearby resident, an unpleasant hazard of living in such an area; and one committed by an Englishman, subsequently arrested for a housebreaking offence and the theft of a night-dress, petticoat, and perfume, who admitted, following his arrest, a number of indecent and sexual assaults which had occurred in the area: he was committed to be detained at a mental hospital under the Mental Health Act.

There were three assaults on police officers, two occasioning grievous bodily harm (Section 18, Offences Against the Person Act), one occasioning actual bodily harm (Section 20); two were in the course of an arrest for larceny offences, and one in the course of making inquiries into a suspected motoring offence. The three assailants were Irishmen.

[1] McClintock et al., op. cit., p. 23.

Two of the possessing-weapons charges involved Jamaicans; the third involved a 12-year-old English boy who was cautioned for threatening a young woman with a knife.

The five assaults arising from domestic disputes consisted of:

(a) An assault by an elderly Pakistani man on the boy-friend of his West Indian tenant following a month of nearly continuous dispute during which the police visited on numerous occasions for what were recorded as minor incidents (see Example 3, p. 49).

(b) An assault by an English prostitute on her Pakistani cohabitee. The relationship had been full of discord and dispute, sometimes involving the police in minor incidents.

(c) An assault by a Jamaican on another Jamaican at a 'party' in Varna Road.

(d) An assault by a Pakistani on an Indian workmate at a local works. It was acknowledged in court that the man had been severely provoked by insult and annoyance for some time prior to the actual outburst (see Example 7, p. 57).

All the above incidents led to wounding charges, of the most serious nature, for grievous bodily harm (Section 18, Offences Against the Person Act).

(e) An Englishwoman who was cautioned after hitting her husband on the head with a bottle when he arrived home drunk and belligerent at 1 a.m. in the morning. She had immediately called the police.

The group of three fights in public houses included two where persons required hospital treatment for cuts but where the assailants were not traced, and a third where an Irishman struck a drinking partner in a local club with a beer bottle.

The group of street fights included six of a fairly mild, 'punch-up' variety following some argument or disagreement, often between strangers, which resulted in a caution or summons (in four cases: three English, one West Indian) or in the charge being dropped altogether; and three which led to more serious charges. One of these involved a 15-year-old English boy stabbing an older boy—a friend and rival—whom he thought was going with his girl friend (see p. 62); a young Englishwoman who attacked and wounded a younger girl; and a young Scotsman who got involved in a fight following a drinking session.

In the 'Other attacks' category were four uncleared mild

assaults on which there was little information; one cleared crime was an assault by the man who committed the sexual assault noted above; the other was an attack by an Irishman on a priest at a local church.

The small number of robberies recorded included three raids on shops or garages where money from the till was demanded forcibly or where there was an actual assault on the shopkeeper; in two cases women in the street were attacked and robbed of their money. One of these was a particularly vicious assault on an insurance collector which left the woman involved permanently disabled: for this offence a suspect—a young man of 19—appeared in court and was acquitted at assizes. Another robbery was that occurring at a large working men's hostel in the area where one tenant set upon another and stole some pawn tickets. The third cleared robbery occurred in Varna Road and involved two Irishmen who set upon someone who knocked on the door in search of a prostitute, robbed him of his money, roughed him up, and threw him out. One of the men involved had featured among those arrested for drunkenness and also among those involved in family disputes of a minor sort.

Sexual offences are included here because frequently they include an element of assault and violence. Six of the recorded indecent assaults occurred in Zone III, most frequently in isolated and open places, near parks or by secluded foot-paths; one such incident was an assault on a boy of 11, the others were on young women. There was one prosecution following a tenant of a lodging-house assaulting the young daughter of his landlady. Four schoolboys were cautioned following an allegation (unsubstantiated) that they had indulged in sex games with a 14-year-old girl. Three cases of unlawful sexual intercourse involved youths and their under-age girl friends. Two of these cases came to light during inquiries which followed the attack on one youth by another noticed earlier (see p. 61).

There was one allegation of rape which had to be formally recorded but which was subsequently treated as 'no crime': it was an unlikely tale concocted by a young Irishwoman whose boy-friend objected to her association with a West Indian. There were no instances of crimes in these categories of sexual offences being recorded and involving immigrants.

This catalogue of offences involving an element of violence

stresses the infrequency of such offences, the mild or technically violent nature of many of them, the way they involve persons known to one another, and how many arise from deteriorating relationships between the parties in areas where violence (un-prosecuted) and disorder are fairly commonplace.

This information is summarized in Table 21.

TABLE 21: NUMBERS OF OFFENCES OF VIOLENCE RECORDED AND CLEARED DURING THE FOUR MONTHS, NOVEMBER 1966–FEBRUARY 1967

Offence category	Cleared	Uncleared	Total
Personal violence	19	9	28
Possessing offensive weapon	3	—	3
Robbery	3*	4	7
Indecent assault	2	6	8
Unlawful sexual intercourse	3	—	3
Total	30	19	49

* Includes one finding of 'not guilty'.

These crimes involved the prosecution of thirty-two persons, of whom twenty-four were adults, three were young persons (17–20), and seven were juveniles. The nationality (birth-places) of these offenders is shown in Table 22.

TABLE 22: NATIONALITY BY BIRTH-PLACE OF OFFENDERS PROCEEDED AGAINST FOR OFFENCES OF VIOLENCE*

Nationality	1 Violence	2 Possessing offensive weapon	3 Robbery	1,2,3 No.	%	Sex offences
Birmingham born	3	1		4	16	7
England and Wales	6			6	24	
Scotland	1		1	2	8	
Ireland	5		2	7	28	
West Indies	2	2		4	16	
Pakistan	2			2	8	
Total	19	3	3	25	100	7

* These figures compare with the over-all figure for violent crime in Birmingham for 1965, as quoted by Birmingham City Police. Of a total of 363, 60 per cent were English, 23 per cent Irish, 12 per cent West Indian, 4 per cent Asian, and 1 per cent other coloured Commonwealth.

Assessing a comparative rate of crime for the different national groups can be seen to be particularly problematical due to the importance of area characteristics which generate the kind of tensions from which violence springs. As has been shown, Irish, West Indian, and Asian immigrants tend to live in certain typical areas and conditions where the level of violence is likely to be greater. They are an over-represented population in those areas which thus lessens the seeming over-representation the above figures imply. Within Zone I, where the majority of violence occurs, and in the three residential areas—Calthorpe Park, Balsall Heath, and Sparkbrook—the Irish make up about 10 per cent of the population, and other immigrants about 16 per cent. These population estimates indicate the extent of the unequal distribution of nationalities of persons; and the processes which promote that inequality produce the same conditions of overcrowding and disorganization of which crime and violent crime are aspects. Such qualifications are necessary correctives to shallow interpretations of statistics of crime.

SUMMARY

The police were not infrequently summoned to assist and advise members of the public in dispute or argument. Forty per cent of these were family disputes, 17 per cent disputes between landlords and tenants, 13 per cent involved tenants of a house or neighbours, and 17 per cent were disputes in the street or near or in a public house or café.

Many such incidents involved an element of personal violence, although not such that the police considered a prosecution by them to be appropriate. One-third involved coloured immigrants and of these a half involved disputants of different races. The 'mixed' disputes are typically landlord and tenant disputes; otherwise English, Irish, or West Indian disputes show a similar propensity to be family disputes. Most occurred in Zone I, and the areas with the highest rates were those where landlord and tenant disputes occur associated with multi-occupied dwelling. The situations and nature of these disputes mirror the situation of much violent crime and thus indicate how the dark figure for violent crime may be due to police discretion not to prosecute in cases of mild violence arising from domestic disputes.

During the four-month period of data collection there were recorded twenty-eight violent crimes, three offences of possessing weapons, seven robberies, and eleven sexual offences. These involved proceedings against thirty-two persons, twenty-four adults, three young persons, and seven juveniles. Of twenty-five violent offenders, twelve were born in England, Wales, or Scotland, seven were born in Ireland, four in the West Indies, and two in Pakistan.

In interpreting violent crime there is particular need to note the extent to which much is mild in character and the result of deteriorating interpersonal relationships in particular areas marked by disorganization and slum conditions. It is also necessary to note the infrequency of such events which constitute less than 3 per cent of all indictable crime.

3. *Street Disorders*

Most of the minor incidents recorded by the police occurred with families or tenants or neighbours in private premises (homes, flats, and rooms). Even if the police role and action depend much on the individual policeman's perception of the situation, only infrequently will he find the situation personally threatening. This is not the case with some of the other kinds of disputes, particularly those in relation to fights and arguments in or near pubs, cafés, clubs, and so on, in which setting the threat of personal violence is always present.

But whereas it was noted that in the case of domestic disputes the difficulties facing the policeman sent to deal with them derived from there seldom being grounds for police action (in the sense of an arrest for an infringement of a law), these other disputes, since more often than not they are in a legally designated public place, provide greater scope for more certain police powers. This does not mean that the policeman necessarily makes use of the power directly, it makes his warning more potent, for those in dispute will usually be aware of (or be made aware of) the policeman's power of arrest.

As with family or other domestic disputes, here too the situational link with violent crime is pervasive. McClintock found that nearly 20 per cent of crimes of violence arose from such settings: 'The largest proportion of felonious woundings in any

one class occurred among attacks and fights in public houses and
cafés and it is in this class also that the greater increase in the
more serious wounding has taken place.'[1]

Furthermore, it is interesting to note that outbreaks of interracial violence and fighting bear a relation to arguments started in
pubs and inflamed by drink.[2] Birmingham police could remember
and describe one such instance of the kind of closing-time tension
and threats which in other cities provoke ugly and violent scenes.

Few licensees of public houses or café owners like to call the
police for it reflects none too well on the character of their
establishments, the quality of their clientele, or the efficiency of
their own managing abilities. Some pubs and cafés seem adept
at coping with a mixed clientele with a minimum of public
disturbance; others manage to eject their rowdier customers into
the cool of the night air where nature or the patrolling policeman
can effectively prevent or control disturbance; but a small number,
and again the area factor is all important, seem to require frequent
police attention, not so much because of drunkenness but because
a licensee is not capable of keeping order in his own house. In
such cases as these a few tactful words from a policeman and the
unruly customer can be persuaded to leave and advised to get an
early night or carry on drinking in another pub. For a good pub
to need the police usually means some special event.

Example 8. Closing-time on Sunday: a call came to attend to a
fight that had started in a pub in Balsall Heath. The car was there
in a matter of minutes to find an aftermath of a christening celebration in full swing, including one or two glasses being knocked
about. The arrival of the police brought jollity to an end and left
the chief entertainer—an unfortunate and unfunny sight in fancy
dress—to explain himself. The licensee was satisfied that hostilities
had ceased, had no wish to prefer any charges, and the police
were quite happy for the revelry to end with the combatants going
home rather than to a police cell to sleep it off. They were satisfied
that, though drunk, the parties would go home quietly if un-
steadily, and waited for a few minutes advising stragglers to
disperse from the pavement and earning the licensee's gratitude.

[1] McClintock *et al.*, op. cit., pp. 125–8.
[2] See also Ruth Glass, *Newcomers* (London, Allen & Unwin, for Centre for Urban
Studies, 1960).

The figures for arrests for being drunk and disorderly testify that hard-drinking does not always end so happily as the occasion cited above. Instances could be cited of occasions when drunken customers were not compliant, when fights were real, and when casualty departments of hospitals and police cells received equal numbers of combatants. Here one could find that reality behind the statistical findings of McClintock that the Irish have maintained their almost traditional pre-eminence in pub fights. Policy seemed to be seldom to make any charges for violence from such occasions (particularly when, as is so often the case, both assailant and assaulted were equally the worse for drink). In such instances, the assaulted would be advised that it is possible for him to summons his assailant for assault privately. Fighting in pubs and drunken and disorderly behaviour, though reported to be declining considerably over the years, are still regular and anticipated phenomena in some areas of the city. The police act quickly to quieten any noisy and drunken people, although in most cases an attempt will be made to get the person or persons concerned to go home quietly before an arrest is made. Here, as elsewhere, the police exercise considerable discretion, and they are more concerned to maintain a reasonable level of peace and quiet in a neighbourhood than to arrest every drunken person. The attitude of the drunken person when told to go home quietly will often determine police action. And no doubt many a drunk staggering homewards has cause to regret being abusive to a policeman who may ask him where his home is. Sometimes the policeman's best endeavours *not* to arrest a man are all for naught.

Example 9. 12.30 a.m.; on patrol in Trafalgar Road (Zone II). We saw a tall, strongly-built man, about 30 years of age, making very heavy weather of the mild incline, his legs following curious rhomboid directions from an obviously clouded but well-intentioned mind. However, it appeared that he was being followed by three younger men about whom the patrolling officer had reason to be suspicious for there had been recent reports of drunks being 'helped' home by well-wishers who had relieved their charges of their wallets for their pains. Accordingly, he decided to speak to the drunken man, find out where he was making for, and whether he was on course so as to assess his capabilities. Also, such a ruse would allow the three men to overtake and go on their way. When spoken to, the man was far from abusive, he mumbled a street name some way hence but was insistent that he could make it and would cause no trouble. Although he was breathing hard, and, slumped uncomfortably against a wall, belied capability for anything but slumber, as the other three had now passed he was told to take care and go on his way. We decided to follow him at a distance. He negotiated two corners safely and caught up with the three who had slackened their pace. He paused to ask them something. We passed on the other side of the road but noticed that the men seemed to direct the man down a cul-de-sac. We turned back, had a curt word with the three men, asked them where they lived, and watched them on their way. We then made our way down the cul-de-sac to find the man stumbling uncertainly back towards the entrance. He was less friendly this time, and was instantly abusive at our approach. When he was told by the P.C. that he would have to be brought into the station he started to shout and argue and cling to the wall which lined the road. The P.C. had to summon a van by radio, bundle the growingly abusive man in, and sit impassively by while the Irishman called him every imaginable name, insulted his race (for he was a Welshman), and begged him to 'put them 'op and fight properly'. In the station, he deigned to have nothing whatever to do with the P.C. and kept up his stream of abuse, while, almost eagerly, answering any question the 'office-man' at the station put to him to fill in the charge-sheet and formally charge him.

Most policemen do not interpret their role as requiring them to arrest every drunken person. If a man is going home quietly and on the pavement, an erratic course is tolerated. Policemen often express concern for the man's safety and will often say, somewhat apologetically, for no great merit attaches to bringing in a drunk, that he had to be brought in for his own safety— the threat of danger coming from motor traffic and from 'drunk-rollers' (wallet-stealers). The police are also very sensitive to the kind of respect that is shown by a man: any abuse or swearing that continues after a warning will almost certainly lead to arrest. Sometimes the reason for arrest is more difficult to explain.

Example 10. About 11 p.m., Saturday evening: a man stumbled into the police station, rang the bell, and was attended to by the sergeant. He held up a slightly cut hand, said he'd fallen over, and wanted attention. He admitted to having been drinking (which was plainly true), insisted that he wasn't drunk and all he wanted was some dressing to his thumb. He was dealt with brusquely, offered 'help', and told to come and sit down round the corner. The man, clearly, I thought, put off by the manner in which he was spoken to, drew back protesting somewhat and said he didn't want to come in, he wasn't going to be arrested, he wasn't drunk. But in he came, was sat down, had his name and address taken, and was charged and in the cell within minutes, bitterly complaining, shouting, and yelling his protest but to no avail. He made rather less noise without his boots on and was given a piece of plaster for his cut thumb. But the 'found drunk' charge was made, and only sleep ended his complaints after about twenty minutes or so. And in the cells he stayed until about 5 a.m. when he could be bailed to appear at court the following Monday morning.

Drunkenness with or without disorder is the major kind of public nuisance and disturbance which the uniformed police officer has to control as part of his duties. The law gives the police adequate powers and they seem resigned to the permanence and regularity of some of their clients—often old and homeless, some of whom may accumulate a series of fines which are never paid but which a short spell in prison will dispose of in a state of greater warmth, better feeding, and increased comfort than is available in the local hostel or lodging-house.

In dealing with street disorders of the kinds referred to above, there is rarely a specific complainant who calls the police: a passer-by may dial 999 if he sees street fighting or finds a body asleep in a doorway; a licensee may, as we have seen, telephone in an emergency; but seldom is there a specific complainant to whom the patrolling officer has to refer. The police patrol and maintain order according to an accustomed pattern, but in the knowledge that if they do not, local residents either singly or collectively may lodge a generalized complaint about the inadequacy of policing in a neighbourhood.[1]

Certain difficulties arise when the police do receive a specific

---

[1] For this, in connexion with the activities of prostitutes, see pp. 75–80.

7

complaint about an event, whether it be a noisy party, a disturbance caused by tenants of the same house, or children playing noisily in the vicinity. In such cases the police will try to reassure the complainant, may appeal to the disturbers, but will acknowledge their limited powers. Although there may technically be a remedy, this is often in the form of an injunction as to future conduct which will do nothing to help the immediate situation; and not infrequently the cause is beyond even that civil remedy.

Example 11. At about 10 p.m. a worried resident from the lodging-house area of Zone II telephoned the police station about a noisy party taking place in the house opposite. This was in a house known to C.I.D. and plainclothes, having recently been purchased by a West Indian whose intention, so the grape-vine said, was to operate an unofficial club holding regular week-end parties. On the night in question, the occasion was thought to be something of a house-warming party. The watch inspector attended, accompanied by a sergeant and two uniformed officers. We found on arrival that although there were people moving to and fro in and out of the house in question there was no undue noise at the scene. We entered and were met by the resident hostess who assumed charge of the proceedings, the volume on the radiogram was lowered slightly, but festivities were in no way interrupted. The house was fairly full; it seemed a good party with music, plenty of people obviously having a good time, helped by a supply of canned beer and dim lighting. The hostess, clearly used to dealing with the police, assured us that everything was in order, pointed out that it was just a party, that they were being careful about the noise level, and so on. She implied that she knew the police would be keeping an eye on the goings-on and gave the impression of being mistress of the whole situation. The inspector explained to her why he was there: he wanted to be sure that they appreciated the feelings of nearby residents who complained, and implied, on his part, that he knew the strength of the situation was perhaps greater than met the eye. We left to visit the complainant opposite. Inside her well-built house, the total absence of noise was apparent and it was clear that she was worried about 'such things going on night after night' and the noise she complained of was that anticipated when the party broke up in the small hours of the morning when she thought car doors and engines would certainly disturb the whole neighbourhood. It was pointed out to her that there was nothing the police could do or should do in this case for it was just another party. She was assured that the police would not be ignoring any new developments in the situation and was told firmly but kindly that her suggestion, that the least that should be done was that all those parked without lights should be 'done', was of no value as far as the police were concerned.

Reassurance and advice, an element of 'showing the flag', and a careful watch on the developing situation are the ways in which the police deal with situations like these.

Drunkenness is the major street disorder the police have to deal with. It is a jurisdiction in which they exercise considerable discretion, only arresting when the circumstances demand, usually attempting to get drunks to go home quietly; those abusive or otherwise acting in disorderly manner or those totally incapable and not infrequently lying unconscious in gutters or doorways account for the majority of such arrests.

Under a local government by-law the police have the power to arrest anyone who commits a disorderly act in a public place. This power was used only sparingly, usually as a last resort measure when persuasion failed. As has been noted, most disorderly behaviour is in connexion with drunkenness. To control singing, shouting, arguments, and other annoyances the police can make an arrest, but the police depend more on persuasion than the exercise of powers—except for crime there is no great value attached to an arrest, so the possession of power to back up a reasonable request is usually found to be sufficient to maintain the peace. Such a use does put a great stress on the policeman's ability to approach, advise, control, and not provoke—in which skills a diversity of abilities was apparent.

Offences of drunkenness, with or without acts of disorder, accounted for 60 per cent of all arrests for non-indictable offences during the four months of the crime survey. In addition there were fourteen incidents leading to the arrest of twenty-nine persons for disorderly acts in a public place made under By-Law 5 of the local Good Rule and Government Act. A further eight incidents involving twelve arrests were made of persons causing wilful damage to property. Over 80 per cent of all such arrests occurred in Zone I (see Table 23).

Within the four areas of Zone I there were marked differ-
ences: there was a lower over-all rate per 10,000 of population in
Sparkbrook (20·5) and the highest rate occurred in Deritend (92).
This could be attributed to the presence in Deritend of a large

TABLE 23: INCIDENTS INVOLVING NON-INDICTABLE
ARREST FOR DRUNKENNESS AND OTHER DISORDER
OFFENCES IN THE THREE ZONES

	Zone I	Zone II	Zone III	'F' division	
	No.	No.	No.	No.	%
Found drunk	106	23	4	133	38
Drunk and disorderly	157	27	7	191	55
Disorderly act	10	2	2	14	4
Wilful damage	7	1	0	8	2
All offences	280	53	13	346	100
Percentage zonal distribution	81	15	4	100	

working men's hostel some of whose tenants seemed to appear
with depressing frequency among those arrested for being drunk.
The area distribution of arrests for disorder and damage was more
even.

TABLE 24: AGES OF OFFENDERS FOR DRUNKENNESS
AND DISORDER OFFENCES

	10–16		17–20		21–30		31+		Total	
	No.	%	No.	%	No.	%	No.	%	No.	%
Found drunk	2	25	7	11	31	25	99	45	139	34
Drunk and disorderly	—	—	44	71	85	68	106	48	235	57
Disorderly act	2	25	10	16	5	4	10	5	27	7
Wilful damage	5	50	1	2	4	3	4	2	14	3
All offences	9	100	62	100	125	100	219	100	415	100
Age distribution (%)	2		15		30		53		100	

The age distribution of offenders in these offence categories
is provided in Table 24. From this it is clear that over 50 per cent
of all such arrests are of older persons, although 15 per cent are
between 17 and 20, and 30 per cent between 21 and 30 years of
age.

Turning to the nationalities (by birth-place) of these offenders,
Table 25 shows the relative proportions. From this there appears

the striking statistic that nearly two-thirds of all arrests for drunkenness are of persons born in Ireland or Northern Ireland. It can be shown that of these, over half are homeless or hostel-livers without a fixed address. It is noticeable that there are very few arrests of coloured immigrants in these categories of offence. Four of the disorder arrests of West Indians arose from a raid on premises where there was thought to be an illicit still operating

TABLE 25: BIRTH-PLACE OF 415 OFFENDERS ARRESTED FOR DRUNKENNESS AND DISORDERS

	No.	%
Birmingham County Borough	65	16
Rest of West Midlands	2	0·5
Rest of England and Wales	44	11
Scotland	29	7
Northern Ireland	46	11
Irish Republic	204	49
West Indies	10	2
India	3	0·7
Pakistan	2	0·5
Europe	7	2
Other or not known	3	0·7
Total	415	100

for the production of a particular alcoholic hooch of a specially favoured Kittitian recipe: the raid was successful and the equipment confiscated by the Customs and Excise police: the offenders' complaints and arguments were such as to constitute disorder.

SUMMARY

Drunkenness is the major kind of street disorder facing the police in the division. Arguments and fights in public houses (or outside) are fairly frequent, though not in every case do the police arrest. Arrests only occur when persuasion to go along quietly fails or is impossible.

Most drunkenness occurs in the area nearest the city centre and a number of arrests are associated with a large hostel for homeless working men in Deritend.

Over half of those arrested are over 30 years old, many are homeless and frequently in court for offences of this kind. Sixty per cent were found to be from Ireland or Northern Ireland.

4. Vice: Prostitution and Drug Trafficking

Research into crime which is concerned with the analysis of crime events has to face up to the fact that reported crime is only a sample of unknown dimensions of all crime. Although with crimes against property it might be assumed that most offences are discovered and reported, the small number of offences which were asked by known offenders to be taken into consideration and for which there had been no complaint notified to the police is a warning against too ready an assumption of this nature (see above, p. 7). Through considering minor incidents it was possible to suggest how recorded violent crime is only a fraction of all violence, where factors of area and class and police procedures affect the final amount recorded as crime. Few offences of drunkenness and disorder are reported to the police for attention. The published statistics are only a measure of police activity; while many instances will go unnoticed, some observed will not be dealt with by prosecution, and those finally recorded, therefore, give no true indication of the extent of the wrong concerned. Explorations of the statistics are fraught with dangers for interpreters.

All these same considerations apply to an even more marked extent in relation to those crimes which are loosely gathered under the general heading of vice—prostitution and allied offences, drug trafficking, and so on, as well as other offences often associated with the vice fringe (e.g., the operations of legal and illegal clubs, gambling and gaming outfits). In some cities the C.I.D. branch of the police, apart from their duties in relation to indictable crime, carry out plainclothes work in this field. In Birmingham investigation is entrusted to divisionally-based squads of men appointed, usually just for one year, from the ranks of uniformed officers. Their duties are directed on a divisional basis by an assistant superintendent and at city level by an assistant chief constable. The kinds of offences with which the plainclothes branch are concerned are often among the most concealed of events. Even if they are visible, they are not any more eradicable. There is an understandable sensitivity about the offences dealt with, for no city wants to publish itself as being vice-ridden and as few of the offences are subject to *specific* citizen complaint an over-active and zealous vice squad can easily bring to light a purely statistical vice-wave. On the other hand, if the police ignore these activities or if the scale of the operation is not in harmony with the demands of the public, generalized complaints can arise which reflect on police activities in this field. Thus this kind of work requires of police organization and administration subtle exercise of discretionary judgement; often this is made acutely difficult by the ambiguities and moral confusion that society at large reflects on these matters. Nowhere is this more apparent than in relation to prostitution.

The activities of prostitutes are restricted to certain areas. On the fringe of the division and included in the area studied is a notorious, nationally-famed area for prostitution, where for many decades the oldest trade has flourished neither unnoticed by the police nor unchecked. Yet its presence and continuity illustrate the curious status of prostitutes and prostitution. Although prostitution is not a crime, to solicit for the purposes of prostitution is an offence. Yet because prostitution is seen as in some way necessary for the health of an imperfect society there is a traditional tolerance of prostitution in certain fairly well defined areas of most cities; the police task is not to eradicate an evil (although in theory this would be legal and possible); by custom their role is a measure of harassment and a continual surveillance lest the evil spread or grow so as to cause nuisance and affront to society at large.

During the period of study there was a total of sixty-five arrests of prostitutes from two main areas. Forty-nine occurred in the Varna Road area of Calthorpe Park or the roads nearby, with a small number from one or two cafés in Balsall Heath which seemed to act as an overspill area at times of great business further down the road; and sixteen occurred in an area of Anderton Park where, in recent years, it would seem that these activities have started up and flourished. The procedure laid down by the Home Office for the arrest of prostitutes is that the girl must be cautioned on two occasions prior to being arrested. This means that arrests can only be made by certain specialist officers who have to maintain observations and records so that third offenders can be identified. It also means that girls from one area are likely to keep on the move, never staying so long in one place as to risk arrest. But arrest and court appearance would seem to be of only slight deterrent value for fines are quickly earned and courts are loath to commit prostitutes to prison: few prostitutes respond to offers of help from probation officers or social workers, although a disturbed and distressed minority, often casual participants in the game, appear among those on probation. The majority of prostitutes would seem to be in many respects adequate and capable people, without any deep motivation to change their way of life.

Similarly, persons suspected of running a brothel are by custom warned that they are suspected and may be the subject of inquiries, observation, and prosecution. The courts seem to demand a high level of proof and evidence which requires the police to continue observations over a period of time and effect a raid only when a known prostitute is entertaining a client and when the brothel-keeper is present and can be shown to know what is happening. Likewise, evidence to prove a charge of living on immoral earnings is frequently difficult to obtain.

The plainclothes branch of the police in maintaining a surveillance effect a steady number of arrests which bear little relation to the true extent of prostitution in an area. In a street like Varna Road some houses are so well known that there is limited need for a prostitute to solicit: at peak times a virtual queue forms and the number of cars circling the area with clients or sightseers is great. The pattern of activity in Varna Road is distinctive from that in Anderton Park. In the Varna Road area, prostitutes and clients use rooms in the houses and solicit from windows, doors, or in the street. The road is busy with customers day and night who arrive by car, lorry, bus, or on foot: some arrive drunk, and assault or accost any woman in sight or knock on doors of houses unoccupied by the girls. Many of the houses in the streets in the area are occupied by immigrant families and their children, who have to live amid the throng and bustle of the prostitutes and their clients.

In Anderton Park it is less intrusive, less obvious: the girls solicit by waiting on street corners for a pick-up from a motorist. They then drive to a secluded spot rather than to a room in a house, although there was one house in the area which the police observed for a time, recently raided, and got a conviction against an Englishwoman for keeping a brothel. One arrest was also made of an Englishman for living off the immoral earnings of his English prostitute wife.

In neither area is there any high-class call-girl style prostitution operating, although it is thought that in the one other area of the city where arrests of prostitutes do occur, prostitution is rather more sophisticated and expensive than that in the squalor and dirt of Varna Road or that which goes on in cars in Anderton Park.

A small number of arrests occurred in Balsall Heath where it was acknowledged that prostitutes worked from one or two cafés and used rooms in nearby houses or solicited for a pick-up from a passing motorist. Prostitution was also known to occur in Sparkbrook, from one or two cafés and using rooms among the lodging-houses in the area; but during the period during which data were collected no arrests were made. It was publicity from the Varna Road area that sparked off considerable public debate in the summer of 1967 about whether Birmingham should sponsor municipally controlled and licensed brothels. Here is not the place to describe that debate at any length, but it is instructive to consider the position of the police. The controversy followed moves by residents in the Varna Road area—largely Indians and Pakistanis—through the local area residents' association, to obtain a larger measure of police action in the area. This led to the Corporation announcing that within two years the area was, anyway, to be redeveloped. Thus the initial cause can be seen as a failure on the part of the police to control prostitution sufficiently. Undoubtedly this was exacerbated by Varna Road being an area traditionally associated with vice and therefore 'tolerated' by residents. The immigrant newcomers to the area markedly changed the social composition of the area but only with time did they articulate an untraditional intolerance of the activities in their neighbouring houses. The situation seems to have been further exacerbated by a small number of immigrants who partially took over the traditional role of brothel-keepers and landlords, whereby the whole immigrant community in the area tended to be imputed to tolerate the activities of the prostitutes. It seems likely that there may have been, if anything, a lessening of police surveillance (due as much to increasing manpower shortage as anything else) which, when sensed by the immigrant majority, led to their complaint.

But the controversy which raged in the columns of the local Press in Birmingham in 1967 was not directly concerned with the appalling conditions existing in Varna Road. It was more concerned with what would happen in nearby Anderton Park when the bulldozers finally put Varna Road on the level. The local Anderton Park residents' association voiced urgent pleas for the saving of their area; not without cause, as prostitution, as the arrest figures suggest, is active in that area even if of a different kind from that in Varna Road. It is likely that brothel-keepers may move in, among whom may be some coloured immigrants. Again, the growth of prostitution may be linked with aspects of decline and decay in an area that people tend to associate with the arrival of coloured immigrants. Again, the white residents in the area may be inclined and encouraged to associate the majority of immigrants with the activities of a minority, and the unwarranted assumption of vice being linked to coloured immigration may be bolstered rather than countered. The attitudes and procedures which allowed the Varna Road situation to develop in the past could repeat themselves. The task of the police would seem clearly to be to impute no tolerance of prostitution to any sector of the resident population and prosecute their task of harassment with vigour. So long as society's view of prostitution remains in its current ambiguous state, the task of controlling and checking its visibility falls to the police. What is intolerable is for residential areas to have to suffer in the Varna Road tradition. Increasingly the housing market is such that certain sectors of the population cannot choose to live where they would but must go where the market allows: thus were the Pakistanis and Indians forced to live among the prostitutes of Varna Road.

The issue of prostitution and its policing shows the way in which a Police Force has to be sensitive to the needs of the community it serves. Without specific citizen complainants the police exercise an administrative discretion in judging what a community needs in terms of police action. What is particularly significant, for the purposes of this study, is that in this instance it was a mixed racial community whose needs have to be assessed; and the same will apply to any police decisions in Anderton Park. The danger is, of course, that the police may be inclined to react to a generalized and invidious racial stereotype and reflect the attitudes of one sector—the white sector—of the community at large.

Prostitution is often linked with immigrants (particularly with coloured immigrants) in a number of ways. The police had some evidence that among those living with prostitutes were a number of Asians and West Indians; there was some evidence

that highly influential among owners of houses used for prostitution in Varna Road, and for controlling the girls' activities, was
one somewhat notorious Kashmiri family. Among the clients of
prostitutes, the great majority would seem to be English business-
men, travelling salesmen, lorry drivers, and so on, with a minority
of Irish and Asian immigrants. The infrequency of West Indians
among prostitutes' clients was remarked upon by observers.

There is nothing surprising in this pattern. Prostitution might
be thought of as normal for a population deprived of other sexual
contact; thus it is a tolerated and normal aspect of garrison and
seaport towns, in wartime, and wherever there is a predominantly
male and transient population lacking a normal home life. Also
needing this service will be a minority, sexually deviant or
inadequate, or who through marital breakdown or for some other
reason are incapable of achieving a normal sexual relationship.
Among the immigrant groups there may be a marked imbalance
in the sex ratio of the group: this is certainly the case with the
Asian immigrant group, where men outnumber women by
seventy-five to one. Among West Indians the imbalance is less
marked and even less marked among the Irish group.

For some coloured immigrants who arrive in this country
with hopes of miscegenation, the prevailing anti-colour social
context may mean that marriage or cohabitation is impossible
except with a deviant or near-deviant minority of white women
among whom may be some prostitutes. And this minority of
women, many of whom are virtual social outcasts, may find it
impossible to obtain acceptance except with members of a male
out-group, of deviants and criminals, or with coloured immigrants.
For some Asian immigrants a temporary liaison during a period
of separation from wife and children left in the homeland may be
required and be obtainable only with a prostitute. For this kind
of reason it is to be expected that in the first years of a large-scale
immigration a minority of coloured immigrants (and it needs to
be stressed that the numbers involved *are* only a fraction of the
whole population) will be associated with prostitutes, particularly
when it is remembered that the housing market operates so that
immigrants are restricted to areas of the city and to a housing type
that are also those providing the only living accommodation for
poor and underprivileged white families, deviants, and social
outcasts.

As for the prostitutes themselves, Table 26 sets out the nationality by birth-place of the sixty-two arrested during the period of study.[1]

TABLE 26: NATIONALITY OF 62 PROSTITUTES ARRESTED FOR SOLICITING

Nationality	No.	%
England and Wales	42	68
Scotland	6	9·5
Ireland*	11	17·5
West Indies	3	5
Total	62	100

* The high proportion of Irish prostitutes compares with the findings of an Irish survey made in 1961 in Birmingham which found among prostitutes the proportion of those of Irish birth to be 12·5 per cent. See Matthew Russell, 'The Irish Delinquent in Britain', *Studies* (University of Dublin, June 1964).

If a prevailing moral ambiguity poses problems for the police in relation to prostitution, uncertainty due to widespread and official ignorance pervades police work in relation to drugs, the other major aspect of the work of the plainclothes police. Unlawful possession of dangerous drugs is the offence, not addiction, but the police are more concerned with the pushers and suppliers of drugs, to check their widespread use. Again, this is a topic which has aroused great controversy and public debate which adds difficulties to those who have to administer the law as it stands. Although many substances of different and disputed degrees and kinds of danger are included in the category of dangerous drugs, it is thought that their illegal distribution shares a common market. Some of the drugs, for example, cannabis, know no legal outlets; others are of widespread manufacture and distribution through normal pharmaceutical channels. Thus the sources may be distinct, even if the illegal outlets are shared: the large number of addicts who have started on the mild non-addictive drugs further testifies to this market link. This is not of course to suggest a causative link in gradation from soft to hard drugs but that the world of contact with the soft also provides contact with suppliers of hard drugs for that minority destined to be dissatisfied with all stimulants except the addictive. The task of

[1] Three of these 62 were arrested on two occasions during the study period, thus accounting for 65 arrests (see p. 75).

the police is to chart this underworld and secure the sources. Their work locally—now supplemented by a city drug squad particularly concerned with hard drug addiction—is in connexion with pills (amphetamines) and with cannabis. These three kinds seem largely to involve distinct populations, though sharing a common black market of distribution.

Amphetamines are widely manufactured, distributed, and prescribed. Their illegal distribution follows thefts from warehouses or from persons managing to obtain large doses through a series of legitimate prescriptions. In connexion with these, local plainclothes police achieved a notable coup in the arrest of two young men, one of whom on no less than three occasions in the course of a few months was able to break and enter a local pharmaceutical warehouse and obtain some seventy or eighty thousand amphetamines. By extraordinarily patient work over several months, the police, by picking up clues and links in cafés and other places, and by skilful use of informants, not only effected the arrests but recovered the bulk of the products. This case did suggest that no small contributor to the current craze for pills is their ease of availability through non-criminal and relatively disorganized outlets.[1]

It is by no means clear whether there are distinct sources and suppliers of drugs for the local West Indian and Asian market and for the increasing numbers of (mainly young) white takers. There are few coloured immigrants among heroin addicts in this country which suggests how the kind of use made of a drug, the way it is supplied, and the purpose to which it is put, are more important than any inevitable and inexorable tendency for takers to graduate from the mild 'high' of 'pot' to the frightening dependence and addiction to heroin. Addicts who report that they started on cannabis are likely to be exposed to sources of more dangerous drugs which they utilize when the mild euphoria of marijuana is no longer sufficient for their need.[2] What does seem distinctive is the use of the drug: among an English population it seems a teen-age or student cult phenomenon associated with rebelliousness and non-conformity. Among immigrants it is a mild

[1] The frequency of such cases has led to recent legislation to enforce stricter security safeguards at pharmaceutical factories, warehouses, and depots.

[2] See T. H. Bewley, 'Recent Changes in the Pattern of Drug-abuse in the United Kingdom', *Bulletin of Narcotics* (October–December 1966).

enjoyment for a minority, is usually associated with clubs and parties, is taken by a fairly normal adult population, in a manner not unlike that of his white neighbour's enjoyment of alcohol.[1] It may be that its distribution is only contemplated and effected by an already delinquent few of that minority of the coloured population prepared to run the risk of the severe sanctions that are liable to follow prosecution. Certainly the nature of the distribution involves the police in much labour for small returns in places where they are as conspicuous as detectives in a bad old film; and they are dependent upon informants and patience to effect the occasional raid. During the study period four West Indians and one Nigerian were arrested for possessing cannabis. The involvement of coloured immigrants in pushing or taking the other kinds of drugs is minimal.

Age rather than colour makes for police conspicuousness in the centres where amphetamine pills circulate. It also seems that quite considerable numbers are taken by prostitutes, and during the period two arrests of persons on the fringe of the prostitution world were made for possessing quite large quantities of pills (probably part of the haul from the local warehouse mentioned earlier).

Heroin addiction poses severe and distinct problems for the police, such that a city-based drug squad is primarily concerned rather than local plainclothes personnel. With the growing stress on treatment rather than punishment for the unfortunate few, the police are increasingly concerned to ferret out the sources, prosecute the pushers, and save the addicts. This requires them to keep a close watch on places where the drugs are likely to circulate—which leads to the other main sphere of activity for the plainclothes police: that concerned with a surveillance of clubs and other places of licensed entertainment.

The use of drugs—especially the socially mild 'dangerous' drugs—is associated in policing with related infringements of our very complex licensing laws. It is the task of the plainclothes police to maintain some kind of check on licensed club premises and a watch for illegal and unlicensed unofficial clubs starting in the area. In association with Customs and Excise agents they must

[1] This whole topic—complex and controversial—has as yet received little systematic inquiry. Rev. Kenneth Leech has investigated the topic and reports a not contradictory opinion in a letter to the Institute of Race Relations *News Letter* (October–November 1967), pp. 424–5.

also maintain a watch for any illicit distilling of home-brewed alcoholic liquor. These are all tasks which require particular skills of patience and perception; few are of the sort that bring specific public complaints demanding police action; all require a measure of police discretion before action is taken for there is scope both to persecute a technically illegal but actually harmless set of socially necessary actions, and to create an aura of a vice area by over-activity. Sometimes the police may seem to act according to the letter rather than the spirit of the law and find themselves in situations which might be thought not to merit police action and hardly improve police–public relations.

Example 12. The problems facing anyone who wants to provide public entertainment on a regular footing *and* serve alcoholic drink to patrons are very great. Licensed houses can charge no entrance fee and few are suited to provide sophisticated modern entertainment which to be high-class requires large fees. One answer is to open a club which, providing rules as to members and visitors are honoured, is free of a great many of the restrictions which surround normal licensed premises. But the more modest the aims of an establishment, the greater the difficulties. In a suburb in the area under study is a club which, under a variety of names, seeks to provide inexpensive entertainment for the young (mainly under 25) clientele *and* serve drinks. In its most recent form it obtained a complicated supper licence which allowed patrons to have a drink before, a drink during, and (perhaps) a drink after the meal. Furthermore, the licence recognized that the establishment was for dining and dancing. For a moderate entrance fee, people were entitled to a fairly plain meal and to listen and dance to the music; drinks were obtainable from a bar. Police observations suggested that the bar was being used by anyone at any time during the evening's entertainment in contravention of the licence. A raid was planned at which, by questioning customers, it was hoped to gain evidence of the contraventions. The plan was to enter the premises, effectively end the proceedings, and question each person present as to what and where and when they had drunk and danced and dined during the evening. Entertainment had been scheduled for 8.00 p.m.–2.00 a.m., the police raid was made between 11.30 p.m. and midnight.

The premises are not very large and on this night in question were well filled, for the group playing were a nationally known local group of great appeal. What followed on the police raid can only be described as pandemonium, for, in an otherwise very well-planned action, the numbers present had been underestimated and in the limited space it was impossible to promote orderly queues to the five or six officers interviewing persons as they left. It was a near impossible task to interview persons pushed and shoved from behind by a mass of persons clamouring to know what was going on. For a quarter of an hour things were unpleasantly chaotic during which a handful of interviewers left, but in which it was by no means clear if the management were refunding entrance monies or hoping to recommence with music and dancing once the police left. A modicum of order was restored when, on the advice of the police, the music was started again, and the crowds eased back on to the dance floor. Throughout, the bar remained busily open. For a time it looked as if the proceedings might be extended in time by the management themselves interviewing each customer and asking for an opinion of how the club was run. This idea was not continued—but the police stayed at their posts and during about two and a half hours managed to obtain some 300 statements from which to assess the extent of any contravention.

It seems not unreasonable to wonder whether the exercise of discretion in this instance to seek prosecution by performing an elaborate raid can be justified as serving any definable social purpose or in any way furthering the needs of a community or reflecting the wishes of anyone but the senior police officer involved. In other aspects of the work of the plainclothes section, such considerations can be seen to be uppermost in determining what police action is socially desirable.

SUMMARY

The work of the plainclothes police in checking on the activities of prostitutes, drug users, and licensees of clubs and other premises is subtle and demanding and particularly unproductive of crime statistics.

The nature of prostitution and its location in well defined areas require that the police balance persecution and permissiveness, and may lead to criticisms by the residents of areas where prostitution occurs. There may be a tendency to associate prostitution with coloured immigrants in a way that ignores the needs of the vast majority of immigrants whose children and families may be forced by the operations of the housing market to live in areas where prostitutes may thrive. Such a situation highlights how Police Forces need to be aware of the legitimate needs and demands of a resident population in traditionally bad areas.

Sixty-five arrests of prostitutes were made during the study period. Because of the rule that prostitutes must be cautioned twice and only arrested on the third or subsequent occasion, such a figure bears no relation to the widespread extent of prostitution, particularly in the notorious area of the division. During the period one person was arrested for living on the immoral earnings of a prostitute and one person was prosecuted for keeping a brothel.

Drug trafficking likewise poses considerable problems for the police who have to operate in places where only a complex game, much dependent upon informers, allows the occasional raid and arrest. Amphetamines involve the police in a largely juvenile clientele in cafés and clubs, although there is also a considerable market for such drugs among prostitutes. Cannabis, although gaining more widespread use with English people, is associated with West Indian and Asian immigrants, a minority of whom in certain defined areas indulge in the use of this drug. Four West Indians and one Nigerian were arrested for possessing cannabis during the four-month study period.

Supervision of licensed premises leads to fairly frequent visits, checks, and raids by the police both to warn proprietors and to gain evidence for prosecutions. Again this is a sphere where there is unlikely to be a complaint to the police which initiates action; it is up to the police to maintain surveillance and judge when and where action is appropriate.

5. *Motoring Offences and Other Crimes*

Jurisdiction of motoring offences is interesting because of the extent of police discretion: it is recognized that if the police chose to prosecute every known driving offender the administrative and court system would be snarled up in a massive traffic jam greater than anything experienced even on the Exeter by-pass. Thus there

8

is considerable selection of offenders and offences to prosecute, a fairly widespread use of the caution, and a great deal of informal warning. Potentially there is scope for discriminatory action by individual police officers in selecting certain categories of offenders for prosecution such that almost anyone can claim to have been picked on for 'special' treatment.

There is in Birmingham a body of police officers with special responsibilities for matters relating to motoring offences, accidents, and road safety. They constitute a special mobile division directed from city Police Headquarters, although they are given patrolling duties which correspond to divisional boundaries, and administrative matters relating to motoring offences are dealt with on a divisional basis. Divisional personnel form a divisional accident inquiry squad who investigate incidents, take statements, and prepare dossiers for the more serious motoring offences like those for careless or dangerous driving. Apart from these specialized units, patrolling officers and the crews of area cars spend a not inconsiderable part of their time with matters relating to motoring offenders. It is a routine procedure at most traffic incidents, whether there has been an infringement of the law or not, to issue the driver of a vehicle with a form requiring him to produce at a police station of his choice, within five days of the event, licence, insurance, and test certificate documents relating to himself and his vehicle, unless he is able to show them to the officer at the time. This procedure brings to light a number of infringements and probably acts as a deterrent for those inclined to risk motoring without tax, licence, or insurance.

An out-of-date road fund licence may attract the attention of a patrolling officer and lead him to trace the owner of the vehicle and make inquiries. Different officers have different attitudes: some seem almost to specialize in such infringements; others remarked that they thought there were more vital aspects to their job and would only bother with vehicles if some particular incident caught their attention. Among the crime data are a number of cases of thefts of road fund licences which came to light through observant patrolling officers finding them fraudulently displayed on vehicles to which they did not apply. It was difficult to discover a common attitude towards this category of motoring offences—it was generally admitted that if the police cared to, they could occupy all of the twenty-four hours of the day dealing with traffic, for checking vehicles and addresses can be a time-consuming business and if you try hard enough you can find *some* infringement. Birmingham, unlike some other cities, requires cars to be parked with lights in all hours of darkness; as there are many more cars than garages or off-street parking places, this measure is popular with no one, except perhaps the manufacturers of parking lights. Occasional purges on some streets were made, and persons cautioned by patrolling officers. But not surprisingly this work is intensely unpopular with all ranks of policemen (many of whom, anyway, admitted parking their own cars outside their own homes without lights).

Area car crews understandably deal with a different kind of motoring offence than do patrolling officers (though such offences may reveal, as I have indicated, other infringements). As with disorderly offences, the police exercise considerable discretion in whom they report for process and whom they caution or warn. Some car crews more than others would stop cars which had manoeuvred badly or behaved oddly to give the driver advice in varying degrees of friendliness; most were more inclined to warn speeders than report them, depending, it seemed, much on the manner in which the person responded. It was interesting to find that the same kinds of considerations as apply to drunks apply to speeding drivers: policemen are prepared to tolerate drunkenness and speeding but not disrespect from either category of person. They would argue that a 'respectful' drunk is making his way home quietly and is not causing any disorder: less plausible is the argument that the respectful speeder is likely to go on his way within the speed limit in future. Such discretionary power is needed, it is argued, for two main reasons: if the police prosecuted every motoring offender, administration would be impossible; secondly, the police jurisdiction of motoring offenders brings them into a frequent contact with a non-criminal section of the public whose support the police need and would lose if they routinely prosecuted all—they want to be seen as reasonable men doing a difficult job and they bargain for respect with the implied threat of 'giving a ticket'.

An attempt to distinguish the work of a mobile area car crew and the patrolling officer or office administration in the jurisdiction of motoring offenders was made in a survey of 500 motoring offenders occurring in the approximate four-month period. These

500 constituted a census of all motoring offences (except speeding offences arising from a radar check, and simple parking and 'no-lights' infringements) which were dealt with by the divisional administrative office. Nationality of the offender was determined by circularizing each officer reporting an incident with particulars of the infringement and asking him to indicate to which nationality the person belonged: English, Irish, West Indian, Indian, Pakistani, European, other, or not known. The circular met with full and prompt response and collection of these data ceased as soon as 500 returned forms were at hand.

Three main categories of offence were noted: (a) those involving just driving offences—speeding or careless driving or failing to stop at a halt sign or other traffic direction; (b) those involving administrative offences—driving without a licence or insurance or a vehicle excise licence; and (c) those involving both kinds of offences.

The distribution of these three categories by the nationality of the offender is shown in Table 27.

TABLE 27: NATIONALITY OF MOTORING OFFENDERS
IN THE THREE CATEGORIES OF OFFENCE

Category	English	Irish	West Indian	Asian	Other	Total	
a. Driving	210	11	12	6	7	246	(49%)
b. Administrative	146	33	12	24	6	221	(44%)
c. Mixed	20	8	3	2	—	33	(7%)
Total	476 (75%)	52 (10%)	27 (5%)	32 (6%)	13 (3%)	500	

There is a marked tendency for Irish and Asian motoring offenders (but not West Indians) to be over-represented in the administrative category—offences for driving without licence, tax, or insurance. All nationality groups showed a similar propensity for straightforward driving offences.

Assessment of comparable rates is, as always, problematical. Not all these offenders were resident in the division, although 256 (51 per cent) were. Not surprisingly, rather more of those prosecuted for administrative offences were residents (64 per cent). On the assumption that the residents are a representative sample of motoring offenders and distinguishing 'motoring' and 'administrative' offenders, some comparisons are possible.

Again it will be noted that there is a more marked over-representation of immigrant offenders in the administrative category of offence associated with patrolling beat officers rather than mobile patrols. There was a marked tendency for more of such offences to occur in Zone I where there is a proportionately greater number of immigrants at risk. But even so there is evidence that all immigrants appear to be more frequently prosecuted for

TABLE 28: PROPORTIONS OF RESIDENT MOTORING OFFENDERS OF EACH NATIONALITY IN TWO BROAD CATEGORIES OF MOTORING OFFENCE (%)

Category	English	Irish	West Indian	Asian	Other	Total	Number of offenders
a. Motoring offences	75	8	6	4	6	100	114
b. Administrative offences	63	15·5	6	13·5	2	100	142
Total	69	12	6	9	4	100	256
Estimated % resident in division	86·7	6·7	3·9	2·7	—	100	

motoring offences than the native population. Without comparable figures for those warned or cautioned it is of course impossible to assess comparative rates of incidence of such offences. But, in so far as offences involving licensing infringements are both widespread *and* unlikely to escape prosecution if observed, the marked degree of Irish and Asian over-representation in these categories shown by the above may be thought to present something of a realistic picture of the situation. If a larger proportion of immigrants are in the car-owning age group than the over-all non-immigrant population, this would reduce any over-representation of the immigrants among the motoring offenders. Both Irish and Asian immigrants (but not West Indians) are over-represented among those prosecuted for failing to tax, insure, or licence themselves or their vehicles. Without further information it is impossible to say whether such evasion of duty is actually more widespread among those groups or whether the system of prosecution selects persons from immigrant areas with a greater frequency than other areas where such infringements may be as widespread but more unnoticed.

During a similar period forty arrests were made which led to charges of driving while under the influence of drink. Of these, twenty were persons born in England, Wales, or Scotland, two were Northern Irish, seventeen were Irish, and one was an Indian. The large number of Irish is very striking and to be seen in relation to the large proportion of Irish among those arrested for drunkenness (see pp. 73–5).

OTHER CRIMES

Also included in the crime survey were certain other offences not dealt with in the foregoing sections.

Thirty-eight young persons—thirty-two English, six Irish—were taken to court for taking and driving away motor vehicles. In nine of such incidents, the persons were also charged with stealing property from the vehicle concerned.

Forty of the persons arrested for non-indictable offences and bailed to make a court appearance failed to do so and were the subject of a further arrest: twenty-six were English, thirteen were from Ireland or Northern Ireland, and one was an Indian.

Three persons were arrested on a warrant and committed to prison for failing to maintain a wife as directed by a Court Order: two were English, one was Irish.

Four persons were arrested for wandering abroad under the Vagrancy Act: two English and two Irish.

One Englishman was arrested for begging.

There was a small number of forgery offences—usually of postal drafts; there was one charge against a man for abstracting electricity illegally by by-passing his meter; one man was charged with offences under the Moneylenders Act by illegally advertising for investors to deposit monies with him.

Not included in the survey were charges relating to infringements of the Licensing Acts (three cases) and charges relating to the illicit distillation of alcohol (one case involving a group of West Indians in Sparkbrook).

There were other sundry charges brought by the police against various persons for such things as depositing litter, discharging a fire-arm in public, keeping a ferocious and unmuzzled dog, failing to have a dog licence, one or two cases of indecent exposure, and one case involving a deserter from the Armed Forces.

CHAPTER 3

Criminal Areas

1. *Migration, Housing, and Immigrant Areas*

The description of the division's crime in a number of points shows the uneven distribution of crime events of various kinds in the different areas of the division. At one level of explanation it is fairly obvious that there will be more thefts from cars wherever more cars are parked and there can only be thefts from gas or electric meters in areas where there are houses with gas and electric meters to be broken open. But if, as can be shown, various kinds of crime and disorder are persistently more prevalent in some kinds of areas than others, such findings can add to our understanding of crime as a social phenomenon and reflect the kind of security and stability, the kind and quality of community that exists in areas of a city. Such findings may also deepen our awareness of the meaning and causes of crime and throw some light on its due social treatment.

If crime is the result of certain typical living conditions, a study of those conditions is necessary for an understanding of comparative rates of involvement in crime of different categories of persons. In assessing comparative rates of crime among immigrant populations there is a need to explore the extent to which the pattern of settlement of immigrants in a city associates immigrants with areas where crime and disorder are prevalent, and whether immigrants share in the life style of an area (and therefore in the crime and disorder) or whether the immigrant life style is distinctive within areas of crime and protects the immigrant group from any widespread criminality.

At the outset of the analysis of the divisional crime profile, eleven areas in three zones were described to provide a convenient basis for a description of crime events (see pp. 8–18). It needs to be stressed that it is not intended that the zonal boundaries or the areas are significant as defining separate natural areas; they are boundaries of convenience, encircling areas which seemed to the researcher likely to show variations in rates of crime and disorder, and provide a means of relating crime and disorder to various other social factors existing in the areas. In what follows these factors are used to describe the area with rather more precision so as to identify immigrant areas of the division; thereafter the variations in crime and disorder between the areas can be explored. Following this, by considering the areas of residence of offenders and their nationalities, it will be possible to explore the extent to which immigrants live in criminal areas and the extent to which immigrants are involved in crime.

The social composition of the division studied can only be understood with some reference to the situation in Birmingham as a whole.

Birmingham has a declining population. It had some 20,000 fewer in 1966 than in 1961.[1] As there was a natural increase of 50,000 more births than deaths in this period, the decline is due to outward migration. At the same time, the population in areas peripheral to the conurbation is increasing substantially: there was a 50 per cent increase from 1947 to 1966 in the areas of the conurbation outside Birmingham and the Black Country County Boroughs. Though there is some dispersal of industry in the West Midlands, it was the despair of the regional study[2] that in the short run there would be little industrial relocation to

[1] Note on 1961 and 1966 Census information.

1961 was a 100 per cent census, while 1966 was a 10 per cent census. Interpretation of the results of the 1966 Census, in addition to the difficulties associated with definitions and reliability of information from individual dwellings, must take account of bias and errors in the 10 per cent sampling. Thus both 1961 and 1966 Censuses may well have underenumerated, for instance, the number of immigrants in individual lodging-houses, who feared official reprisals for reported overcrowding. But results published to date for the 1966 Census suggest, in addition, that something less than a 10 per cent sample was taken, and there was probable over-all underenumeration in the order of 1–2 per cent of the total population. It is suggested that errors derive chiefly from the sampling frame, which was the 1961 Census, supposedly brought up-to-date with additional rateable dwellings since 1961. Errors are likely to have occurred either in relation to new buildings or in relation to subdivision of existing buildings.

All figures from the 1966 Census used in this study are multiplied by a factor of 102 per cent, to make them more comparable as a whole with the 1961 Census. But the distribution of error between different sorts of housing and different sections of the population can only be guessed at. Figures must therefore be treated with great caution. Implications of possible bias are discussed in the text.

[2] Department of Economic Affairs, *The West Midlands: a regional study* (London, H.M.S.O., 1965).

complement the urgent need for dispersal of population from the overcrowded centre of the conurbation. The study could only suggest perpetuating and rationalizing the existing tide of commuter development. But not all can afford to buy or rent new housing outside Birmingham, and cover the costs of the long journey to work. Hence a situation arises in which a sustained demand for labour continues to attract lower-paid workers to work and live in overcrowded Birmingham, while the more affluent move out and commute.

Something of the contrast implied in this process is shown in Table 29 which sets out the proportions in four socio-economic class groups of the population moving into Birmingham in the year 1960–1 compared with those for the population moving out of Birmingham into the adjoining Municipal Borough of Solihull.

TABLE 29: PERCENTAGES IN EACH OF FOUR CLASSES AMONG MOVERS INTO BIRMINGHAM COMPARED WITH MOVERS FROM BIRMINGHAM TO SOLIHULL IN THE YEAR 1960–1.

Area	Professional and managerial	Intermediate and junior non-managerial	Skilled manual	Semi and unskilled manual
Into Birmingham County Borough	11	17	36	24
From Birmingham to Solihull Municipal Borough	45	23	20	6

Source: 1961 Population Census.

This tendency is mirrored in the pattern of movement within Birmingham, where there is considerable internal migration of persons from one part of the city to another and substantial migration of persons into the city. But the areas of these two kinds of migration are fairly distinctive, as is indicated in Maps 3 and 4. Migrants into Birmingham from elsewhere were moving in the main to parts of Calthorpe Park, Balsall Heath, and Sparkbrook, Anderton Park and Moseley, and Hall Green. Movers within Birmingham were more widely distributed; large areas show between 20 and 30 per cent population change; some specific areas—in Deritend, Calthorpe Park, and Balsall Heath (but in

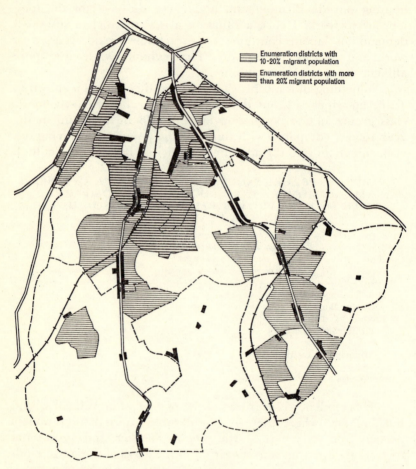

Map 3. Areas of migration (1): persons moving *into* the local authority area during the five years prior to the 1966 Census.

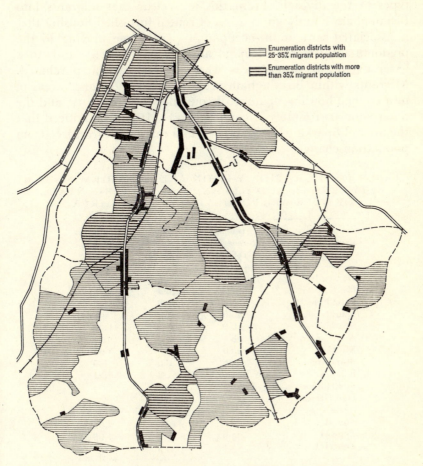

Map 4. Areas of migration (2): persons moving *within* the local authority area during the five years prior to the 1966 Census.

different parts from the other movers), in Moseley, Billesley, and Fox Hollies—show a rate in excess of 35 per cent. This pattern is rendered somewhat more explicable if compared with Maps 5 and 6 which show the distribution of the principal housing tenure types in the division. From this it is clear that migrants into Birmingham mainly go to areas of rented furnished housing that is associated with multi-occupation (with some moving to the predominantly owner-occupied area of Hall Green), and, to a lesser extent, to outer areas where houses can be purchased. Migrants within Birmingham are associated with inner areas of new council housing, 'patched'[1] council-owned property, and the outer suburban estates of council houses. It will be noticed that the area of Sparkhill in Zone II is, to a marked degree, free from population change.

TABLE 30: MIGRATION WITHIN AND INTO BIRMINGHAM
BETWEEN 1961 AND 1966 AND IN 1966—PERCENTAGE
OF OVER-ALL POPULATION IN EACH AREA

Area	Within Birmingham 1961–6	Into Birmingham 1961–6	Into or within April 1965– April 1966
Deritend	33·1	5·5	11·3
Calthorpe Park	32·5	20·2	24·9
Balsall Heath	30·0	12·8	14·8
Sparkbrook	20·8	11·1	9·4
Sparkhill	16·8	8·5	9·7
Anderton Park	28·3	22·8	21·0
Moseley	27·8	11·9	14·2
Brandwood	23·6	6·0	8·6
Billesley	24·5	2·8	8·2
Fox Hollies	23·3	4·3	7·7
Hall Green	19·6	10·0	7·7
Zone I	26·0	11·5	12·5
Zone II	23·9	12·2	13·5
Zone III	23·1	5·3	8·1
Division	24·2	8·9	10·8
Birmingham County Borough	23·8	6·9	10·1

[1] 'Patched' houses are old houses which have come into council ownership and are used to house some categories of council tenants. The houses are frequently sub-standard houses in development areas.

Table 30 sets out proportions of the population who have moved in the five years preceding the 1966 Census, together with a measure of population change in the year preceding the 1966 Census. This latter figure suggests how there is a considerable movement of population in Calthorpe Park and Anderton Park.

TABLE 31: PERCENTAGE OF HOUSEHOLDS BY FOUR TENURE CATEGORIES IN THE ELEVEN AREAS IN ZONES AND DIVISION COMPARED WITH THE OVER-ALL PERCENTAGE FOR THE CITY, 1961 AND 1966

	Owner-occupied		L.A. rented		Privately rented unfurnished		Privately rented furnished		Number of households	
	1961	1966	1961	1966	1961	1966	1961	1966	1961	1966
Deritend	2	1	70	83	18	9	3	1	3,450	3,120
Calthorpe Park	24	20	9	21	16	16	47	42	1,939	2,200
Balsall Heath	17	20	33	40	33	23	14	13	5,370	4,180
Sparkbrook	25	31	6	19	51	34	15	13	12,196	11,270
Sparkhill	51	54	5	6	33	33	8	4	5,963	6,030
Anderton Park	30	28	3	3	26	25	39	42	2,599	2,330
Moseley	52	50	8	11	23	21	14	16	8,052	9,070
Brandwood	49	53	34	34	13	8	2	3	10,034	10,210
Billesley and Fox Hollies	28	26	64	65	6	6	2	1	17,328	17,830
Hall Green	81	84	2	3	13	10	2	2	4,677	5,660
Zone I	20	23	22	33	39	26	16	15	22,955	20,780
Zone II	48	48	6	8	27	26	16	16	16,614	17,420
Zone III	42	44	45	45	9	8	2	2	32,039	33,700
'F' Division	36	39	29	33	23	17	10	9	71,608	71,900
Birmingham County Borough	35	38	35	39	21	16	6	6	333,033	339,470

Table 31 sets out the percentage area and zonal distribution of the four main tenure types in the division for both the 1961 and 1966 Censuses. Apart from indicating distinctions in the pattern of migration, Table 31 is interesting in the light it throws on the state of housing that is available for those attracted to work in Birmingham.

Table 31 notes a marked reduction in households in Zone I with increases in the other two zones. In each of the areas of Zone I the proportion of council house tenants increased as the council provided new houses and flats or bought up old terraced houses, formerly in owner occupation or privately let. Deritend, Calthorpe Park, and part of Balsall Heath are subject to comprehensive redevelopment; Sparkbrook, though subject to much purchase by the council of old terraced properties to let to tenants, is not subject to any planned redevelopment, hence the steady rise in owner occupation as tenants of formerly privately let properties buy their houses or move to better areas. Council housing has

Map 5. Tenure (1): areas of owner occupation and council housing in the division.

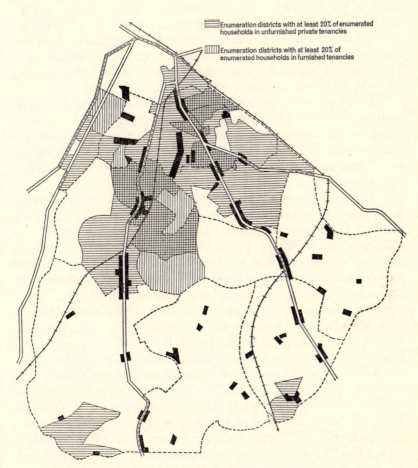

Map 6. Tenure (2): areas of private unfurnished and furnished housing in the division.

increased in Moseley due to a certain amount of 'in-filling' of vacant building plots, but over-all, Zone II is not an area of council-owned property. In Zone III council housing accounts for 45 per cent of all households in the two large settled estates at Billesley and Fox Hollies, and in Brandwood where the estates are smaller and within an area of mixed property types (see Maps 5 and 6).

Owner occupation has increased in most places wherever land was available for new housing—Hall Green, Brandwood, Moseley, and Sparkhill—and where formerly rented property was sold—Sparkbrook and parts of Balsall Heath.

Table 31 suggests how vital in the provision of low price housing is the role of the local authority. Only in Sparkbrook were cheap small houses being purchased for owner occupation and many of these will have been purchased by sitting tenants. Otherwise, house purchase is only possible in the suburban and relatively expensive estates.

Table 31 also records the decline in the availability of unfurnished lettings as sitting tenants or the council purchase such properties. Nowhere was there an increase—only in Sparkhill and Calthorpe Park did the proportion remain constant, and in all other areas there was a marked decline. The privately-rented terraces which formed the basis of working-class housing at the beginning of this century have been disappearing with increasing rapidity since 1945. Before 1945 new working-class houses to rent were already being built, largely by local authorities, but since then a large proportion of privately-rented cheaper houses have either been demolished in slum clearance or sold for owner occupation. The 'blame' for the diminishing of this private provision to rent is laid either at the door of restrictive Rent Acts, or the availability of more lucrative forms of investment. The 1965 Rent Act enabled tenants of privately-rented furnished properties (conspicuously the large old city houses converted to multi-occupation) to apply to rent tribunals for review of their rent. But such tenants only have one month's, or at most six months', security of tenure, and the scarcity value of furnished lettings (and the unauthoritative social position of many tenants) maintains the profitability of this small and often bitterly attacked provision of housing. The recent resurgence of housing provision by charitable or non-profit-making housing associations is most welcome, but is not yet a large contribution.

It is difficult to discuss trends in private furnished lettings as these dwellings were the most susceptible to sampling errors in the 1966 Census. Many subdivisions within large old houses may have been missed. Indeed, the substantial over-all drop in enumerated households in the multi-occupied area of Anderton Park is open to great suspicion, as acquaintance with the area suggests little reason why this should be so. It must, therefore, be sufficient to note the continued high concentrations of furnished lettings in Calthorpe Park and Anderton Park, and similar concentrations in parts of Balsall Heath, Sparkbrook, and Moseley. Particularly interesting is the absolute increase of enumerated households in furnished lettings in Moseley, as observation suggests an appreciable growth of conversions to multi-occupation in large houses close to Moseley village.

In such a situation it might have been supposed that the local authority is left with responsibility for those persons and their families who come to Birmingham for work. But the widespread hope and belief that each family has a right to a home compromises the market situation in housing and anyway is not acted upon by the local authority in Birmingham who define social need to exclude anyone who has not lived in the city for at least five years. The accumulation of responsibility for housing persons displaced by public works, persons with special medical needs, closely defined homeless families, and, above all, persons displaced by slum clearance currently adds up to a waiting list of 35,000 families applying for council houses or flats. So although over-all Birmingham is a declining population, as slum clearance, over-spill towns, and affluence depopulate the city, those remaining are in an increasing number of households indicating a higher proportion of families wishing to live in dwellings of their own. Therefore the demand for housing is not diminished at all, and is actually greater both because of the slum clearance programme, which temporarily depletes the available housing stock, and because the over-all decline masks the arrival into Birmingham of considerable numbers over the last years into vacancies in Birmingham's thriving industries and services. These, having neither the capital to purchase houses nor the qualifications necessary to satisfy the local authority for a council house, are forced into flats, mostly furnished in multi-occupied lodging-houses.

9

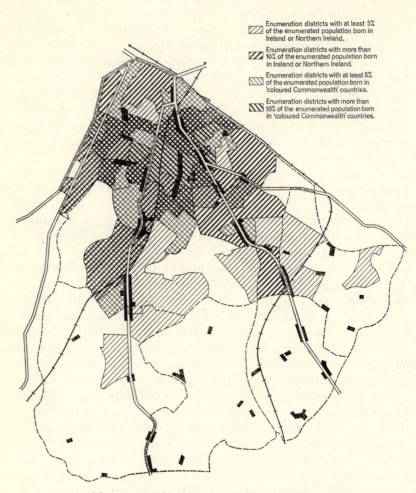

Enumeration districts with at least 5% of the enumerated population born in Ireland or Northern Ireland.

Enumeration districts with more than 10% of the enumerated population born in Ireland or Northern Ireland.

Enumeration districts with at least 5% of the enumerated population born in 'coloured Commonwealth' countries.

Enumeration districts with more than 10% of the enumerated population born in 'coloured Commonwealth' countries.

Map 7. Areas of immigrant residence in the division.

This process of migration and housing availability is the essential factor in understanding and explaining immigrant areas in the city, for immigrants (from Ireland, the West Indies, and Asia) are one particular category of migrants to the city.

Table 32 shows what proportion of the population in each area was of Irish or Commonwealth birth-place as enumerated in the 1961 and 1966 Censuses. Map 7 marks the enumeration

TABLE 32: PERCENTAGE OF POPULATION OF IRISH AND COMMONWEALTH BIRTH-PLACE IN THE ELEVEN AREAS, THREE ZONES, AND THE DIVISION COMPARED WITH BIRMINGHAM AS A WHOLE, 1961 AND 1966*

	Enumerated population		% Irish† in each area		% Commonwealth‡ in each area	
	1961	1966	1961	1966	1961	1966
Deritend	12,568	11,900	9	9	3	3
Calthorpe Park	6,676	8,040	17	14	22	26
Balsall Heath	18,540	15,000	10	10	7	18
Sparkbrook	41,173	38,760	13	10	6	15
Sparkhill	18,651	18,260	11	11	2	5
Anderton Park	7,468	7,340	14	11	9	16
Moseley	24,179	25,200	5	7	2	3
Brandwood	31,473	30,810	3	3	0·5	1
Billesley and Fox Hollies	56,494	55,720	2	3	0·2	0·3
Hall Green	13,375	15,530	1·8	1·3	0·3	1·2
Zone I	78,957	73,700	12	10	7	15
Zone II	50,298	50,800	9	9	3	6
Zone III	101,342	102,060	2·2	2·8	0·3	0·6
'F' Division	230,597	226,560	7·1	6·7	3·2	6·4
Birmingham County Borough	1,107,187	1,085,500	5·5	5·3	2·5	4·7

* Other groups of persons born outside the British Isles were not large. Australia, Canada, or New Zealand was the birth-place of 1,430 (0·13 per cent) of Birmingham's 1966 Census population; foreign countries and at sea, 11,040 (1·02 per cent).

† i.e., Northern Ireland and Irish Republic.

‡ i.e., Commonwealth countries outside the British Isles, excluding Australia, Canada, and New Zealand: approximating to 'coloured'.

districts with fairly high proportions of Irish and Commonwealth migrants to allow rather greater precision in locating immigrant areas. Extreme caution is necessary in using these figures. Comparing the 1961 Census with estimates of immigration from other sources, Peach concluded that the Census underestimated the West Indian-born population in the United Kingdom in 1961 by at least 20 per cent.[1] Underenumeration of multi-occupied properties makes it unlikely that the 1966 Census was appreciably more accurate for immigrants. The figures should, therefore, be taken chiefly as an indication of the areas in which most immigrants live, and only large changes should be treated as significant.

It is interesting to note that there are few areas of high coloured immigrant residence that are not also markedly Irish areas. Coloured immigrants, though numerically now equal with the Irish in the division, are more concentrated in the central areas, whereas the Irish are now fairly widely dispersed in Zones II and III but not, it is to be remarked, in the council estates in suburbia.

Map 7 indicates Irish concentrations in Deritend in the areas associated with recent council housing; the small number of coloured immigrants live in 'patched' council houses or in the old terraced houses awaiting slum clearance.

The Irish are fairly evenly distributed throughout Calthorpe Park but the coloured immigrant population is concentrated in one particular part of the area, in the large three-storey houses in Varna, Princess, and Alexandra Roads. Over-all this area is 40 per cent immigrant and shows the highest density of coloured immigrants in the division (26 per cent).

Balsall Heath, with 10 per cent Irish and 18 per cent coloured immigrant, has more immigrants at its southern end in the streets of large houses which are not scheduled for redevelopment. But in addition there are signs that both Irish and coloured families are housed in some of the 'patched' council-owned terraced houses in the development area to which they have been rehoused by the council; this applies especially to the northern end of the area around Belgrave Road.

In Sparkbrook coloured immigrants occupy the large multi-occupied houses in the lodging-house area around Farm Park, which was the subject of Rex and Moore's study, but by now they also occupy the small terraced houses between Moseley Road and Stratford Road and the somewhat larger houses towards Sparkhill in one of the few areas where reasonably priced older-

---

[1] *Sociological Review* (Vol. 14, No. 1, March 1966).

style family houses not in a redevelopment area will have been for sale.

In Zone I, 25 per cent of the population is immigrant—10 per cent Irish, 15 per cent coloured Commonwealth. While the Irish are evenly dispersed throughout the zone in all kinds of housing, the coloured population is concentrated in furnished terraces in the three areas of multi-occupied lodging-houses, with some in 'patched' houses or owner-occupied houses in Balsall Heath and central Sparkbrook. Within the zone were enumerated 10,710 coloured Commonwealth immigrants or over 70 per cent of the division's coloured population.

In Zone II lived 4,500 Irish and 2,870 coloured immigrants who together constituted 15 per cent of the population.

In Sparkhill the Irish were evenly dispersed throughout and comprised 11 per cent of the total population. Coloured immigrants were found mainly in one small part of the area between Anderton Park and Sparkbrook and to a lesser extent in a mainly lodging-house area between Stratford Road and Warwick Road.

In Anderton Park, the main density of immigrants was found in a group of streets at the northern end, although throughout there were at least 5 per cent of both Irish and coloured immigrants in each of the enumeration districts constituting the area.

In Moseley, the Irish were widely dispersed with a particular concentration near the Alcester and Stratford Roads. Coloured immigrants were only present in two districts—the large houses in Alcester Road, south of Moseley Village, and in the large multi-occupied houses to the immediate west of the Alcester Road, near Balsall Heath.

The number of immigrants in Zone III is small: just over 600 coloured immigrants and nearly 3,000 Irish. The Irish were found in owner-occupied houses in Brandwood and on council estates in Fox Hollies as well as small numbers in owner-occupied Hall Green. The coloured immigrants, few in number, were about equally distributed in owner-occupied and council house areas.

Interpreting the trend in immigrant residence between 1961 and 1966 on the basis of the Census information is fraught with difficulty due to the uncertainty of the figures' reliability. But the large over-all increase in population in Sparkbrook and Balsall Heath, the large proportional increases in Calthorpe Park, Anderton Park, and parts of Sparkhill, and the way the pattern of increase is restricted to certain areas, confirm the basic finding of Rex and Moore's Sparkbrook study that the housing market forces the majority of coloured immigrants into certain typical housing conditions in certain areas—those where there are lodging-houses or houses that can be purchased and used for multi-occupation. Where dispersal has occurred it is within the central area into 'patched' council-owned houses or small terraced houses that can be purchased for owner occupation.

Although large numbers of coloured immigrants have now lived in the city for more than five years, there is little or no evidence that more than a handful have obtained council tenancies on the outer estates or in the new council flats near the city centre. Irish immigrants have achieved house purchase in areas where more moderately priced housing is available in Sparkhill, parts of Moseley, and Brandwood. Coloured immigrants have only obtained small houses to purchase to a limited extent in Sparkbrook, otherwise the houses purchased are larger houses which can house large numbers to assist the high mortgage repayments. Not surprisingly this places immigrants in conditions where overcrowding is widespread and amenities are frequently restricted.

The Census also provides an indication of the scale of overcrowding and makes some assessment of the adequacy of amenities available to households. This information is summarized in Table 33.

The high rate of overcrowding in Calthorpe Park and the only slightly lower rate in Anderton Park, both predominantly lodging-house areas, suggest how this is the key factor. But in Deritend it will be noted 17 per cent of the population is living in overcrowded conditions which suggests—with reference to housing type and age structure—that this is due to large families in slum housing still awaiting rehousing to adequate accommodation. Undoubtedly lodging-houses in Balsall Heath and Sparkbrook account for the high figure there. It will be noted that in Zone I as a whole three times as many persons live in overcrowded conditions than the city average. As for amenities, the high figure for Moseley suggests that lodging-houses by definition will appear as lacking in amenities and the high figures for Calthorpe Park and Anderton Park confirm this. But the very high rates for Balsall Heath and Sparkbrook testify to the presence of old slum

TABLE 33: OVERCROWDING AND AMENITIES,
1966 CENSUS: PERCENTAGE OF PERSONS LIVING AT
OVER 1½ PERSONS PER ROOM AND PERCENTAGE OF
HOUSEHOLDS WITHOUT EXCLUSIVE USE OF CERTAIN
AMENITIES IN EACH AREA

Area	% persons living at over 1½ persons per room	% households without exclusive use of hot tap, fixed bath, or w.c.
Deritend	17	44
Calthorpe Park	21	62
Balsall Heath	15	77
Sparkbrook	11	65
Sparkhill	3	33
Anderton Park	15	51
Moseley	3	27
Brandwood	2	9
Billesley	4	3
Fox Hollies	5	10
Hall Green	1	5
Zone I	14	64
Zone II	5	32
Zone III	3	7
'F' Division	7	30
Birmingham County Borough	5	27

houses which have not been modernized but still house substantial numbers of the whole population.

This survey of the characteristics of the division studied can be concluded with reference to the age and class structures of the areas. Table 34 sets out the proportions of the population in four age categories as enumerated in each area at the 1966 Census, together with a measure of males aged 15–44 as a proportion of the total population.

Table 34 suggests that there is a preponderance of young adults and small children in central areas, the elderly and teen-agers in the suburbs, and a more adult population in the inter-mediate zone. The lodging-house areas, Calthorpe Park and Anderton Park, stand out for their high proportion of young adult males. Their populations have a significantly higher proportion of males than females, but they are not without young children. The terraced housing of Balsall Heath is experiencing appreciable migration in its final days, and shelters families with many children. In contrast, the settled respectable terraces of Sparkhill house many more elderly and many fewer under 15 years old. The component areas of Sparkbrook are too varied to provide a meaningful composite age structure, and similarly for Moseley.

TABLE 34: AGE STRUCTURE 1966: PROPORTIONS OF THE POPULATIONS OF THE AREAS IN EACH OF FOUR AGE CATEGORIES AND THE PROPORTION OF THE POPULATION WHO ARE MALES AGED BETWEEN 15-44

	% of population within each area between the ages of:				Males 15-44 as % of area population	Population
	0-14	15-19	20-44	45+		
Deritend	42	9	30	20	21	11,890
Calthorpe Park	26	7	43	24	33	8,040
Balsall Heath	36	8	34	21	22	15,000
Sparkbrook	26	7	34	33	23	38,760
Sparkhill	22	7	33	38	21	18,260
Anderton Park	24	6	50	20	32	7,340
Moseley	19	7	34	40	20	25,200
Brandwood	21	7	32	40	19	30,810
Billesley	23	10	28	39	19	27,710
Fox Hollies	19	9	27	45	18	28,000
Hall Green	18	6	30	47	18	15,530
Zone I	31	7·4	34	27	23·7	73,700
Zone II	21	6·8	36	36	22·0	50,810
Zone III	21	8·3	29	42	18·7	102,060
'F' Division	24	7·6	32	36	21·1	226,560
Birmingham County Borough	24	8·4	32	36	20·6	1,085,500

The areas of council-built housing differ considerably. The re-development properties in Deritend have large young families and few elderly persons, though the striking number of children may be explained by the size of many families in temporarily remaining slum properties. Billesley and Fox Hollies, established council estates, have high proportions of older people, and 15 per cent of the population of Fox Hollies is in fact over 64. They have a higher proportion of teen-agers than any other area. Hall Green is characterized by the elderly successful who have moved out to buy nice houses. The younger successful people who live there have smaller families than the council tenants at Billesley and Fox Hollies. Brandwood is a mixture of tenure types but its new building in public and private sectors gives it a higher proportion of young adults than other suburban areas.

Table 35 sets out the proportions of the active and retired male population in each area in each of the main socio-economic groupings.

TABLE 35: SOCIO-ECONOMIC GROUPS OF ACTIVE AND RETIRED MALES, 1966: PROPORTIONS OF THE MAIN CATEGORIES IN EACH OF THE ELEVEN AREAS

	% professional and managerial	% skilled manual	% semi-skilled and un-skilled manual	% inter and junior non-manual	Total active and retired males
Deritend	7	42	40	10	3,980
Calthorpe Park	6	29	56	8	3,250
Balsall Heath	5	44	40	8	4,870
Sparkbrook	4	41	44	8	14,190
Sparkhill	8	41	34	14	6,650
Anderton Park	16	36	24	22	2,610
Moseley	23	35	19	20	8,570
Brandwood	16	38	21	22	10,590
Billesley	9	47	25	15	9,830
Fox Hollies	8	42	31	18	10,250
Hall Green	28	31	9	30	5,590
Zone I	5	40	45	8	26,290
Zone II	16	37	26	18	17,830
Zone III	14	41	23	20	36,260
'F' Division	11	40	31	16	80,380
Birmingham County Borough	10	44	29	15	381,240

Skilled manual occupations, which are much the largest group in Birmingham and command a wide range of remuneration and status, are spread surprisingly evenly throughout the division. Predictably, Zone I has a high proportion of semi-skilled and unskilled manual workers, and Zone III has a contrasting high proportion of professional and managerial, and non-manual workers. Zone II has more in common with Zone III than Zone I.

The lodging-house areas are quite distinct in this respect, despite similarities in tenure and migration, race and age of population. Calthorpe Park, with 40 per cent immigrant population, has almost two-thirds semi and unskilled manual workers. Anderton Park is over-represented at all levels of non-manual occupations, indicating the variety of persons seeking short-term residence in its multi-occupied properties.

Balsall Heath retains the class composition of an old working-class area, divided equally between skilled and semi or unskilled manual workers. Despite its tenurial variations, Sparkbrook emerges with a similar class composition. Sparkhill has rather fewer semi and unskilled manual workers, and a proportion of non-manual occupations approaching that of the suburban local authority estates, but not the areas of owner occupation.

Moseley, which, it will be remembered, is a mixed area with not inconsiderable furnished lettings for its immigrant population, has few manual workers and high proportions of non-manual workers which suggests how its lodging-houses cater for a professional trainee and student population.

The local authority areas are again contrasted. They are each strongholds of skilled manual workers, but Deritend supplements them with more semi and unskilled manual workers; while Billesley and Fox Hollies have a higher proportion of intermediate and junior non-manual workers than Birmingham's average. An impression that Billesley is a slightly higher-status estate than Fox Hollies is supported by the differential of skilled and semi and unskilled manual occupations.

Brandwood's mixed tenure profile is reflected in its relatively high proportion of non-manual workers, while Hall Green, predominantly owner-occupied, is predominantly non-manual having the highest over-all proportion of both professional and managerial persons and those in intermediate and junior non-manual occupations.

Immigrant areas in the division are, therefore, restricted to a crescent-shaped zone coinciding with the presence of multi-occupied housing: Calthorpe Park, the southern end of Balsall Heath, Anderton Park, the fringe of Sparkhill, and Sparkbrook west of Stratford Road. To a lesser extent the crescent encircles a zone of smaller houses where in the past five years there has been some increase in the numbers of coloured immigrants. The Irish population, although well represented in the crescent zone, are more widely dispersed beyond its confines.

TABLE 36: NUMBERS OF THE MAIN EVENT CATEGORIES IN EACH AREA EXPRESSED AS A RATE PER 10,000 OF POPULATION, ALSO FOR ZONES AND THE DIVISION AS A WHOLE*

Area	Population	Minor thefts		Major thefts		House thefts		Dispute and violence		Disorder		All events	
		No.	Rate	No.	Rate	No.	Rate	No.	Rate	No.	Rate	No.	Rate
Deritend	11,900	174	147	192	164	45	38	74	54	111	93	551	453
Calthorpe Park	8,040	43	54	61	77	54	68	61	76	27	34	183	230
Balsall Heath	15,000	89	61	175	118	119	80	93	63	59	39	416	280
Sparkbrook	38,760	117	31	327	86	176	43	169	44	83	21	696	183
Sparkhill	18,260	50	28	72	40	34	19	47	26	13	7	182	100
Anderton Park	7,340	33	47	10	10	54	73	39	55	20	27	162	220
Moseley	25,200	87	36	104	42	70	28	42	17	20	8	253	108
Brandwood	30,810	56	19	76	25	44	14	203	8	7	2	162	54
Billesley and Fox Hollies	55,720	77	14	97	18	48	9	34	6	5	1	213	39
Hall Green	15,530	33	22	28	18	7	4	6	4	1	1	68	45
Zone I	73,700	423	57	756	102	394	55	397	54	280	38	1,846	250
Zone II	50,800	170	33	246	48	158	31	128	25	53	10	597	118
Zone III	102,060	166	16	201	20	99	10	63	6	13	1	443	44
Whole Division	226,560	759	35	1,203	54	296	29	588	26	346	15	2,886	128

* Minor thefts do not include forty-one for which an area location was inappropriate; house thefts are those major thefts occurring in residential premises; dispute and violence include twenty-eight crimes of violence; disorder includes offences of drunkenness, disorderly act, and wilful damage. Total figures are of all those listed in the table excluding house thefts which are already included in major thefts.

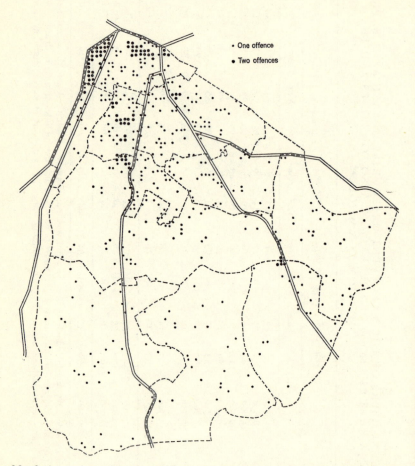

Map 8. Approximate locations of thefts of cycles and motor vehicles and thefts from motor vehicles reported to the police and occurring November 1966 to February 1967.

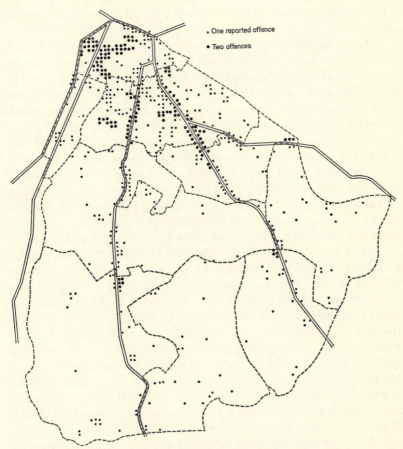

One reported offence

Two offences

Map 9. Approximate locations of thefts or 'breaking' offences from shops, factories, warehouses, etc. (but not from residential premises or from or of motor vehicles), reported to the police and occurring November 1966 to February 1967.

2. *Area Characteristics of Crime and Disorder*

It was noted in an earlier chapter that about two-thirds of all the events recorded in the major categories occurred in Zone I. In discussing the various kinds of offences it was possible to note some of the area variations within the over-all zonal pattern. Table 36 brings together those various data into a single composite table.

Table 36 shows that the rate of occurrence of events in Zone I is more than twice that in Zone II and nearly six times that in Zone III. The most marked disparity between Zones I and III is in relation to dispute and violence, and disorder, and the most even distribution is in minor thefts. The series of maps on which various event categories have been spot-marked can give further precision to the area characteristics of crime and disorder. Map 8 marks the location of every minor theft involving a theft of a cycle, motor cycle, or other vehicle, or theft from parked motor vehicles; these constitute 75 per cent of all minor thefts. Map 9 marks all major thefts from non-residential premises and Map 10 marks all major thefts from residential premises. Map 11 marks all minor incidents; Map 12 marks all arrests for drunkenness.

Within Zone I it will be noted that Deritend, the area nearest to the city centre, has the over-all highest rate of crime; it ranks highest in all categories except those relating to dispute and violence, and thefts from houses. Reference to Map 8 shows a great preponderance of vehicle thefts in Deritend associated with the fact that many cars are parked in the area during day and evening; and Map 9 shows a large number of non-residential thefts in the industrial area. As was shown, the houses and flats in Deritend are relatively secure; the high rate of disorder offences is explained with reference to Map 12 by the mass of arrests occurring in the centre of the area where a large hostel for elderly homeless working men provides a large number of such arrests.

Deritend is exceptional in Zone I as being the main attracting area for offences against property; Calthorpe Park and Balsall Heath both have rates which rank over-all third and second among the areas. The maps suggest certain contrasts between the areas.

A large measure of Balsall Heath's minor thefts is due to larcenies from vehicles and of vehicles, whereas in Calthorpe Park it is non-vehicular thefts which occur. Both areas have the same rate for thefts from houses; in Calthorpe Park these are thefts from fairly large multi-occupied houses in the Varna Road area, whereas in Balsall Heath much of the theft is from the small houses in the heart of the area, many of them thefts of money from meters; it is noticeable that the area near the southern boundary of Balsall Heath, an area of large houses, many owned by coloured immigrants and occupied by tenants and families, is relatively free from crime. Calthorpe Park is predominantly residential and this is reflected in almost all of its major thefts being thefts from houses; Balsall Heath's shops at Moseley Road, Edward Road, and the cafés and shops in the Cox Street area get fairly frequent visits from thieves which inflates its over-all crime rate.

Again there is contrast in the nature of disputes: in Calthorpe Park it is landlord and tenant disputes which predominate, in the same central area around Varna Road; in Balsall Heath it is family disputes which account for a high proportion of the over-all rate. Both areas were equally inclined to generate drunk and disorderly behaviour: some in Calthorpe Park, where there are not a great many pubs, will be among sightseers and clients of the prostitutes in Varna Road; in Balsall Heath, where there are a great many public houses, drunk and disorderly behaviour is more normal.

It will be noted that Anderton Park in Zone II has an over-all rate in excess of that of Sparkbrook and similar to that in Calthorpe Park. Sparkbrook's relatively low rate for most categories masks certain areas of concentration. Thefts from motor vehicles and minor thefts are fairly evenly scattered; it is noticeable on Map 10 how there are fairly frequent thefts in the lodging-house areas near the boundary with Anderton Park to the south and to the west of the Stratford Road. The shops along the Stratford Road and at the junction in Warwick Road account for a proportion of the non-residential major thefts. The disputes are located more evenly between the small terraced central part of the area and among the lodging-houses; the public houses along the Stratford Road generate a certain amount of drunkenness.

In Zone II Sparkhill and Moseley share a common pattern, while Anderton Park generates about twice as much crime and disorder. Again it is noticeable that the lodging-house area of Anderton Park is the centre of considerable thefts from houses, whilst the better houses of Moseley attract a quantity of thefts at a rate much more marked than in Sparkhill. The rate of minor

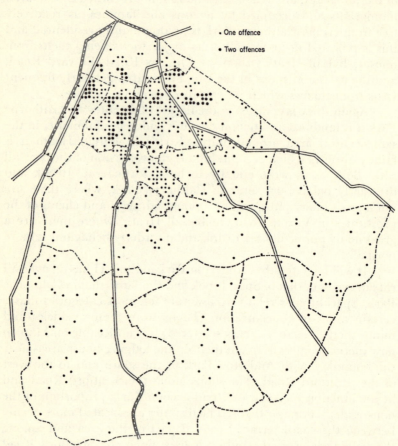

Map 10. Approximate locations of thefts or 'breaking' offences from residential premises reported to the police and occurring November 1966 to February 1967.

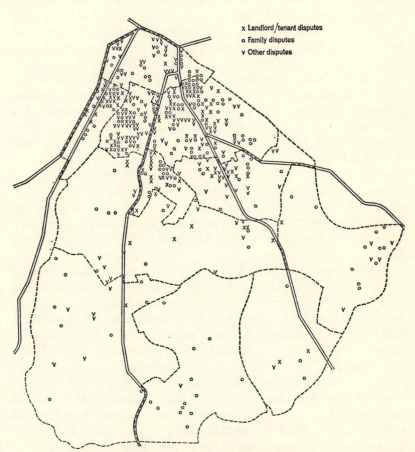

Map 11. Approximate locations of minor incidents reported to the police and occurring November 1966 to February 1967.

incidents is similarly twice as high in Anderton Park than in the other areas of the zone, many of which can be attributed to disputes between landlords and tenants.

The pattern in Zone III is much more even: the slightly higher rate for minor thefts in Hall Green can be attributed to a number of thefts of and from cars or vehicles parked at a car park by a Technical College near the Stratford Road. Hall Green, the settled, suburban area is almost entirely free of thefts from residential properties while some thefts do occur in the shops in the area. Disputes and disorder are very infrequent throughout the zone. It is interesting to note that rates for most categories are higher in Brandwood than in the other areas. Brandwood is a much more mixed area in terms of housing type and social class. Over half of its thefts are from houses widely scattered throughout the area. It may be that if much crime is petty and local an area like Brandwood with less settled older council estates close to good owner-occupied areas provides more opportunity in the form of theft for delinquent youth in the area whereas on the large estates in Billesley and Fox Hollies, where it can be shown there live more delinquents, opportunities are further afield (see pp. 45 and 251–2).

The major points of interest in the area characteristics of crime occurrences relate to the central area, being the attracting area both for petty crime and for rather more ambitious offences against factories and warehouses. Apart from Deritend, the highest rate of crime is in Balsall Heath associated with the remaining slum area of the division. Next are the two predominantly lodging-house areas of Calthorpe Park and Anderton Park, both areas where overcrowding, poor amenities, and a highly mobile population make for marked instability and disorganization. Middle-class Moseley and working-class Sparkhill share below average levels in most categories of offence and disorder but have over-all rates that are twice that for the other areas of the suburban estates.

Thus far the analysis has been concerned with occurrences of certain kinds of events to show how geography and social conditions promote complex variations within an over-all rate of crime. Areas have been spoken of to show how they generate or attract crime. A somewhat different kind of analysis is required when the extent to which the areas are areas of criminal *residence* is examined.

During the four months a total of 503 persons were proceeded against for indictable offences, of whom 307 (60 per cent) were resident at the time of the offence in the area. During the same period 616 persons were arrested for non-indictable offences of whom 324 (53 per cent) were residents. Among the crime offenders were ninety-seven juveniles (under 16); among the non-indictable offenders ten were juveniles. Table 37 sets out the variable rates of crime and delinquency based on these figures of residence. The

TABLE 37: COMPARATIVE RATES OF DELINQUENCY AND CRIME IN THE TEN AREAS AND THREE ZONES BASED ON THE OFFENDERS RESIDENT EXPRESSED AS A FRACTION OF 1,000 OF ESTIMATED POPULATION AT RISK FOR THE AGE CATEGORIES

| Area | Juveniles* | | | Adults† | | | | |
| | Estimate of male juvenile population | No. of offenders | Rate per 1,000 | Estimate of male 15–44 population | Crime | | Disorder | |
					No. of offenders	Rate	No. of offenders	Rate
Deritend	2,500	8	3·2	2,500	14	5·6	26	10·4
Calthorpe Park	1,050	2	2	2,650	18	6·8	37	14
Balsall Heath	2,700	13	4·8	3,300	29	8·8	43	13
Sparkbrook	5,000	23	4·6	8,900	49	5·5	77	8·6
Sparkhill	2,000	7	3·5	3,850	15	3·9	29	7·5
Anderton Park	800	4	4·5	2,450	16	6·8	36	14·6
Moseley	2,400	9	3·7	5,100	21	4·1	32	6·3
Brandwood	3,250	19	5·8	5,800	12	2·1	10	1·7
Billesley and Fox Hollies	3,200	22	6·9	5,250	31	5·9	23	4·4
Hall Green	1,400	—	—	2,750	5	1·8	1	—
Zone I	11,400	46	4	17,500	110	6·3	183	10·4
Zone II	5,200	20	3·8	11,200	52	4·6	97	8·6
Zone III	10,600	41	3·9	19,000	48	2·5	34	1·8
Whole division	27,000	107	4	47,700	210	4·4	314	6·5

* Includes ten offenders charged with non-indictable offences.
† It was unavoidable to include a small number of women among both the crime and disorder categories.

only available population estimates for the areas unfortunately include all children under 15 years of age; for the adult population, as the great majority of offenders are between 17 and 44, this is the base used, distinguishing the two categories of offenders. The rate is expressed per 1,000 of the male population at risk.

Table 37 shows how juvenile offenders are fairly evenly

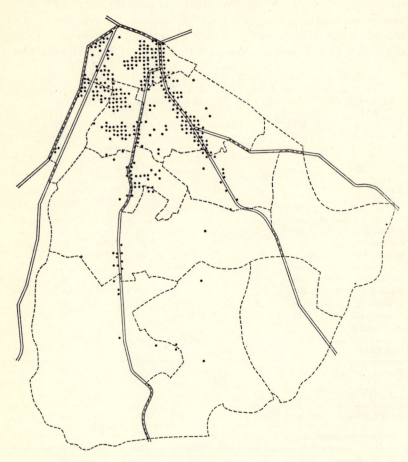

Map 12. Approximate locations of arrests following street disorders (drunkenness, disorderly act, wilful damage) occurring November 1966 to February 1967.

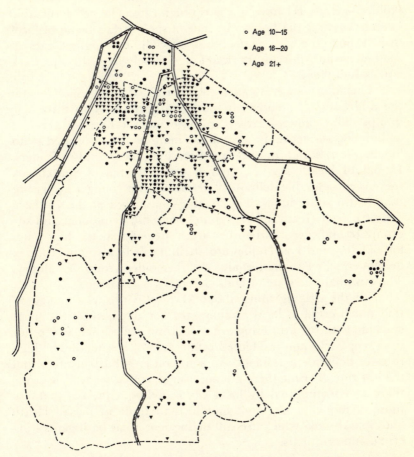

Map 13. Approximate locations of home addresses and the ages of all persons proceeded against for offences committed November 1966 to February 1967 who were
at the time resident in the division.

dispersed throughout the division with the highest rate of juvenile delinquency in the two outer suburban areas. Among crime offenders the highest rate is in Balsall Heath, followed by Calthorpe Park and Anderton Park, and with Billesley and Fox Hollies in Zone III having a fairly high rate. The non-indictable offenders reflect the preponderance of such arrests being of local drunks near the city centre; but over-all, the highest rate of residence is in Anderton Park followed closely by Calthorpe Park and Balsall Heath.

This information is joined together on Map 13 which locates the addresses of offenders in both categories and in three age groups. This shows clearly the three main centres of areas of delinquent residence in the three main areas associated with lodging-houses and multi-occupation and young adult offenders. In Balsall Heath and the central terraced area of Sparkbrook there is considerable delinquent residence of a younger age group than in the other areas. The lodging-house area at the southern end of Balsall Heath appears quite markedly delinquent and the groups of markings in the other areas suggest that the high rates for Billesley and Fox Hollies are attributable to a young group of delinquents in Fox Hollies and a rather older group in Billesley. The criminal-free state of Hall Green is very striking.

But the striking thing about Map 13 is the way it suggests that much crime is local in character, for the areas of residence coincide with the attracting areas of crime occurrence, except for the exceptional non-residential crime area of Deritend. The high rates of delinquent residence in some outer suburban areas and the low rate of crime there not only suggests that what little crime there is, is committed by local young delinquents, but that also those delinquents are more mobile than those in Balsall Heath and Sparkbrook, which are still delinquent areas both generating crime and criminals.

3. *Crime in Immigrant Areas*

It is very apparent that the housing market operates in such a way that immigrants, and particularly coloured immigrants, live in certain typical conditions and areas, one of whose features is high rates of crime and disorder, both in terms of occurrence of crime events and in terms of residence of criminals and delinquents.

The four areas covered by the crescent where coloured

immigrants live—Calthorpe Park, Balsall Heath, Anderton Park, and Sparkbrook—have the four highest over-all crime rates for the various categories defined (excepting the special area of Deritend); they also have high rates of criminal and delinquency residence. It was also noticed that they were areas with the highest indices of overcrowding and lacking in amenity; they were also the areas where the population was most mobile, between 10 and 25 per cent having moved in the year preceding the 1966 sample Census.

Typically, crime here means petty theft from houses in multi-occupation, thefts from which situation account for an estimated 10 per cent of all indictable recorded crime. In Calthorpe Park, and to a lesser extent in Anderton Park, prostitution is a common and visible indicator of area decay and demoralization. Overcrowding and poor living conditions provoke hostility between landlords and tenants, place great strains on the stability of personal relations, and can lead to argument, fighting, and violence. The nature of crime and disorder is such that it underlines the stark reality of the disorganization and instability which are features of conditions in such areas. The security and stability reflected in the data from Sparkhill and Moseley and from the outer area of the division highlight the inequalities and conflicts that are visible in the city. The evidence that crime rates of all kinds are higher in the old slum areas of Balsall Heath (and to a somewhat lesser extent in Sparkbrook) serves as a reminder that much of the crime and disorder is petty theft and drunkenness in slum areas; that organized crime is still the exception rather than the rule; and that violent crime is not premeditated viciousness but the outcome of domestic dispute and strife or a pub brawl. The typical criminal and delinquent is no success figure making a living from theft or skilled criminality; he is someone who steals small articles from parked cars, or rooms in houses— the young, the unemployed, the failed, or the failing account for the majority of persons proceeded against for crime.

Crime and disorder are fairly common features in certain areas of the city; resident in these areas are the great majority of the coloured immigrant population and many immigrants from Ireland; in all the areas the majority of the residents are persons born in England or Wales or Scotland. If the crime that is cleared up is typical of all crime that occurs (and it must be remembered that the majority of crime is *not* cleared up), coloured immigrants are very much less involved in the crime and disorder that surround them in the areas where they live than their white neighbours. The evidence for this is presented in Table 38 which sets out the ages and the nationalities of persons proceeded against for the indictable crimes and non-indictable offences that have constituted the profile of crime in a division of the city.

TABLE 38: NATIONALITIES OF OFFENDERS IN THE NUMBERS AND PROPORTIONS

Birth-place	Indictable crime: all offences									
	10–16		17–20		21–30		31 +		All ages	
	No.	%	No.	%	No.	%	No.	%	No.	%
Birmingham	97	85	67	58	59	37	31	29	254	50
Rest of England, Wales, and Scotland	6	5	29	25	48	30	40	36	123	24
Ireland and Northern Ireland	5	4	18	15	49	30	27	24	99	20
West Indies	5	4	1	1	3	2	5	4	14	3
Indian	—	—	—	—	—	—	—	—	—	—
Pakistan	2	2	1	1	—	—	2	2	5	1
Other	—	—	—	—	2	1	6	5	8	2
Total	115	100	116	100	161	100	111	100	503	100

It is interesting to note that whereas 50 per cent of indictable crime is attributable to persons born in Birmingham, only 19·5 per cent of disorder offenders are locals born and bred. It is difficult to know or measure what proportion of the current Birmingham population was born outside: the net migration rate of persons moving into the Birmingham area in the five-year period 1961–6 was nearly 7 per cent. In areas of high adult criminal residence rates (Calthorpe Park, Anderton Park) it was over 20 per cent. It seems likely that migrants into Birmingham as a group are rather more prone to crime than the over-all population, particularly among the older age groups; it is to be noted, however, that in the younger age groups the Birmingham-born predominate, which confirms what is suggested by the maps of residence, that some areas are delinquent areas due to the presence of old established Birmingham slum families among a minority of whom are delinquent children and young persons; other areas are delinquent due to the presence of a large number of migrants into the city, often young men living alone in hostels or lodgings, among whom a minority engage in thefts.

Among such migrants are, of course, the Irish and it is noticeable that the proportions of Irish offenders rise with age, suggesting how time may sift out a less capable minority who fall into petty theft and criminality. It is of course very difficult to assess truly comparable rates because there is no means of adjusting the proportions of immigrants in an area for the vitally significant factors of age (the great majority of offenders are

TWO MAJOR CATEGORIES OF OFFENCES, WITH THE
IN FOUR AGE GROUPS

| Non-indictable offenders: all categories | | | | | | | | | | | All offenders all ages | |
| 10–16 | | 17–20 | | 21–30 | | 31+ | | All ages | | | | |
No.	%	No.	%	No.	%	No.	%	No.	%		No.	%
12	75	48	43	30	14	33	12	123	19·5		377	34
2	12·5	26	23	49	23	63	22	140	22·5		263	23·5
1	6	32	29	118	55	155	56	306	49·5		405	36
1	6	1	1	8	4	8	3	18	2·7		32	2·8
—	—	1	1	2	1	2	1	5	1·4		5	0·4
—	—	1	1	1	0·5	2	1	4	1·2		9	0·8
—	—	2	2	5	2·5	13	5	20	3·2		28	2·5
16	100	111	100	213	100	276	100	616	100		1,119	100

between 17 and 40) and of ratio of men to women (the vast majority of offenders are men). Nevertheless, it is apparent that the Irish are over-represented as a population among both categories of offenders.

The extremely low rate of involvement in crime and disorder among coloured immigrants, West Indian and Asian, when also adjusted for age and proportions in either sex, would appear actually much lower. This finding is the more striking bearing in mind, as has been shown, that there is more crime committed in areas where immigrants live than in other areas; and more offenders live in the areas of high immigrant population density than in other areas.

4. *Nationalities of Offenders*

(i) *The Irish.* Twenty per cent of those proceeded against for indictable offences during the period of study were born in Ireland or Northern Ireland; 75 per cent of these were over the age of 21. Irish offenders were 20 per cent of those proceeded against for property offences and 23 per cent of those proceeded against for violent crime.

Of those proceeded against for non-indictable offences, 49·5 per cent were Irish; 90 per cent were over the age of 21. The great majority were arrested for offences of drunkenness, of which group they accounted for 60 per cent. In addition, 42 per cent of those arrested for being drunk in charge of a motor vehicle were Irish. Seventeen and a half per cent of arrested prostitutes were Irish.

Thirteen per cent of minor incidents to which the police were called involved Irish persons, and a further 5 per cent were incidents where one of the parties was Irish. The great majority (62 per cent) of these were disputes between members of the same family.

The analysis of crime and disorder offered in the foregoing pages points to the need to acknowledge that crime is prevalent in certain areas and arises out of certain typical social conditions. These are the poorer areas of the city where depressed classes of persons live and there is a highly mobile population in poor class housing. Much of the theft is petty and much of the violence arises from domestic or other disputes. The Irish, though in over-all terms accounting for nearly 7 per cent of the population in the division studied, account for 11 per cent of the population in the four areas where crime is most prevalent and where relatively large numbers of offenders live. Most crime is committed by males between 15 and 44 in which groups there will be a higher proportion of the Irish than of the native English population. But even making these allowances and recognizing that a greater proportion of the Irish are in lower-paid occupations than other populations, it would seem that there is a greater propensity for crime among Irish immigrants than among other immigrants and than among the native English population.

The reasons why this should be so are complex and beyond the scope of this study. But one or two facts are worthwhile noting.

Later, in Chapter 8, it will be suggested that the Irish are *not* markedly over-represented among juvenile and young offenders and, as has been noted, the majority of Irish offenders are adults. Furthermore, it needs to be noted that the dispersal of the Irish population in the division is fairly marked and in Sparkhill, where 11 per cent of the population is Irish, rates of crime and criminal residence are low. Also, it must be remembered that the proportion of the Irish population who are involved in crime is small; the vast majority settle in the city, work, marry, raise families, and obtain housing in better areas of the city without ever getting into trouble. Left behind in the poor areas are a relatively higher proportion than the native population among whom are some who commit crimes. The age of this group is older than a 'normal' native criminal or delinquent group; many it would seem are single working males in poorly paid insecure occupations who have assimilated to, rather than risen above, the conditions in the areas where they live.

Crime rates in Ireland are very low. A close-knit family life and the overarching influence of the Catholic Church undoubtedly exert potent controls against wrongdoing and law-breaking. The process of immigration removes these controlling influences. For some families they are replaced by the new controls of the host society in areas where family and Church continue to enhance the sense of community, security, and stability for the members. For others the loss is more total and release from the stringent controls of the home society provokes something of a reaction which finds expression in relatively greater crime and disorder, theft, and drunkenness—the expression of those for whom immigration has not brought economic security, stable family relations, and other signs of success in the new country. Failure means poor living conditions and poor occupational attainment in areas where overcrowding and disorganization are common, and the contingent crime and disorder. Relatively more Irish immigrants fail in these terms than other immigrants or similarly placed English persons. The Irish are over-represented among the urban poor and so over-represented among the ranks of offenders.

(ii) *The West Indians.* During the period of study fourteen persons of West Indian origin were proceeded against for indictable crimes; six of these were under 21. Together they account for a mere 3 per cent of all offenders. This number includes nine prosecuted for property offences, three for offences of possessing offensive weapons, and two for violent offences.

At the same time, eighteen were arrested for non-indictable offences: five were of offences for possessing cannabis, ten were of offences of disorder, and three were arrests of prostitutes.

Together they accounted for less than 3 per cent of all non-indictable offenders.

In addition, 10 per cent of minor incidents to which the police were called involved West Indians and a further 4 per cent were disputes in which one of the parties involved was West Indian. Again, the majority of these were family disputes.

The same factors which were necessary to qualify any interpretation of the proportion of immigrants of Irish birth apply here. It has been shown that in the four 'criminal' areas live 75 per cent of the division's coloured population, who comprise 17 per cent of the population of those areas. Over-all in the division, the 1966 Census enumerated just over 14,000 coloured immigrants who comprised 6·4 per cent of the population. More of the West Indians can be assumed to be working males between the ages of 15 and 44 as compared with the native population. These factors further magnify the *under*-representation of West Indians among the population of offenders.

In a later chapter it is shown that this under-representation is matched by a similarly low proportion of West Indians among the younger age categories of offenders (see Ch. 8). It is suggested there that in contrast with the typical English delinquent and his family, the few West Indian delinquents appear to come from families with high aspirations and ambitions. West Indians in general are aspiring and ambitious; many are acutely aware of the poor status that attaches to the kinds of areas and houses in which they live and are ambitious for a better way of life. They are not part of the failure that life in such areas means for many. They seek success within the general framework of values and generally rise above the delinquent and criminal standards prevalent in the areas where they live.

Clearly the danger is that if their legitimate aspirations for betterment in terms of employment and housing opportunity are not met, with time the crime and disorder which surround them will contaminate their life style and lead in years to come to a crime rate that matches that of their neighbourhoods. Such influences may particularly infect and misdirect their children's achievement and undermine their chances for success and mobility.

(iii) *The Asians*. During the period of study three young Pakistani boys were proceeded against for minor property offences; two adult Pakistanis were convicted of offences of violence; and five Indians and four Pakistanis were arrested for non-indictable offences, mainly drunkenness. Together they comprised just over 1 per cent of all offenders.

Five per cent of minor incidents involved members of Asian communities and a further 14 per cent were incidents in which one of the parties involved was Asian. Typically, such incidents were disputes between landlord and tenant.

It will be apparent from what was said in relation to West Indian offenders that, like them, Asians are substantially under-represented among all categories of offenders.

Within this over-all pattern of low involvement of coloured immigrants in crime, three factors are of considerable significance.

In the first place, the relatively large number of minor incidents which involve immigrants illustrate something of the disorganization and instability that can affect immigrant groups. Many of such incidents reveal the effects of overcrowding in poor standard housing. Such conditions provoke argument and hostility among and between tenants and neighbours; many family disputes suggest how the comforts and stability of normal home relations break down under the strain of living in rooms and lodgings and substandard housing; the frequency of disputes between landlord and tenant indicates the insecurity which attaches to living in multi-occupation. Many such incidents are potentially violent; violence may be seen as a last resort when other means of resolving disputes fail. Unless people subject to such conditions are offered some alternative to violence as a means of resolving such disputes, the subcultural prevalence of violence in these areas will increase and underline the fundamental insecurity of residents and families in the areas. All such incidents involve the police in situations which to ignore or treat merely and routinely as *minor* may only increase the sense of frustration and despair of the persons involved who may be justified in thinking that 'nobody cares'. Inaction by authority both to the total situation and to individual incidents can only add to the sense of disorganization and absence of community in such areas. Coloured immigrants may become enmeshed in a slum culture where family life and secure personal relations are impossible. A minority who fail to withstand the pressures of disorganization and resort to violence and disorder may gain for the majority an unenviable reputation for poverty, depravity, and viciousness.

Secondly, it must be recognized that a minority of coloured immigrants, Asian and West Indian, are involved in the distribution and use of the drug cannabis. Although use seems largely restricted to certain places and situations—in clubs (official and unofficial) and parties—such activities involve the police in considerable effort to trace and arrest the offenders. The prevalence of such activities in areas of high immigration whereby the deviant minority are living in close contact with the law-abiding majority may again mean that a group stereotype of drug taker evolves which increases suspicion and hostility among the races, for the prosecution of a minority may be seen to indicate a willingness to persecute the majority, none of whom escape from the suspicion of involvement. In a somewhat similar way, the involvement of a minority of coloured immigrants, Asian and West Indian, with prostitutes, either as brothel-keepers or ponces, may suggest to the police and to white opinion that all immigrants condone such activity. This may be exacerbated by immigrants and prostitutes being forced to occupy similar kinds of housing in certain typical areas.

Both these factors point to the need for the police to be particularly sensitive in their operations in areas of high immigration, areas which are likely to be the focus for not inconsiderable police activity, being areas where crime and criminals are prevalent. How the police act in such a situation is explored in the chapters which follow.

The third factor grows from a concern for the kind of family life which is possible under the conditions which immigrants live. If such conditions make family life less stable and secure, children of immigrant families may be exposed in a crucial way to the criminal and delinquent influences in the area. This aspect is explored in the third section of this report and is concerned to note the extent of family breakdown and the involvement of immigrant children in delinquency.

Part II: The Police

CHAPTER 4

Policing in the City

1. *Introduction*

The analysis of crime events in the division points to the need to treat crime as a complex multi-dimensional concept. 'Crime' used by different persons in different contexts can mean a variety of things. Not infrequently use of terms like 'the crime wave' or 'the war against crime' in discussions can be misleading because of the way they suggest, imply, or treat crime as a simple uniform fact. Nowhere is this imprecision so invidious as when crime and the proportions that are said to be cleared up are used as a measure of police efficiency. As has been shown, there is a great deal more to crime than the word often implies: so, too, there is very much more to police work than clearing it up.

Of the 3,000 events which have constituted this census of police work, only about 2,000, or 66 per cent, are events of the kind that find their way into the criminal statistics. Crudely this should make it clear why rates for crime cleared can be but a poor indicator of police efficiency. Furthermore, the events which have constituted this census do scant justice to the range and diversity of tasks that the police undertake, many of which are as important as they are time-consuming, and as constructive as they are unproductive of paper records that can provide convenient grist for the researcher's mill. Another fact which is of importance is that the process of clearing up crime is itself a complex and (to the outsider) bewildering assortment of several procedures, mainly carried out by the C.I.D. (see pp. 39–43). This further detracts from the value of clear-up rates for measuring the efficiency of the work of the uniformed branch.[1]

---

[1] Members of the uniformed branch are, of course, directly concerned in clearing crime by arrests they make on the street. Of 200 arrests for crime made during the four-month study period, 50 per cent were recorded as arrests by uniformed officers (see p. 40).

The extensive duties of the police that have little to do directly with crime and criminals are those which in an area where many immigrants live require of the police actions that affect or perhaps reflect the existing state of relations between the races. To understand the role of the police in race relations terms is to grasp the significance and complexity of police work as a whole; and it is just that totality of police work that is missed in the usual discussions of police efficiency in terms of clear-up rates of reported crime.

The terminology used in describing police work is as variegated as it is vague. Law enforcement, crime detection, crime prevention, maintaining law and order, keeping the peace, and so on, none of these, nor 'policing' itself, are words and phrases that can easily be given an operational definition. Even in a sphere where one might have supposed the police role (expected and effected) to be clear-cut and specific, that with regard to motoring offences, in practice the extent of such duties is so great that any instructional specificity is modified quite severely due to operational discretion. In addition the police are called upon to perform a whole variety of administrative tasks—from relaying hospital messages, checking on aliens, and receiving lost property, to checking the references of prospective restaurant licence holders. These and many others, routine and exceptional, constitute the whole gamut of the police enterprise. Much of the work is by no means dangerous, or exciting, or recognizably productive; most of it brings members of the Force into daily contact with all sorts and kinds of people in a complex of different roles and situations.

If amid this variety there is a favoured role situation, a valued aspect, then, not surprisingly, it is in terms of the police as law enforcement officers (catching and prosecuting criminals); other functions and duties are seen as adventitious to this central purpose and not proper police work. This ideal is certainly reflected in the training of policemen which is still largely devoted to law studies and first aid, while social studies and subjects loosely defined as 'human relations' feature hardly at all.

My argument is that the higher evaluation of law-enforcement duties above other more time-consuming aspects of a policeman's work sets up tensions within individual policemen and the Police Force as a whole which mitigate against the efficient exercise of the total police enterprise. These other aspects are a variety of tasks which can be seen to bring police and non-criminal public into frequent contact. The nature of this contact largely determines the nature of police–public relations which are recognized to be crucial for good policing in all its aspects, including crime prevention, law enforcement, and the detection and prosecution of offenders.

Mr. Robert Mark, formerly a chief constable, noted for his forthright exegeses of police problems and now promoted to the Police Inspectorate, has suggested that there may be a need arising 'to consider some change in the relationship between the uniformed branch of the Police and the C.I.D., creating in effect an order police—a uniformed body responsible for public order and the sort of job that the police do in uniform today—and a C.I.D. or criminal police'.[1] Such a change would certainly go some way to recognizing a fundamental duality in the nature of police work and allow both aspects to develop, not in isolation, of course, but in harmonious conjunction. Certainly such a development would free the way to a more realistic appraisal of efficiency and of the crime problem.

At the moment there is reason to believe that public confidence in the police as an institution is not great; and policemen sense this. It is interesting to consider the evidence of the Social Survey's inquiry carried out by the Royal Commission into the Police of 1962. As Ben Whitaker shows,[2] the Commission itself placed a curiously complacent interpretation on its Survey's findings:

For some reason which is not easily apparent the Commission seems to have ignored the police's views whenever they were in conflict with those of the public; although each policeman interviewed is both trained to observe and report and in daily touch with the public, whereas many of the members of the public, who were chosen at random may well have had little or no recent contact with any policeman. Furthermore Police Forces and police spokesmen are continually asserting the need to forge a better relationship with the public and seem to be experimenting with vigour and imagination new ways of bringing this about.[3]

[1] Notably in a televised discussion with Sir Peter Rawlinson, entitled 'Do we Need a National Police Force?'; see *The Listener* (25 August 1966), p. 261.

[2] Ben Whitaker, *The Police* (London, Eyre and Spottiswood and Penguin Books, 1964), Ch. 1.

[3] Some of the new systems of beat patrolling are described in a working party's report in *Police Manpower, Equipment and Efficiency* (London, H.M.S.O., 1967).

The need for and value in good police–public relations is greatest where the police function in terms of 'order': it is helpful, but of secondary significance perhaps, to the functional efficiency of the C.I.D. As preservers of peace and order the uniformed police carry out an essential public service to the community, or better put, perhaps, to local *communities*. To the extent that the community accepts and understands the police role and to the extent that the police understand the needs of the community in police terms there is a basis for sound police–public relations. To the extent that the public interpret the police merely as authoritarian thief catchers and to the extent that the police project themselves as authoritarian law enforcers, there is a basis for recrimination, resentment, and complaint.

Most of the crime in such communities is petty thieving, with the occasional crime of violence arising usually from a complex domestic entanglement or from a pub brawl. Much of the thieving is almost insoluble,[1] a good proportion is the work of deprived, disturbed, delinquent youth, most of it committed by local people and not the sort of person to figure as cannon fodder in any war on crime. Yet, unfortunately, the 'war on crime' epithet tends to be compounded with 'order' and community police work, whereas it seems more appropriate when attached to crime police.[2] For, among this local crime there is the occasional job that is the work of well-organized criminal gangs.[3] Few of the criminals and delinquents who find the way to police stations and the courts really figure as men challenging the whole basis of our orderly civilized life, the only lives whose order and stability are challenged are unfortunately their own. Yet, increasingly, it is being recognized that 'in sharp distinction to the usual criminal, a demonstrably successful criminal class is emerging, a minority

---

[1] It was shown earlier that 44 per cent of crime that is 'cleared' is so not by dint of any skilled detection on the part of the C.I.D. but because persons caught for another offence admit their part in previous enterprises.

[2] For an unambiguous use of the 'war on crime' epithet, see B. N. Bebbington interviewed in the *Police Federation Newsletter* (Vol. VI, No. 1, January 1957). 'Consider ourselves as an army, having ground cover to hold the enemy and task forces to attack him . . . the enemies of society such as criminals and the dangerous drivers.'

[3] Among the cleared crimes in this study is an innocent-looking receiving charge for some electrical equipment stolen from a local warehouse. This in fact is a holding charge against a number of suspects involved over several months in a very large number of well-organized and well-planned raids. 'The biggest thing in the Midlands for years', was how a local C.I.D. man described it.

of importance far beyond their numbers, of persistent professional criminals who are caught by the police, only infrequently, if at all, and who thus carry on committing more offences more or less with impunity'.[1] It is suggested that perhaps throughout the country there are fewer than 200 or 300 leaders of criminals and professional receivers. But also it is suggested that there may be emerging in this country an 'opportunity structure' for criminal activity, based on gambling and gaming outfits, clubs, protection, and prostitution, that is such a feature of crime in American cities. It is in these fields of activity that the war against crime can be fought and where developing a strong crime police is an urgent necessity. Newspaper reports suggest that the regional crime squad experiment is proving successful in this field.[2] Such measures, requiring co-operation between Police Forces, demand new systems of financing police activities and are leading to more realistic expenditure by public authorities, who in the past have tended to parsimony over all aspects of policing.

There is also recognized a need to present crime statistics in such a way to distinguish the planned depredation by a criminal minority from the mass of petty thieving of local delinquents. Together, it might be supposed, these measures will promote a fuller understanding of what tasks our police undertake and lead to reforms in procedures and attitudes to facilitate both a more efficient 'crime' police and a well-administered 'order' police, both aspects enjoying the necessary support and confidence of the public.

The distinction between 'order' and 'crime' police is useful in exploring some of the criticisms levelled at the police and in starting to present a picture of police work in its public service *and* criminal-catching aspects. The analysis of the crime data has attempted to demonstrate how within our areas of study there are meaningful and distinct patterns of crime and, therefore, of police work. In different localities there are distinct differences in police operations. These area differences suggest that police work— order police work—must be locally adaptable and sensitive to the particular needs of particular localities. The survey also showed the extent to which crime and socially dislocating acts are phenomena of the inner areas of the city and to what extent they are

---

[1] N. H. Avison, in an address to the British Congress of Crime, September 1966, reported in *Observer* (11 September 1966).

[2] See the *Guardian* (20 January 1967).

caused by local residents. It is in this 'local' policing of an area that the role of the police in race relations terms is most crucial. It has been shown that the involvement of the coloured immigrants in crime (indictable or non-indictable) is very small, yet this does not mean that there is no contact between police and coloured immigrants. In terms of order policing, the demands on the police from the coloured immigrant are not inconsiderable. Like their English and Irish neighbours, West Indians and Pakistanis alike bring their problems and arguments to the police —a considerable number of minor incidents involved the different immigrant groups. It has been noted how immigrants live in areas where much crime occurs; and immigrant houses seem as much prone to attack from the petty thief as 'white' houses. The police have contact with the immigrant community as much when they are complainants as when they are complained about. To understand police-immigrant relations is, then, to understand the whole of the work of the Police Force in serving a community by preserving order and peace and justice.

The police have a direct role to play in the community that is affected by and itself affects the general state of relations between races. The nature of police work brings policemen into daily contact with citizens of all races. This contact, in so far as police action is discretionary rather than strictly bound by rules, provides opportunity for actions that may be discriminatory in the invidious sense. To the extent that the police organization is sensitive to dangers and aware of the possibilities for discrimination, and depending on the way management and education and adaptations in training and operations are exercised by Police Forces, so the police can make a constructive contribution to improving relations between the races.

2. *General and Routine Duties*

The problems the police face which involve them in issues of race relations are those which are central problems of policing: what relation between police and community will allow maximum police effectiveness and how can that relation be achieved? To approach the role of the police in race relations is to understand the complex totality of the police role in general. In the pages that follow an attempt is made to describe that role, laying stress on those aspects which seem to the researcher to have implications for our particular concern. The analysis of policing is derived from a series of observations and conversations made during a four-month period, during which data for the research were collected. An attempt was made to obtain a systematic coverage of normal police duties: observations were made in the five police stations during five week-ends (Thursday–Monday) from 6 p.m. to 2 a.m.; this allowed the researcher to appreciate the range of incidents with which the police are concerned, to see something of police organization, to have the opportunity to discuss various aspects with officers of all ranks, and to provide a general orientation to the area and its police. These observations were followed by ten successive evenings and nights spanning two week-ends with patrol cars in the area. A number of cars patrol the division day and night responding to emergency calls from the public monitored through the central H.Q. information room. Cars are in continuous radio contact, are in frequent touch with police stations and patrolling officers, and are constantly dealing with a wide variety of incidents. Each evening would provide observations with two different car crews and over the period the researcher had contact with several different crews and was able to spend considerable time listening and learning about their approaches to their tasks. Observations were concluded by three successive week-end evenings and nights out on patrol from each of the sub-divisional stations with officers assigned to the area. Each period provided contact with different men and during the week-ends considerable time was spent with a number of officers. In addition to these observations a number of evenings were spent talking with C.I.D. men and men in the plainclothes section. Regular data collection took the researchers into each station once or twice each week for varying lengths of time when it would be unusual not to be involved in wide-ranging discussion. Throughout the period frequent contact was maintained with officers of every rank who were generous with their time and interest in informing the researcher about all aspects of policing. It should be clear, however, that the impressions gained are only impressions; observations of this kind are only an element in sound objective research; and in what follows my interpretation may be open to modification —it is offered as a basis for discussion and description, not to provide any final analysis.

Crime and arrests for indictable and non-indictable offences, the minor incidents to which the police were called, the problem of motoring offences and offenders, are only a small part of police duties. Routine duties are such that in the mornings there may be busy road junctions requiring traffic direction during rush hours, school crossings may need checking, and busy shopping thorough-fares may need regular patrolling. Here the police presence is less to command and enforce, more to help and advise. There may be routine inquiries to be conducted from other Forces and areas about persons reported missing or 'lost' but innocent of any crime or offence. There may be witnesses to a road accident or crime event from whom a statement is required. In the outer suburbs where traffic wardens are yet to be appointed there will be parking regulations to enforce.

In recent years there has been widespread acceptance of the view that there is a viable role within the Police Force for police-women, who today in Birmingham, apart from supplementing many normal and routine police duties within most branches of the Force, function in liaison with local social workers in an important capacity with families and children—particularly in the poorer and less stable areas. As such the policewomen indicate how broad and extensive are legitimate police services within a community.

Routine duties facing the police also bring them into contact with members of the public at times of stress and anguish. Police attend to the scene of every turn-out by the fire or ambulance brigades, to check the circumstances and to offer assistance. The police are used by hospitals to deliver urgent messages to the relatives of the sick and dying. All are situations requiring a measure of tactful sympathy: the role is not authoritarian but helpful.

The unpredictable nature of police work is perhaps its most important component: it is probably easier to predict the type of crime that is going to occur than the kind of incident to which the police are called. What the papers treat as astonishing and sensational—talking down a suicide attempt from a window ledge, or having an arm broken trying to restrain a violent suspect—are less remote to the policeman among whose colleagues are the men who carried out the task. Just as the individual policeman has to be ready for anything, so does the Police Force as a whole. I well remember when on almost the first evening of observations for this research a large fire at a factory on the division disrupted normal policing for several hours. Almost every available man had to leave his area and assist in the many additional tasks that such an event brought—redirecting traffic, controlling sightseers, evacuating nearby residents, manning additional patrols after the fire to deter looters, and so on. The sense of readiness to undertake the unusual, perhaps dangerous, always necessary tasks frequently unrelated to crime prevention and law enforcement is a permanent feature of police operations. A few weeks later a bad train disaster in another part of the city similarly placed an additional burden on the Police Force requiring swift and confident redeployment of manpower to help mitigate the effects of disaster.

During the day routine duties require frequent contact with all sorts and kinds of people in a hundred different situations: at night-time the task is more specific—premises to check, pubs to be 'turned out', and trouble-spots to keep an eye on. In the era of beat work, the policeman's most constant enemy at night must have been boredom, for on some beats the likelihood of anything happening is remote and the chances of the policeman happening to be there when it does, infinitesimal. In more recent enlightened times, the sheer plod of the beat is avoided: more cars, better radio contact (and the forced necessity due to manpower shortage) have seen the decline of this kind of work. What remains is the state of readiness to attend whenever required.

Day or night, 'routine' for the police is a routine unpredictability and uncertainty; a readiness to go to the service of and help those in need or distress at any time of the day or night.

Perhaps the most difficult thing for an outsider to grasp, particularly when there is so much stress on the police being engaged in a 'war against crime', is the variety and complexity and extent of duties which have little to do with crime and criminals: the nature of the police role cannot be understood in terms of crime, law enforcement, arrest, and proceedings, for such misses the major part of what policemen actually do. To begin to understand the whole of the police enterprise, there is a need to consider aspects of police organization and how the police set about their multifarious tasks; there is a need to explore what is implied in the valued concern for close police–public relations; and there is need to inquire into the nature of police 'failure' which can appear as brutality and violence. Most important of all there is a need to explore the idea of 'discretion' and appreciate how its use has developed. Furthermore, policing and police organization are not static, they are contemporary responses to immediate needs which can modify the traditional police role or seem to recapture elements of an earlier policing system. These issues and others must be considered before it is possible to explore the role of the police in terms of race relations. In the pages that follow certain ideas that evolved during the course of observations of the police in action, with some reference to writers, British and American, who have dwelt on contemporary problems facing the police, will seek to provide some such perspective. Three important points are to be noted arising from the description of certain aspects of police procedure that were necessary for an understanding of crime statistics.

First, the nature and variety of police tasks differ from area to area within the division; certain key problems are focused distinctly in just one or two localities. Areas where crime is most frequent are also those where other non-crime police work is most demanding. Police organization needs to be sensitive to these area differences and acknowledge that to achieve a functional police–public relations in the 'problem' areas demand different kinds of approaches and techniques from those required elsewhere.

Secondly, in the normal line of their duties policemen exercise considerable discretion. At every point the policeman's judgement has to be in play with frequently complex sets of facts; the nature of his judgement will determine the action he takes. This discretion is a valued aspect of the policeman's work for it encourages individuality of response to situations where advice and persuasion are more effective instruments than orders and demands. But it is at odds with officially articulated police values which favour a role situation of 'law enforcement officer' where procedures can be governed by rules. The operational setting tends, I believe, to exert a stronger influence than the official recognition or orderly rule-bound procedure: nowhere is this shown more clearly than in the arrest and questioning of a suspect for a minor crime—an incident where police action is that of law enforcement officer (see pp. 36–7).

Thirdly, and very much related to this, there is a need for a better measure of police effectiveness than the frequently cited clear-up rate. Concern for a rising crime wave, reflected in the oft-cited epithet of the need to wage a war against crime, has encouraged police spokesmen and senior officers to stress the crime-catching function of the police to the detriment of other duties. Much local crime is petty, unplanned, 'lucky-dip' thieving, easier to prevent than detect. *Real* crime is the work of skilled professional gangs, mobile and ambitious, and as such is remote from the work of local police. The nature of much local crime requires of the police actions aimed at crime prevention. Fundamental to a preventative function is the achievement of sound police–public relations which are moulded by the way police carry out their everyday duties. Thus there is a need to attach value and worth to all aspects of police work if efficiency in prevention and detection is to be achieved.

Each of these three related aspects have implications for those concerned with race relations. Coloured immigrants live in areas and form communities which pose difficulties for the police, who need to gain the respect and esteem of members of *all* communities, if they are to extend to all communities an equitable degree of protection and supervision against crime and disorder.

3. *Aspects of Police Organization*

The formal structure of police organization reflects a fundamental duality in police work—the division between the uniformed branch and the C.I.D. Both branches have different systems of working in terms of duties and hours, and although there is a similar area and divisional pattern, personnel are deployed through distinct but parallel structures and there is not much interchange of personnel. All recruits spend a week with the C.I.D.; during a young P.C.'s first probationary years he may be selected to spend a period on C.I.D. duties after which he may have an opportunity to join the C.I.D. Thereafter it seemed exceptional for a C.I.D. man to revert to the ranks of the uniformed branch.[1] Older police officers were wont to express satisfaction that they had not joined the C.I.D. where the long tours of duty and the tradition of a long, uncertain, unpredictable pattern disrupts any family life more markedly than other normal police duties. Younger men, particularly the unmarried, expressed strong ambitions to join the C.I.D. Many saw this as *real* police

---

[1] Significantly, perhaps, returning to uniformed duties is, it seems, used as a disciplinary measure against errant or failed C.I.D. officers.

work. The impression was given that the C.I.D. are something of an *élite* and there are some signs of competition between the two branches to outdo each other, success being measured by number of crime arrests.

Within these two branches there is a shallow hierarchy of ranks and relatively little internal specialization. Specialized detective functions are reflected in the city and regional crime squads and in the more technical aspects of detective work. Local policing remains largely undifferentiated.

Formally, the demands on routinization are very great; reports have to be submitted in certain ways and are checked for correctness at a number of stages in the hierarchy. This, it should be noted, is an *ex post facto* supervision rather than operational direction for, as has been indicated, in the exercise of his duties the policeman is in a situation where he is allowed extensive discretionary powers.

The Second Report of the Home Office Working Party on 'Operational Efficiency and Management' has pointed to the need for the achievement of improved communications within the Force, and greater emphasis on man management. Many officers spoken to were critical of certain elements in day-to-day police organization, which would support the Working Party's contention:

We think that there has in the past been a tendency for senior ranks to overlook the need to pass on information; as a result rumours tend to circulate unchecked. . . .[1]

But in many ways the demands on routine within the Force which tend to minimize the scope for individuality and responsibility accompanied by an operational setting which maximizes individual response, only underline the contrast between the officially articulated police role as law enforcement officer, and the actually observed police role which is something much more complex and less amenable to rules of routine and order. The problem of management in the Police Force seems to derive from an insufficiently broad view of what are proper police duties and functions. If senior officers stress crime aspects of police work to the detriment of other duties, significance and authenticity are

[1] *Police Manpower, Equipment and Efficiency* (London, H.M.S.O., 1967), p. 124.

imputed to only a small number of the things that policemen are expected to do.

The founders of the modern Police Force created an organization modelled on the army but involving many important modifications. Certain aspects of this heritage are prominent in the style of contemporary police organization: parades, marching, saluting, drill training, a uniform turn-out, and so on. Many of these are essential and valuable but certain side effects can, I think, be seriously questioned. It is valuable to strive for a disciplined Force where actions are orderly and where efficient exercise of duties is effected. But the stress on routinized internal relations within the Force is at odds with the demands for unroutinized individual and discretionary relations between police and the public they serve. The use of a man's number rather than name by officers is a source of some criticism. It is one way in which the organizational style tends to depersonalize the setting in which police operations are planned. As interpreted by some officers, certain of the forms of organization seemed to conflict with the function of police organization. For the organizational style that results, far from joining men in a collective enterprise where the policing function is a shared responsibility of all concerned, increases the private and individual nature of the interpretation each man has of his duties and is a barrier to the supervision, direction, and control of senior officers.

Senior officers are in a peculiar managerial position: they are only involved when the men under them bring them a report, a person, or an incident to manage. Only in a specialized event like a co-ordinated raid or special plan of action do they designate specific actions and purposes to individuals. As now conceived, a managerial exercise is exceptional. Normally the 'manager' is remote and only involved by his men in specific incidents. This is of course exaggerated: some officers clearly made a point of keeping in contact with everything going on during their watch and actively participating in the day-to-day and hour-to-hour actions of their men. But this seemed somewhat exceptional, the 'expected' function of the watch-inspector seemed to be the more remote and uninvolved variety that has been described.

Such elements as these seem more important than the generally antiquated aspect of much police administration and organization: the old and dotty typewriters, the laborious typing efforts of non-typist officers; the mass of undifferentiated paper work on every imaginable subject from a request for a new door handle at a single man's quarters, to a request for leave or change of duties or a notification of a person reported for a minor motoring infringement. Professionalism in the sense of clear directives, confident exercise of duties, efficient administration of internal aspects of the Force, separated from efficient administration of policing matters, seemed lacking in day-to-day affairs of the Police Force. What was apparent was a keen awareness of the short-comings and malfunctioning of the police expressed in bitterness, tension between personnel, and trenchant criticism. Not surprisingly, and to some encouragingly, internal dissension if not conflict about how the Force is run seemed to matter more than problems facing policemen in the exercise of their duties.

4. Police–Public Relations

The policing needs of different areas, among different communities and sub-communities, are suggested by the uneven distribution of crime and disorder in the various areas of the division. For much crime the notion of detection is irrelevant: the function of the Police Force is to prevent crime not merely by advising people to lock up their possessions and their daughters to prevent theft and assault, but by establishing relations with communities whereby a sense of well-being and security is enhanced. Such a relation requires policemen as individuals and Police Forces as organizations to appreciate the needs of different communities, to understand people and families, their disputes and arguments, as well as to appreciate the kinds of living conditions in which crime and disorder are prevalent.

Michael Banton[1] has explored the importance of considering how the way a policeman exercises his powers is much affected by his participation in the society he polices. British policemen, he suggests, 'feel socially isolated . . . less because the public rejects them than because both the public and the police themselves require such conduct of officers that they are bound to feel set apart'.[2] This sense of isolation is furthered by a tendency on the part of the public to identify all individual policemen with

---

[1] Michael Banton, *The Policeman in the Community* (London, Tavistock, 1964).
[2] Ibid., p. 119.

their occupation to a greater degree than is the case with doctors, clergymen, or representatives of any other occupations. This, Banton suggests, is because of the public ideal of the policeman as peace officer and the recognition that his authority derives from his responsibilities as a citizen. Following the American sociologist, W. F. Whyte, he notes: 'the contradiction between formal obligations and the relationships he needs to build up in [the] community if he is to keep the peace. The policeman who takes a strictly legalistic view of his duties cuts himself off from the personal relations necessary to enable him to serve as mediator of disputes in his area. Yet the policeman who develops close ties with the local people is unable to act against them with the vigour prescribed by the law.'[1] This is a particularly significant remark, for Whyte is describing the police role in an ethnic and culturally distinct slum area of an American city.[2]

In the British setting the policeman's sense of isolation may be changing in nature. It must have been at its greatest when and where policemen were housed together, sometimes in virtual barracks, at other times in fairly well defined colonies of police houses. Yet it can be argued that this social isolation was not disfunctional to the exercise of a policeman's duties because the desired police–public relation was formal and legalistic. So long as society remained fairly homogeneous the policeman could establish a relationship with 'his' community that served the ends of policing for the policeman's position was accepted by all concerned.

Change has taken place on two fronts. There has been a reaction against the idea of police 'colonies' as increasingly policemen have sought pay and status that match their middle-class aspirations. Housing is perhaps the most important aspect of this shift in ideals where policemen seek an equitable position for themselves and their family along with the skilled worker and the lower middle class: policemen have sought—and in Birmingham it would seem they have attained—a move to the suburbs. This is the second aspect, for in so doing policemen have kept pace with their social equals who since the 1930s and especially since the Second World War have moved away from the poor and old decaying central areas of the city for the new suburban estates.

---

[1] Banton, op. cit., pp. 138–9.
[2] W. F. Whyte, *Street Corner Society* (Chicago, 1943).

These moves have left the policemen still somewhat isolated due to occupation but not geographically from their proper neighbours. But it has rendered them remote geographically and in terms of involvement and identification from those areas where crime is most marked and the demands on the Police Force most constant: the poor and decaying areas of cities (Zone I in the division surveyed).

This, it seems, is the most pressing problem facing the police today; how to establish the right kind of relationship with communities and in areas where police neither choose nor desire to live. These are areas where the calls on the police service are greatest and the need for the older, more mature, and experienced men most noticeable. Yet it is likely to be the policeman who is married and with a family who is least inclined to live in the area. Banton's concern is to show how the traditional role of the policeman—the somewhat remote but respected figure policing his own community (i.e. that where he lives) being able to take for granted a shared value system—is increasingly anachronistic as the problem of maintaining order becomes more severe. Less and less can be achieved by formal controls and routine patrolling, more and more will depend on co-operation between police and public and in the general recognition by police and public that the maintenance of order is a co-operative venture rather than a delegated function. Thus it can be seen how the need for police–public relations is greater now than ever before, but the barriers to such relationships are most intense just where the need is greatest.

The recognition that crime is just one adjunct of declining areas where dislocation and disorganization are visible in a number of aspects of the social conditions in those areas; and the recognition that the policing needs for such areas are distinctive from the needs of the more settled, relatively crime-free, suburban areas of the city, must undoubtedly have been behind the major recommendation of the recent Home Office Working Party on police 'Operational Efficiency and Management'[1] which called for more flexible systems of policing urban and suburban areas. In Birmingham this has led to the introduction of an entirely new system of local policing: the unit system of local policing.

What is by no means clear is how far-reaching the actual

---

[1] *Police Manpower, Equipment and Efficiency*, op. cit., pp. 109–48.

changes will be. Many of the arguments for such a change were in terms of better use of limited manpower resources. The system did not, to my knowledge, involve the men in any major programme of re-training. Proponents of the system, in their public utterances, have continued to stress its value as a new weapon in the current war against crime. There are no signs as yet that it will lead to any new measure of efficiency although in an appendix to the Working Party Report, which outlines the duties of the area constable, it is noted that 'his effectiveness will be judged by the amount of information he feeds into the collator'.[1] This certainly suggests a move away from clear-up rates as a measure of police effectiveness and places a strong value on the area constable maintaining a close relationship with the community he serves. What is left unresolved is the central uncertainty in police organization of relations between C.I.D. and uniformed branches, between 'crime' officer and 'peace' officer, and between detection and prevention. If information from the area man is only seen as valuable if it refers to crime and criminals, if the area men are encouraged to become area secret agents to the neglect of the traditional duties on the police *service* front, the system may be of doubted value. Certainly its impact on Birmingham has been considerable, where it is generally thought to have boosted morale among policemen.

There were fears that men would be expected to live on their areas, an idea which prospective beat men on the poor areas did not welcome, and there were doubts that some senior officers would accept the new levels of freedom, initiative, and responsibility that the system requires. Unit policing is interesting because it can be seen as an affirmation of police work in the peace-keeping tradition and as a response to particular needs locally. It places demands on the quality of manpower and leadership of the Force, on the training and guidance offered to beat men, while leaving unchanged most of the operational actions that the Police Force undertakes. The kind of changes that emerge from the analysis that Banton provides may be seen as a logical extension and outcome of the administrative changes effected by the introduction of such systems.

[1] *Police Manpower, Equipment and Efficiency*, op. cit., p. 142. The collator is an office-based man who receives information from the beat constables in the areas, processes it and records it, and makes it available for C.I.D. men, other constables, and so on.

The police needs of a settled community are not great: crime is infrequent and would seem to be reported quickly. The police function would seem to be supportive rather than active: to patrol in the old way regularly each night is both unnecessary and irrelevant. People require to call the police rather as they might an ambulance or fire brigade in an emergency. The police can be left to concentrate on quite particular problems—related to juvenile vandalism, the needs of the busy local shopping centre, or special attention to areas where outbreaks of petty theft (i.e. stealing from parked cars) might seem likely. The relation between police and public in such an area is quite distinct and would seem to provide scope for developing each policeman's personal involvement in the community he serves, which is also the community in which he lives. As the need for *authoritative* police intervention is slight, so the opportunity to establish a close *rapport* and respect exists. This opportunity may mean that the traditional stereotype of the policeman will be changed, and from the patrolling beat officer whose *presence* is preventative of crime and whose availability brings security, the police will become more actively engaged in community life—promoting a respectful understanding of police work, advising in security and road safety, participating in youth clubs and other community organizations. What is needed is to explore ways in which the public can recognize that the police can usefully serve a community in a variety of ways, of which perhaps the least important is arresting criminals, and a recognition by the police that such advisory and supportive functions are central to their role within the community.

The greater problems attach to the less settled communities in the city where the crime figures reveal the extent of disorder and demoralization and the need for policing is very evident. The problems of urban decay and declining areas of cities are many and complex: much of the crime can be sufficiently explained as being characteristic of areas where social controls are slight and a sense of community almost non-existent. Clearly, crime is but one aspect, or one indicator, of a complex set of social conditions, and it would be unwise to suppose that the agencies of law enforcement can counter the social forces. To treat crime as a thing in itself unrelated to its social context can only render the police role oppressive and ineffectual. If the interpretation of the police role is merely in terms of law enforcement, the police may tend to contribute to the process of neglect and decay by treating the symptom and not the disease. A preventative role, however, would stress positive police functions in supporting the inhabitants of the area in their struggle to maintain order and decency. But such a role would require a much greater understanding of the processes and problems of social decay than is shown at present and would require the police to work in close liaison with other agencies working in the area. The situation is complicated by the fact, noted earlier, that the policeman understandably will lack any sense of personal involvement in the community or area because, participating as he does in the general value systems of the city, he and his family will want to escape from such areas to the more pleasant, cleaner, more settled, better schooled suburbs. Police work in the decaying areas is acknowledged to be more difficult and more interesting by many men, but it is accompanied by a rejection of the area as a place to live. How the police serve such a community will depend on their participation in it, and such participation, in contrast to their participation in the settled areas, must necessarily be more professional and less a part of their normal community and social life. But it is no less vital if the police are to be constructively effective as an agency of social control in such areas that the nature of participation and the nature of the police–public relationship reflect an awareness of social needs and a wide interpretation of the police role.

What further complicates the situation in policing such areas is, of course, that to a marked degree these are the immigrant areas of the city. The analysis of the division's crime demonstrates quite clearly the extent to which areas with the highest rates of crime and the highest rates of criminal residence are also those areas where coloured immigrants live. The analysis also showed to a very marked degree how coloured immigrants in particular are far less criminal than their English or Irish neighbours. This requires of the police a particularly sensitive response to the needs of immigrant communities and to the general climate of opinion prevailing among the white community lest they participate in, or are seen by the immigrants to contribute to, general prejudices and discriminatory activities. Not only must the police face up to what may be termed technical problems of achieving a meaningful relationship with minority ethnic groups, distinguished not only by colour but by language, culture, morality, and custom, they must also be aware of processes which hasten or hinder the integration of immigrant minorities and recognize that immigrants may be ignorant of their citizen and civil rights and duties.

5. *The Police Force and the Handling of Complaints against the Police*

One of the most important qualities a policeman must have, or acquire by training, is the ability to make swift decisions appropriate for complex and unpredictable situations. A rule book cannot guide a policeman through the sea of social muddles and interpersonal crises with which he is confronted daily. Although in many instances advice, persuasion, and assistance are sufficient action, they will usually be sufficient because of the authority the policeman represents, for the policeman possesses power to discipline, restrain, or arrest. In some situations arrest is the only action possible, while in others it is only an ultimate possibility among many alternatives. Many of the incidents with which a policeman must deal are potentially or actually violent: the quarrelling family, the drunken brawl, disorderly youth, the fleeing suspect, all these include a violent element. In recent years civil disorders and demonstrations have brought police into sometimes violent conflict with some groups in the community. This element of danger and violence implicit in much police work justifies training policemen in the use of force, for to the police is granted the only legitimate use of force in civil society. The legal recognition that there is a legitimate use of force by the police goes hand in hand with a recognition that in the use of force there lies a major risk and danger for police management and personnel because of the difficulty in practice in distinguishing illegitimate and legitimate uses of force. The danger is that the experience of violence in everyday duties, the inevitable involvement of the use of force in maintaining law and order can lead to a situation in which the police exceed the legal use of force and enlarge the area in which violence is used.

Between the legitimate and illegitimate police use of force is an operationally grey area. The police literature in America has frequent reference to police lawlessness. 'Third degree' measures to exact confessions, and the 'alley-court' in which justice means a police beating rather than arrest and court appearance; these seem to have been commonplace events in years gone by. While these obvious abuses may be now largely things of the past, accusations and allegations of police brutality are still frequently heard in the United States. This brutality can refer not only to individual violence to suspects, but to aggressive patrol tactics, harassment of suspects, arrest on suspicion, verbal insult, or other demeaning behaviour. These complaints and arguments of how they should be handled by the police are part of the chaos and distrust in police-community relations in America, where to a far greater extent than in Britain the use of force by the police is both an operational prerogative and necessity.[1]

The situation in America shows very clearly the way the use of force by the police is implicit in everyday police duties and also how in practice the demarcation between use and abuse is unclear. It also shows how insufficient controls on illegitimate use can grossly impair the basic trust between police and community that is a prerequisite of good policing. In Britain the situation presents a marked contrast. The greater measure of support for and confidence in the police, the lack of any history of police corruption and lawlessness, and the less violent context in which the police operate have meant less need for the police use of force and more effective controls on its illegal use.

Yet the contrast should be seen as one of degree rather than of kind. The context of violence and danger is still a reality for the British policeman. 'You won't be a good copper until you've suffered a hiding', was how one man expressed it to me, implying that once he has felt the reality, a policeman will know how never to be faced with a second defeat. And there is a sharp distinction between the use of force to control and assert authority in a violent or potentially violent situation and the use of force against a suspect. Clearly force must be used against a bunch of unruly drunks punching it up in the bar or street at closing-time on a Friday evening. But if after arrest and in the police station disrespect and abuse flow from the arrested towards the police, the use of force to win silence and submission is, despite the provocation, clearly unjustified.

Obviously instances where the use of force is necessary are very many; but so are opportunities for improper or illegal police

[1] For a full account of the use of force by the police in America, see William A. Westley, 'Violence and the Police', *American Journal of Sociology* (Vol. 49, 1953), pp. 34–41.

force. Restraint can turn into retaliation; threats might turn to punishment. These potential occupational hazards of policing call for special training from management if they are to be overcome.

Example. The police were on the look-out for a young Irishman who some days previously had assaulted a policeman quite severely while being questioned by him in the early hours of the morning in connexion with a motoring offence. A young P.C. off duty spotted the man in a pub in an adjoining division and took him to the nearest police station for interview. A C.I.D. man was called from the division to identify the man and conduct the inquiry. I was told by a number of policemen that a senior divisional officer had instructed that the man *not* be brought to the home station where the assaulted P.C. was based (as would be normal procedure). It was suggested that this was to minimize any risk of the assaulted P.C.'s colleagues getting at the man.

A number of men on duty were critical of the senior officer's actions (some went so far as to say that 'it was none of his business to interfere'—presumably implying administrators should administer, not try to be policemen). They suggested that the man deserved a hiding and deserved to get from a policeman as good as he gave to the assaulted man: an understandable but illegitimate attitude—and one which called for, and got, firm neutralization from the senior officer in question.

The consequences of managerial weakness can be extremely severe, as was revealed in the inquiry that followed two Sheffield detectives appealing their dismissal from the Force.[1] The case in question involved two suspects who were severely beaten in an attempt to exact a confession. But the most serious thing the inquiry revealed was the extent to which violence as an almost normal practice seemed an accepted means within the local C.I.D. The inquiry discusses a briefing given to C.I.D. men who were to form a special crime squad, by a detective chief-inspector who hinted that they might need to use a 'lie detector'. 'By this he certainly meant an instrument used to extract a confession by violence . . . we have come reluctantly to the conclusion that the admitted reference to a "lie detector" did contain a veiled hint to those who wished to take it that force might have to be resorted

---

[1] *Sheffield Police Appeal Inquiry*, Cmnd. 2176 (London, H.M.S.O., 1963).

to. . . .'[1] One of the appellants, the inquiry reports, 'told us that he held views that criminals are treated far too softly by the Courts, that because criminals break rules, police may and must do so to be a jump ahead, that force is justified as a last resort as a method of detection when normal methods fail'.[2] Of the detective-inspector's testimony, the report comments: 'He made use in evidence of two revealing phrases: "These things go off fairly frequently don't they", relating to the skirmish, and "You can't have kid gloves on when detecting crime." '[3]

Many C.I.D. men work under the same pressures of overwork, and the same demands for results, that were offered as mitigation for the Sheffield affair. The extreme and unrepresentative response to the pressures that occurred at Sheffield shows very vividly the dangers and pitfalls that beset the police. The most vital shortcoming found by the official inquiry was the insufficient leadership and control exercised by senior officers.

But perhaps a more important aspect of the Sheffield affair was the way it showed that all too easily an impenetrable curtain of secrecy can be thrown between police and public. The affair only came to public notice when one of the officers involved appealed against the sentence of his Force's disciplinary board. Had he accepted that finding there was no reason for any publicity to have been attached to the matter which till then had been dealt with entirely as an internal matter.

A second case provides a useful illustration of this aspect. In 1958 a Press photographer covering the Guy Fawkes night celebration in Trafalgar Square was arrested for obstruction. Arrested at 9.30 p.m. he was released on bail at 1.30 a.m. He was found guilty on this charge and fined £5. In the meantime he had issued a writ against his arresting officer, a chief inspector, alleging assault and battery, trespass, and false imprisonment. When eventually heard in October 1960 this writ was dismissed. The appeal of this case, *Meek v. Fleming*,[4] brought to light that while the case was pending, the defendant was charged before a police disciplinary board with offences involving the deception of a court of law. On these charges he was reduced in rank from chief inspector to station sergeant. This altered status was not revealed at the trial where the plaintiff's case turned against that of the

---

[1] *Sheffield Police Appeal Inquiry*, op. cit., p. 4.   [2] Ibid., p. 5.   [3] Ibid., p. 7.
[4] (1961), 3. *All England Reports*, p. 148.

defendant and other police officer witnesses. The counsel for the police officer, who was aware of his client's reduced status, laid great stress on the experience, status, and credibility of his witness. The judge and jury clearly agreed. Only after the case did the defendant learn that for almost a year the man he had thought a chief inspector was in fact a sergeant; accordingly the case was appealed. As one of the appeal judges stated: 'The fact that the defendant's advisers were prepared to act as they did showed the great importance which they attached to the facts concealed.'[1] A retrial was ordered.

These two cases underline the frequent absence of effective *public scrutiny*, the difficulties which are likely to face someone with a complaint against the police, and hence the importance which must be attached to the mechanism whereby complaints are handled.

The current situation provides for the internal investigation and hearing of complaints. In the event of a serious case, the investigation may be conducted by a senior officer from some other Police Force or division than that to which the complaint refers. Chief constables, who usually act as chairmen of hearing tribunals, must depute supervision of complaints investigation to some other senior officer so that his impartiality of the hearing is not impaired. The current method undoubtedly produces investigations that are thorough and complete. Nonetheless there is a case for the investigating tribunal to be properly independent of the police. In arguing the case for an ombudsman, *Justice* named three reasons which apply to the case of police tribunals:

(a) No department or authority should be judge in its own cause; (b) a complainant has a natural sense of frustration if he has his complaint rejected without being given the opportunity of putting his facts before an impartial tribunal and without being informed of the evidence by which his complaint was refuted; (c) if complaints are impartially investigated, the department and its officers are able to clear themselves of wild and unfounded charges made against them and a greater degree of confidence and mutual respect is established between public servants and the public.[2]

Some genuine complaints against the police may come from criminals or near criminals whose word and opinion may not be

[1] *All England Report*, op. cit., pp. 148–57.
[2] As cited in Whitaker, op. cit., pp. 151–2.

accepted in court, or whose evidence the police might be inclined to prejudge at an internal hearing. As the Sheffield inquiry noted, the police may be more inclined to resort to violence and illegal methods only with one who 'would be unlikely to complain or to be believed if he did'.[1] The other reasons noted above—the strong position of the police in court, and the possibilities which exist for reducing public scrutiny—all can become strong arguments for independent tribunals. Furthermore, an independent tribunal might be expected to protect the police from excesses of misplaced loyalty while also acting as a better deterrent to misconduct than the existing system of inquiry, rather than by deliberate intent.

The main objections to the establishment of independent tribunals seem to be twofold. In the first place, there is the large number of complaints among which undoubtedly many are trivial if not maliciously intended. In Birmingham in 1966, 178 complaints were received, of which 145 were unsubstantiated. Of the thirty-three substantiated, in twenty-seven instances 'the Officers were given a warning and suitable advice'[2]; six cases resulted in disciplinary proceedings. Clearly, unless an independent system is to be overburdened with trivia, some process of selection is required. But to whom should be entrusted the selective task? Criticisms of the framework in which inquiries are conducted are to be distinguished from criticisms of the inquiries themselves. The thoroughness and excellence of the inquiries themselves is nowhere in doubt.

Secondly, the purpose and motives of complainants must vary a great deal. Few people probably wish to risk an expensive court action in pursuit of damages, few cases are likely to involve or require criminal proceedings. Yet for the police officers concerned a great deal is at stake, not least their reputation and standing within the Force and their prospects for success in their chosen career. As Whitaker comments,

It would be better if both civil servants and policemen felt that they were allowed to admit that they are human, and that to do so would not necessarily prejudice their job . . . an independent inquiry should make every allowance for mistakes committed in the public interest.[3]

[1] *Sheffield Police Appeal Inquiry*, op. cit., p. 8.
[2] Birmingham Chief Constable's Report for 1966, p. 41, which is also the source of the figures cited.
[3] Whitaker, op. cit., p. 150.

Clearly the introduction of a system of independent inquiry would demand complex machinery. What is not doubted is that complaints are other than investigated thoroughly and vigorously under the present system. Whitaker argues strongly that an independent inquiry mechanism would be a better deterrent to malpractices and would, moreover, be welcomed by the majority of policemen. The merits of the present system are administratively and actually very many, yet the aim of a visible system of justice is not done. If it is true that an increasing number of complaints are made by coloured immigrants, as Lester suggests,[1] the need for a demonstrable and visible impartiality in police inquiries is increased, for this sector of the population may not share the hallowed trust in 'the system' shown by the long-established citizenry. With sectors of the population unaccustomed to the particular position of the police in British society, the opportunities for misunderstanding and wrong are many and confidence in the police may only increase if a non-police body, an independent tribunal, can effect understanding and clarity.

These several aspects of police work and organization point to the particular way in which individual policemen can exercise a discretionary judgement in carrying out their duties. Although intelligent management can effect a measure of supervision and direction, the uncertainty of policing, the unpredictability of incident, and the inappropriateness of rules to govern each and every complex situation in which a policeman finds himself lays great stress on the training, education, and qualities of manpower and the way the Force as an organization evolves its own traditions and mores and customs which are the most influential of directives. The values an organization expresses, the opportunities that are made available for different kinds of police work will of course affect the nature of police operations in an area, but by and large the most vital aspect of police–public relations is that which concerns an individual officer in contact with a 'client' whether law-abiding or law-breaking. This element of individuality in the exercise of what are discretionary powers, and how they are applied, interpreted, and used by the individual and by the police organization is the subject of the following chapter.

[1] See p. 177. Such allegations were the repeated concern of C.A.R.D. in the autumn of 1967, see the *Guardian* (6 November 1967).

CHAPTER 5

Discretion, Professionalism, and the Prevention of Crime

The office of constable is much older than the Police Force. To an ancient office over the years have been added a great number of diverse tasks. Since 1829 the form of administration, the setting within which the constable works, has been that of the modern Police Force. Also older than the Police Force have been arguments and proposals for limiting and restricting police powers. The legal philosophy of democratic society sees police activities as potentially threatening to individual liberty and implying a danger of arbitrary interference. Accordingly the police are subjected to a host of restrictions concerning the ways they carry out their tasks. '[The] interplay between ends and means', Michael Banton suggests, 'is much more complex than in most organizations. The efficiency of the police may, therefore, be less important than their responsiveness to the community they are required to serve.'[1] The previous chapter discussed how the police are faced with most intense problems of 'responsiveness' in areas of the cities where most of their work occurs and which are also immigrant areas. What has been said so far of police work has intended to suggest the wide variety of contacts between police and public, few of which require authoritative police intervention but where the individual policeman can exercise considerable discretionary judgement before deciding what action is appropriate. Through the exercise of discretionary powers policemen and Police Forces are enabled to achieve the desired kind of relationship with communities, for it makes possible less formal relations between police and public than would follow from the idea of strict duties of law enforcement. But the use of discretionary powers can be seen to be police modifications of the regulations

---

[1] Banton, op. cit., pp. 105–6.

which are supposed to constrain policemen and reduce the extent of an *arbitrary* interference with individual liberty. Thus the use of discretion is a contentious issue. Some writers and police officers tend to deny the significance of discretion and suggest that as law enforcement officers policemen impartially administer the law according to the rule of law itself. Other writers recognize the operational necessity of discretionary procedures but also recognize the way such procedures can undermine police responsiveness to the rule of law.

Most of the literature concerns the American situation where an unenviable tradition of corruption and lawlessness within the Police Force and the considerable political control that is exerted locally on police administration, have led to far greater emphasis on legal controls and checks against police practices and malpractices than is apparent with reference to the British police.

Joseph Goldstein[1] has defined the concept of enforcement with some precision. He distinguishes between 'Total Enforcement' and 'Full Enforcement', between which falls the dark figure of unreported crime. Full enforcement means:

(1) the investigation of every disturbing event which is reported to or observed by [the Police] and which they have reason to suspect may be a violation of the criminal law; (2) following a determination that some crime has been committed, an effort to discover its perpetrators; and (3) the presentation of all information collected by them to the prosecutor for his determination of the appropriateness of further working the criminal process.

Goldstein shows, however, how full enforcement is not a realistic expectation and that between full enforcement and *actual* enforcement, decisions not to invoke the criminal process are made both by the police and by prosecutors. He argues that:

The mandate of full enforcement under circumstances which compel selective enforcement has placed the municipal police in an intolerable position. As a result, non-enforcement programmes have developed under cover, in a hit-or-miss fashion, and without regard to impact on the overall administration of justice or the basic objectives of the criminal law. Legislatures ought to consider what discretion, if any,

---

[1] Joseph Goldstein, 'Police Discretion not to Invoke the Criminal Process. Low Visibility Decisions in the Administration of Justice', *Yale Law Journal* (No. 69, March 1960).

the police must, or should, have in invoking the criminal process and what devices, if any, should be designed to increase visibility and hence reviewability of these police decisions.[1]

Wayne La Fave[2] has distinguished various types of situations in which observed instances of law-breaking are not followed by prosecution:

(i) Where the legislature is thought not to desire enforcement either because of ambiguity in the wording of the law, or where the noticed infringement does not come within the vice that the law is intended to check, or instances of laws which for a variety of reasons have fallen into disuse and whose strict enforcement would be anachronistic.

(ii) Where resources available to the agencies of legal administration are limited and where selectivity applies to exclude the trivial offender, or the conduct is thought common among the offenders section of the population (i.e. Negro violence) or where the victim is unwilling to press charges.

(iii) Those instances where prosecution would achieve nothing or would cause the police loss of public respect, or where non-invocation is planned to bring greater rewards elsewhere or which would cause, for offender or victim, unnecessary hardship. La Fave notes, however, that these are not hard and fast instances whose non-enforcement always applies. Particular cases where process would not normally be invoked can on occasion lead to arrest.

Both these American writers note the essential usefulness of discretionary non-enforcement, while remarking on the dangers into which it can lead police organizations. For England and Wales, where the police are themselves prosecutors, their remarks are of direct relevance. Many of the situations defined by La Fave have parallels in the incidents described in earlier chapters: it was noted that in some domestic violence, in cases of drunkenness, and in relation to motoring offenders, the police decline to prosecute in every case of known infringement. It was suggested that with motoring offenders, although there is great justification

---

[1] Goldstein, op. cit.
[2] Wayne La Fave, 'The Police and Non-Enforcement of the Law', Parts I and II, *Wisconsin Law Review* (January and March, 1962).

for discretionary procedures because of the chaos that full enforcement would bring to administrations, in determining who is actually selected for enforcement, the manner of the person when questioned can be of no little importance. This also applies in some instances of drunkenness where a man can either talk himself into or out of a charge. In both cases the danger lies in the manner of the suspect becoming of greater importance than the observed infringement, which can lead to the selective enforcement (or non-enforcement) of certain *categories* of person. Potentially such a basis for discretionary judgement is discriminatory.

More important are those instances where the police decide on other grounds that a prosecution is inappropriate. It was noted that there are a number of assaults which do not lead to prosecution: the manner and extent of the assault, the relationship of the parties, the willingness of the complainant to take the matter to court, the social standing of the persons, and the nature of the area in which the event occurred; all these considerations count in deciding whether a charge should be made. Goldstein[1] found that in America too there was widespread use of the discretion in cases of domestic assaults. He found that it was common police practice not to invoke any process unless the victim of the assault signed a complaint. This leads to the police persuading victims not to prosecute and is justified as saving work for the police, for it can be argued that such violence reflects an accepted means of solving disputes (particularly among Negroes), and also, the police argue, that it is right and proper to anticipate the dismissal by judge and district attorney of cases in which the victim is an unco-operative witness. Similar arguments would appear to apply in this country: the police feel that they would be criticized by magistrates, judges, and others if they brought trivial domestic violence to court; they also feel that a great many of the victims are seeking not a court case but an immediate cessation of violence, for which end police presence is sufficient; reflecting the different systems, instead of persuading victims not to sign a complaint as happens in the U.S.A., in England the police can point out that the victim can himself institute proceedings and summons the assailant thus releasing them from unnecessary and tiresome work. The question raised by Goldstein is relevant here.

[1] Goldstein, op. cit.

If assaults are made criminal in order to reduce threats to community peace and individual security, should a victim's willingness to prosecute ... be relevant to the exercise of police discretion ... can the individual police officer, despite his own value system, sufficiently respond to officially articulated community values to be delegated broad powers of discretion?[1]

The above instances of discretion come within the category of 'low-visibility' cases of police non-enforcement, so called because they are not subject to review by prosecutor or judge. A less contentious form of discretion operates following an incident where a police officer observes an infringement of the law and informs the person involved that a report will be submitted as a result of which charges may be laid. This may be termed administrative discretion whereby the police as prosecutors decide whether process is appropriate and if so what process is appropriate. The submitted file is seen by senior officers at several levels in the police hierarchy before a decision is reached.[2] A difficult case may be referred to the Police Force's prosecuting solicitor for comment and at any point the upward movement through the hierarchy can be halted for queries, recommendations, re-draftings, and so on, to be effected. The final recommendations can be for (a) filing the papers, in which case no action is taken; (b) for a caution in cases where there is a clear admission of guilt but where court process is thought inappropriate[3]; or (c) for summons in which case an 'information' is laid before a magistrate to effect an eventual court appearance. This is the common procedure adopted for many minor larcenies like shop-lifting offences and for cases involving juvenile offenders.[4] During the survey period 112 such process files were submitted and led to some police action: thirty-nine resulted in cautions, the remainder were dealt with by summons. Forty-three of the sixty-two juvenile cases were dealt with in this way.

[1] Goldstein, op. cit.

[2] It was not possible to judge at what level the crucial decision was made.

[3] In some areas, but not Birmingham, selected juvenile offenders are supervised following a caution under the Juvenile Liaison Scheme. In some cases, the attitude of the complainant (i.e. the shopkeeper in the case of a shop-lifting offence) may be significant in determining whether process will be by caution or by summons.

[4] It is also the procedure for motoring offences, except that the papers go to a special administrative unit for process rather than through the hierarchy of senior officers.

This well-structured system of review in minor cases is to a certain extent mirrored in the procedure following an arrest for a crime, except that an arrested person has to be brought to court very quickly, usually within twenty-four hours. In all but the more serious cases the local C.I.D. man will handle the case in court, although increasingly prosecutions are dealt with by the prosecuting solicitor. In more serious cases the first court appearance will be brief in order for the police to obtain a period on remand to prepare their case fully and provide opportunity for the arrested person to prepare a defence. The kind of discretionary actions open to the police at the proceeding stage of a case lies beyond the scope of this essay,[1] but it should be noted that following arrest some scope for discretion does exist, for the police as prosecutors can determine how seriously to interpret the offence through the way they present it in court and, in some instances, in the choice of section and statute under which they bring the proceedings. What needs to be borne in mind is that the police are not bound to prosecute all offenders of which they have knowledge. 'It has never been the rule in this country that suspected criminal offences must automatically be the subject of prosecution. Public interest is the dominant consideration.'[2]

By and large, the police themselves are interpreters of this 'public interest' although checks on police interpretation do exist from the magistracy (who have to approve summons, and grant warrants for arrests and for raids on suspected premises) and in certain fairly well defined instances from the Director of Public Prosecutions. But these checks are largely of an *ex post facto* nature requiring police initiative for them to become operative. This is perhaps the most important of all aspects of discretion, that which derives from police organization itself in determining what level of policing to apply to what areas, how to deploy personnel, and what significance to attach to certain specialized police duties in enforcing 'non-complainant' infringements whose prosecution depends entirely on police initiative. Commonly these special duties relate to prostitution, drugs, illegal gambling and gaming clubs, and infringements of licensing laws. As was implied earlier,

---

[1] An excellently clear account is provided in the relevant chapters of R. M. Jackson, *Enforcing the Law* (London, MacMillan, 1967).

[2] Hartley Shawcross, when Attorney-General, quoted by G. L. Williams, 'Discretion in Prosecuting', *Criminal Law Review* (No. 223, 1956).

police administrations are often faced with extraordinarily difficult tasks to perform balancing and bolstering the moral ambiguities of the nation: nowhere is this clearer than in jurisdiction of
prostitution. Such a range of duties, reflecting, as has been said,
an organizational discretion, also provides scope and in many
ways invites operational discretion from those specialist officers
assigned to the various tasks. La Fave makes the point that it is
just in relation to these non-complainant offences that discretion
is most open to abuse for only the parties concerned can know
about it. La Fave,[1] Goldstein,[2] and Jerome Skolnick[3] all pay
particular attention to narcotics law enforcement to illustrate their
arguments. They report a fairly complicated system of bartering
with informants and suspects which reveals a toleration of minor
infringements of the narcotics laws in the quest for hard evidence
against the big-time operators. The police guarantee immunity
to a known offender in return for leads and information concerning
others. In this country the state of drugs control has probably yet
to reach this stage and it might be hoped that the critics of the
American system are given careful attention. It is possible to see
a somewhat analogous situation here in relation to prostitution
and within the informant system as a whole. A degree of immunity
can be extended to a prostitute in return for information about
the men who may be living off her or others' earnings. In a situation where there is something of a link-up between prostitution,
illegal clubs and gaming, and distribution of drugs, informants
implicated in one aspect of these activities can be rewarded by a
let-off, a reduced charge, or an assurance of the blind eye, for
good information. Persons known to be infringing the law (i.e.
prostitutes) can be approached with a carrot of modified surveillance if they will work for the police and aid and abet their
inquiries. The American authors draw attention to a number of
discretionary techniques employed by the police: bargaining with
a number of 'rewards' for information or a high clear-up rate.
Within this aspect of police jurisdiction lie most of the dangers
and hazards of abuse and corruption that face the police. These
bartering discretionary techniques require detectives to enter into
something of a client–customer relationship with the persons
involved and from them arise opportunities for bribes, protection

---

[1] La Fave, op. cit.   [2] Goldstein, op. cit.
[3] Jerome H. Skolnick, op. cit., pp. 139–64.

money, and so on. These are also the areas where complaints are heard concerning 'planting' of incriminating evidence and other 'unfair' or illegal means of obtaining evidence. Not only are police administrations faced with formidable decisions as to how to organize and deploy manpower, they are also faced with formidable managerial and supervisory difficulties to ensure high standards of policing that balance efficiency with legality.

This is the contentious nature of the use of discretion: because it is an invisible procedure it tends to violate a principle of good justice: 'A regularized system of review is a requisite for insuring substantial complaint by the administrators of justice on [the] rule-of-law principles.'[1] Because operationally it is most needed in relation to non-complainant offences, it rapidly becomes associated with police corruption and police illegality, for the discretionary procedures discussed are police modifications of the legal restrictions aimed at maintaining a proper level of police legality. Goldstein suggests that the extent of discretion is increased by the unreal demands of full law enforcement in excess of what is actually attainable (see p. 160). The use of police discretion is, then, a means of increasing police efficiency in terms of law enforcement.

The way a Police Force and police personnel exercise discretionary judgement will very much determine the nature of the police role. The link with police efficiency forces a return to the question, mentioned earlier, of the validity of present measures of police efficiency which are in terms of clear-up rates of reported crime, that is in terms of the police as an agency of law enforcement. The description of police work has demonstrated how much of it requires some other justification than law enforcement. This justification for the variety of police duties lies in terms of achieving close relations between police and public to enhance crime prevention and the maintenance of order from which better law enforcement in terms of detecting criminals can follow. Such duties, it was noted, frequently require of police officers and police administration the exercise of discretionary judgement whereby they are seen to perform a public service that is akin to social work rather than the exercise of legally defined and legally rule-directed law enforcement. Banton[2] suggests that to achieve effective policing in the traditional crime preventing manner can

[1] Goldstein, op. cit.   [2] Banton, op. cit.

be seen to require an untraditional professionalism in administration, training, and operations, which would build on the many opportunities of a discretionary nature that exist in that day-to-day work of uniform police officers.

I have suggested, however, that current police ideology, despite notable experimentation with new systems of policing urban and suburban areas, in its stress of the war against crime and clear-up rates seeks a professionalism in terms of law enforcement and as an agency of detection which would seem to value techniques of crime control rather than improved police–public relations. Hence it was not uncommon to find senior police officers denying that significance of discretion as described above, and advocating an ideal of policemen as law enforcement officers devoted to full enforcement as defined by Goldstein. But as Banton notes, such full enforcement would require policemen to be 'far more detached from society than is possible under the present system'.[1]

At this juncture it is useful to consider a recent major treatise on the police by Jerome H. Skolnick,[2] which, though based on the American experience, draws frequent parallels with British policing and explores many issues which are relevant to both countries. Skolnick sees 'the principal problem of police as a democratic legal organization' to derive from the fact that 'the police in democratic society are required to maintain order and to do so under the rule of law'.[3] The legal philosophy of democratic society sees police activities as potentially threatening to individual liberty and accordingly hedges the police about the legal checks and barriers to arbitrary acts. On the one hand, the police are required to work within a firm set of rules, while on the other, they are invited to develop individual skills and techniques akin to those of professionalism, to organize along the lines of bureaucratic enterprise. The conflict has been intensified by the growth in problems of crime and its control. 'In the effort to introduce fairness, calculability and impersonality into an American administration of criminal justice, often riddled with corruption and political favouritism, most writers who have seriously examined police have tended to reforms based on the managerial conception of professionalism.'[4] But, Skolnick believes,

---

[1] Banton, op. cit., p. 131.   [2] Jerome H. Skolnick, op. cit.
[3] Ibid., p. 6.   [4] Ibid., p. 236.

'such a conception of professionalism not only fails to bridge the gap between the maintenance of order and the rule of law; in addition it comes to serve as an ideology undermining the capacity of police to be accountable to the rule of law'.[1] He quotes one version of police work which stresses the non-mechanical nature of the policeman's art. '[This] consists in applying and enforcing a multitude of laws and ordinances in such degree or proportion and in such manner that the greatest degree of protection will be secured. The degree of enforcement and the method of application will vary with each neighborhood and community. There are no set rules, nor even general principles, to the policy to be applied. Each policeman must, in a sense, determine the standard to be set in the area for which he is responsible. . . .'[2] The logic of this argues for a 'system of organization which allows officials to initiate their own means of solving specific problems'.[3] And such a system, Skolnick finds, is particularly relevant to 'the task of enforcing crimes without citizen complainant'. But he also finds that the actual system adopted means that 'the police are increasingly articulating a conception of professionalism based on a narrow view of managerial efficiency and organizational interest'. He argues:

The needed philosophy must rest on a set of values conveying the idea that the police are as much an institution dedicated to the achievement of legality in society as they are an official social organization designed to control misconduct through the invocation of punitive sanctions. The problem of police in a democratic society is not merely a matter of obtaining newer police cars, a higher order of technical equipment or of recruiting men who have to their credit more years of education. What must occur is a significant alteration in the ideology of police, so that police 'professionalism' rests on the values of a democratic legal order rather than on technical proficiency.[4]

Skolnick is himself pessimistic about such a transformation being achieved in America for he sees all the pressures making for managerial efficiency rather than *legal* professionalism. He finds that the official system of 'justice without trial' is one

---

[1] Skolnick, op. cit., p. 237.
[2] B. Smith, *Police Systems in the United States* (New York, Harper, 1960), p. 19, quoted by Skolnick, op. cit., p. 237.
[3] Ibid., p. 237.   [4] Ibid., pp. 238–9.

permeated by the negation of the presumption of innocence. He finds communities expressing fears, not about violations of due process but about a seemingly rising crime rate and the ability of the police to cope with it. Continually the police have to respond to the pressures of the dilemma of having two sets of ideals thrust upon them.

As an institution dependent upon regards from the civic community, police can hardly be expected to be much better or worse than the political context in which they operate. When the political community is itself corrupt, the police will also be corrupt. If the popular notion of justice reaches no greater sophistication than that 'the guilty' should not go free then the police will respond to this conception of justice. When predominant members of the community become far more aroused over an apparent rise in criminality than over the fact that Negroes are frequently subjected to unwarranted police interrogation, detection and invasions of privacy, the police will continue to engage in such practices. Without widespread support for the rule of law, it is hardly to be expected that the courts will be able to continue advancing individual rights, or that the police will themselves develop a professional orientation as *legal* actors, rather than as efficient administrators of criminal law.[1]

British criminology needs to resist temptation to draw over-hasty parallels from American studies, but it would seem many aspects of Skolnick's work apply over here. The duality that Skolnick finds in the demands of maintaining order and operating within the rule of law is mirrored for the British police in the conflicting demands of crime prevention and crime detection. As Skolnick finds an ethos of managerial professionalism undermining notions of legality, the British researcher finds the demands for a better clear-up rate undermining notions of crime prevention. As Skolnick finds value being placed on technical proficiency and more modern equipment to match modern techniques, the British researcher finds value being attached to organizational and equipment modifications without any great rethinking of how to improve police–public relations. American and British settings share the same propensity for the guilty plea to be valued more than the judicial inquiry into guilt. In both countries the spectre of a rising crime rate seems to distract attention from the social

[1] Skolnick, op. cit., p. 245.

conditions and the setting of human relations of which those crime rates are a reflection. In both countries the police are seen as responsible for law and order as a delegated function, not as a shared enterprise between police and public. The description of the policeman's art is equally applicable to the art of English policing. And underlying both systems, but in both countries in danger of being overlooked, is the need to safeguard the liberty of the individual. In both countries the nature of discretion and the task of the police in enforcing non-complainant infringements highlight the problems of a just and proper policing of our towns and cities.

The transformation of police ideology that Skolnick sees as vital to the proper functioning of the police in a democratic society bears a close resemblance to the analysis provided by Banton in stressing that responsiveness to community needs must take priority over efficiency. Both see as essential functions of police work, the idea of sharing in a value-oriented enterprise of administering justice within a community. But if Skolnick is pessimistic of the outcome in America, Banton's analysis suggests why in England there is cause for optimism. Compared with America, policing in Great Britain enjoys some prestige and a great tradition of community service. The kind of work that the police undertake and the fact that the traditional ideal type of policeman is the uniformed 'peace' officer give strength to the argument for the police role to develop along these lines. Indeed in unit policing it is possible to see some of the ideas expressed by Banton made operational. Furthermore, the lower volume of crime in Britain and its less serious nature reduce the pressures for results of the kind that Skolnick found in America. Again, the freedom of the British police from a reputation of corruption and lawlessness means that there is less sensitivity about police interference with freedom and intrusion into privacy and a more confident trust in the police use of discretion. Skolnick's analysis of American policing is valuable because it reveals very clearly the tensions and ambiguities in policing from which it is possible to gain a clearer understanding of the place of the police in British society and the role they perform in relation to British communities. Both Banton and Skolnick provide an analysis of the police function in relation to immediate problems facing the police and serve to explain something of the current ambiguity in British policing deriving from no clear rationale and adminis-tration that reflect the contrasting needs of maintaining order and catching criminals, of crime prevention and crime detection.

Until this ambiguity is resolved, the possibility of the police achieving the kind of area flexibility described in the previous chapter recedes and the probability of increasing detachment of police from immigrant communities and of policing in its narrow legal definition being seen as an adjunct of a hostile and dis-criminatory white society exacerbating racial hostility, may be thought to be greater. Such is the logic of Skolnick's argument.

The insights provided by Jerome Skolnick's sociological treatise on the American police and the analysis provided by Michael Banton in his comparative study of American and British Police Forces could be seen to confirm the interpretation of current police work in terms of conflict between preventative and detec-tive functions. Another dimension to this situation is provided by those who have wondered and worried over the constitutional position of the Police Force and police constables and described a situation of uncertainty about the constitutional position of the police as an organization.[1] An historical study like that provided by Charles Reith[2] in an interesting way can contribute to the present debate.

The ancient office of constable derived from the collective duty of each hundred and township to apprehend criminals. In each township and hundred it was the custom for this responsi-bility to fall by yearly rotation to an appointee who came to be called constable. Local parish constables were obliged to make yearly presentments of their work to the local hundred courts, the court leet, or petty sessions. The duty effectively gave the con-stable of the hundred (the high constable) some superintendence over the local parish constables.

Originally the appointment was achieved by election among local residents then later by the courts. During the course of centuries it became the custom for the justices of the peace to appoint them, for, as the nature and extent of local bureaucracy grew, the justices of the peace took over the duties of the high

[1] For this aspect, see Geoffrey Marshall, *Police and Government* (London, Methuen, 1964).
[2] Charles Reith, *A New Short History of the Modern Police* (Edinburgh and London, Oliver and Boyd, 1956).

constable in the hundreds and assumed superintendence over the local parish constables.

Thus the local character of the office of constable and its effective subservience to local justices are of ancient establishment. The nineteenth-century statutes by which Police Forces were created preserved this relationship of constables to the justices. And the precursors of the modern police, the Bow Street runners, were organized bands of full-time constables employed by the Bow Street magistrates and acting under their immediate direction.

During a period of centuries the tasks that constables undertook expanded considerably as the importance and duties of the local justices of the peace increased. Originally entrusted with the task of apprehending criminals and bringing them before the court, the constable increasingly became a general factotum carrying out myriad tasks for the local justices. This itself might not have happened if, again from an early date, the original elected representatives had not found the task unpopular and inconvenient and resorted to paying deputies, often men simple, illiterate, poor (and therefore cheap), to fulfil their duties for them.

By the nineteenth century constables of all sorts and kinds, appointed by different justices to fulfil different duties, served in a chaos of ways, cheaply and inefficiently and without any over-all co-ordination and direction. The effect of Peel's 1829 Metropolitan Police Act was to end this muddle and confusion in London by transferring the power to appoint and control constables to two special justices, the Police Commissioners. Thereby the modern Police Force inherited a wide range of duties from the past to which was added the new and urgent one of making the metropolis safe for its inhabitants. Initially the London magistrates retained their power to appoint and direct their own constables: these, the direct followers of the Bow Street runners, had a quite limited function in aiding the prosecuting magistrates as a detective force.

The first years of the new police were by no means easy. Peel's reforms were monumental but achieved more by cunning and clever political manoeuvre, and were effected against widespread opposition both in Parliament and from the public; and the way the reform was designed, arbitrarily transferring jurisdiction over constables from the magistracy to two Commissioners of unexplained status and authority, aggravated relations with the magistrates. The police were attacked in Parliament, given grudging support by Home Secretaries and under-secretaries, opposed by the magistrates to whom they bore no well defined relation, and vilified by a public which saw them as a political force aimed at crushing their expression of political opinion.

Yet within a few decades the idea of policing and the style of Police Force established in the metropolis won wide acceptance and was extended throughout the country. The success of the police against considerable odds in its first years owes much to the influence of its first Commissioners who enunciated very clearly what kind of policing was to be achieved. The first paragraph of the first handbook of 'General Instructions' for the Metropolitan police officers is worth noting:

It should be understood, at the outset, that the principal object to be attained is the Prevention of Crime. To this, great and every effort of the Police is to be directed. The security of person and property, the preservation of the public tranquillity and all other objects of a Police Establishment, will thus be better effected, than by the detection and punishment of the offender, after he has succeeded in committing the crime. . . .

To effect better relationships both within the Force and with the public the first Commissioners broke with tradition in whom they employed as constables. Traditionally the Dogberry-type figure was uncomfortably near the mark, but probably more amiable than the reality. Jennifer Hart, in her history of the British police, cites a remark in Blackstone: 'considering the class of man who commonly acted as constable, it was just as well that he remained in ignorance of the powers which were entrusted to him by the law'.[1] The first Commissioners declined to employ the sundry suitors, hangers-on, and grafters that the powerful, as was common and expected practice, recommended to them for favour. They sought men of a different class and calibre, for their interpretation of policing required a close and respectful relation between the police and public.

It is possible to see in these reforms how the particular position the police occupy in society today and the extent to which the uniform peace officer provides the ideal of policing owe more

[1] Jennifer Hart, *The British Police* (London, Allen & Unwin, 1951), Ch. 1.

to the decade 1829–39 than to the often asserted antiquity of the role of constable. The modern police though statutorily welded (and very uncomfortably) to the traditional model would seem to be more important in its new aspects than its traditional ones.

Success came because the police were effective: security was achieved to some great measure, and by a careful unarmed deployment riots were controlled without the police gaining a reputation for oppression. Public favour was courted because it was seen as fundamental to the tasks of maintaining order and controlling crime; and within a decade a firm foundation was laid from which modern policing derives.

What Reith finds left unresolved is the problem of who controls the police. He finds a confused muddle of shared responsibilities stemming from the first reformers who never gave clear thought to where the police should stand in relation to other authorities. 'There is no defect of police administration from which the public and police suffer more seriously than its consequent voicelessness, in the absence of any established authority with full responsibility and obligation to speak for it, and for the Police, to Parliament and to the Public.' From such a defect derives, Reith believes, a loss of purpose in the police administration which has meant the loss of a clear-sighted principled direction of police actions that so marked the formative years of the first Commissioners. The main effective failure has been shown in an unpreparedness to spend money. 'Insufficient pay leads to insufficient man-power; to enforced reliance on mechanization; to concentration of detection and neglect of prevention; to loss of contact with the public; to loss of police power.'[1]

It is interesting to find Reith's analysis in accord with those of Skolnick and Banton. Reith is alarmed at the kind of bureaucratic organization into which the police has grown where detection is valued above prevention and where police answerability to the rule of law is undermined by there being no clear relation of police to other authorities. He also recognizes as fundamental to good policing the firm establishment of close and respectful relations between the police and the communities they serve: an aim he sees threatened by the growing superiority of the detective ethos. In this way all three writers would concur that current trends in policing which aim at efficient law enforcement are in

[1] Reith, op. cit., Ch. 7.

conflict with a broader, more traditional, and by no means anachronistic definition of the role and functions of the police. A description of police work shows that elements in the broader version, whatever the current official ideology may suggest, continue to occupy a significant place in day-to-day police operations. The disjunction between expressed purpose and aims and actual operations can be seen as a defining element in current police practice which is marked with ambiguity and uncertainty.

CHAPTER 6

The Police and Race Relations

1. *Policing Immigrant Areas*

The kind of role the police can be expected to play in race relations terms depends on the kind of role the police perform for society in general. An interpretation of policing that values police–community relations highly and seeks to establish meaningful levels of confidence between police and public may be expected to play a positive part in race relations terms, for such a role will require some structure of communications and liaison between police and immigrant communities. A legalistic interpretation of police work stressing law enforcement aspects might be seen to involve a detachment in relations between the communities and multiply the occasions for misunderstanding or worse.

As might be expected the actual situation reflects elements of both interpretations.

Immigrant school children in Warley and Birmingham when asked about policemen spoke in terms of the help and advice and friendliness they had received: in no way did they identify policemen with punitive or other unpleasant measures.

A police officer in London talking to a mainly West Indian class at a girls' school was met by the unanimous assumption that everybody who went inside a police station was beaten up.[1]

In West Bromwich the local Caribbean Association presented a silver cup to the local West Midlands Police Force in appreciation for the way the Force, and particularly the detective-sergeant who had been acting as liaison officer, had helped them. The chairman of the Association is reported as saying: 'The Police at West Bromwich have done so much for us. They have helped to organize peace and contentment. The cup is a small representation of the high esteem and goodwill between us.'[2]

[1] Reported by Colin McGlashan, 'Growing up with Pinky', *Observer* (10 September 1967).
[2] *Birmingham Post* (25 April 1967).

In April of 1967 *The Times* carried a prominent story, under the headline, 'Police Accused of Racial Brutality',[1] of a report of instances of racial discrimination brought to the attention of the Campaign Against Racial Discrimination and published by them. The C.A.R.D. Report cites forty-three instances of discrimination in a number of fields—five relate to police brutality. 'Complaints of brutality or ill-treatment by the police occur with disturbing frequency. They are invariably denied', the Report states. The Report states further: 'It is not our contention that all these complainants are blameless in every respect. In two of the cases it is quite possible that the complainants were involved in situations which were, to put it at the lowest, suspicious. But if we are permitted to make that deduction, we are also permitted to deduce that the behaviour of the police, if these allegations are accurate, was on all these occasions less than exemplary.' 'It is not altogether surprising', the Report concludes, 'that immigrants do not on the whole regard the police force as a body to whom they can turn with any kind of confidence.'[2]

Writing in the *Sunday Times* Anthony Lester—a barrister and then legal adviser to C.A.R.D.—has noted:

In some places, complaints by coloured Britons of police misconduct outnumber those on any other subject. The hostility which many West Indians in particular feel towards policemen may often spring from previous experiences in the Caribbean rather than here. But what matters is that allegations of police brutality and harassment are readily believed in the coloured community, and that in the absence of any independent machinery to investigate complaints, this vital area of race relations will fester.[3]

Much official regret is expressed at the paucity of coloured recruits to the Police Force. A common attitude found among members of the Force is that 'the police are not yet ready to recruit coloured policemen'. Maureen Cain has noted a variety of reasons offered of varying plausibility: 'Never . . . is it mentioned that there would be internal difficulties which is obviously

[1] *The Times* (17 April 1967).
[2] Campaign Against Racial Discrimination, *Report on Racial Discrimination* (London, C.A.R.D., April 1967), p. 5.
[3] *Sunday Times* (30 July 1967).

the real case.'[1] A survey[2] carried out in a Police Force in an area where there was very little coloured immigration asked policemen of all ranks whether 'coloured recruits should be sought in areas of high immigration'. A majority thought not, although a significant number of higher ranking officers approved the idea. The usual formal barrier to recruitment is level of education and, particularly, language ability, although no published figures show whether a higher proportion of immigrant applicants fail than the over-all population of applicants. It needs to be borne in mind that there is also extreme shortage of the good white recruit.

An interesting innovation in police administration is the appointment in some areas of liaison officers with special responsibilities for establishing fruitful relations between police and coloured communities. It is a measure which gains widespread approval and has been the subject of official recommendation from the Home Office.[3] Undoubtedly there is great variation in how the liaison officers interpret their tasks, but their work and appointment are a first recognition that to establish proper police–coloured community relations requires exceptional measures. There are, after all, no police liaison officers for Irish or other minority groups, nor special officers with liaison duties with difficult or problem white 'areas' or communities.

The survey of crime in the division demonstrated the extent to which immigrant areas of the city are problem areas for the police and thus the establishment of fruitful relations between the police and residents of immigrant areas can be seen as a general problem facing Police Forces overlaid with additional special problems of prejudice and discrimination. Traditionally the policeman was a part of the community he policed: if not actually a native of the area, he would most probably have grown up in the same kind of area. It could be expected that he would know the people and their ways. And over the years the police can be thought to have established a working relation with these primarily working-class communities whereby these expectations were shared. With the advent of a wider range of housing opportunity since the 1930s and the general movement of the successful and

---

[1] Maureen Cain, in Whitaker, op. cit., p. 101.

[2] P. Moodie and J. Lambert, unpublished research carried out at the Cambridge Institute of Criminology, 1966.

[3] Home Office Circular to all Chief Constables, *The Police and Coloured Communities* (Home Office, London, 7 July 1967).

established working class to suburban areas, in which movement police personnel participated, the policeman moved away from the areas in which most of his work was, and has continued to be, centred. Increasingly these are the only areas where newcomers to the city can find homes, while remaining as the areas of refuge for the 'failed' old inhabitant, the 'problem' family, the poor and the socially more deprived, the delinquent, and the down-and-out. The transformation has been neither total nor rapid and there are sufficient links from the past to make the traditional police relationship still visible. But change there has been: older policemen would remark the change in attitudes of the residents, the increasing difficulty in the police being accepted, although in terms of disorder and violence, their comments suggested that there had been a decline.

What would seem to have happened is that increasingly these old areas have suffered from neglect and decay and from a decline in the old sense of 'community' as the resident population has changed. Matching this neglect has been a loss of police contact and effectiveness and a rise in the incidence of crime. City administrations, successful inhabitants, and the police have, to a greater or lesser extent, defined them as bad areas and treated the inhabitants as an out-group. Only recently have the consequences of this neglect, the chronic urban decay noticeable in Balsall Heath and Sparkbrook, begun to be faced. The urgency of the problem is now great because these areas have proved the only areas where considerable numbers of coloured immigrants can find places to live. The danger is that, because of the area in which he lives, the immigrant will be treated as one of an out-group and the *area* neglect and discrimination of the past will create, through racial discrimination, slum ghettos in the not too distant future.

The general problem of the police in these areas is the general problem facing the city administration and it is a problem of racial prejudice, racial discrimination, and the problem of how to find a meaningful actual integration of culturally and racially diverse elements into a multiracial society.

2. *Policing and General Levels of Prejudice and Discrimination*

The fact that coloured immigrants can live in only certain areas of the city is of fundamental importance. Rex and Moore, in their important and controversial study of Sparkbrook, argue cogently

that what they observed in Birmingham was 'a process of discriminative and *de facto* segregation which compelled coloured
people to live in certain typical conditions and which of itself
exacerbated racial ill-feeling. It was this process which provided
the framework of the race relations problem in Birmingham.'[1]
The authors are concerned to relate our ideas of prejudice and
discrimination to the competition for housing that operates in the
city. Through their analysis of the housing situations they distinguished a number of housing classes created within a social
system in which living in suburbia is valued highly but which
denies equal access to all. There is, the authors argue, a class
struggle over the use of houses: through house purchase the middle
classes achieve owner occupation; through attaining a council flat
or house the working class achieves its version of the move to the
suburbs. The 'notion of a certain style and standard of housing
as a right has meant that there is a primary problem of allocation
of resources as between the public welfare sector and the private
house-owner'.[2] Newcomers to the city, poor families, the inadequate, the social misfit, and others are unable to benefit from this
system of allocation: for them a second-class housing system—
lodging-house, multi-occupation, undesirable old houses, and poor
standard council housing in poor areas—fulfils the need. The most
numerous and most visible of this population is the coloured
immigrant who is thus forced into certain areas and who may be
accused of causing urban decay and whose distinctive life style
may become an additional source of conflict.

The several housing classes are differentially placed to one
another by area, housing type, and life style, and are the reason
for varieties in urban living that were noted in the description of
the division studied. The conflict in the system is that it can be
seen to be in the interest of the established residents to preserve
the situation and prevent undue competition for the limited
number of good class houses; but at the same time, newcomers
to the city aspire to move from their primary areas of residence
and share in the value system of the city as a whole. 'The long-
term density of a city which frustrates the desire [of the new-
comers] to improve their status by segregationist policies is some
sort of urban riot.'[3] What Rex and Moore see happening in

[1] Rex and Moore, op. cit., p. 20.
[2] Ibid., p. 273.   [3] Ibid., p. 9.

Birmingham is a process whereby the coloured newcomer is being forced, by discriminatory procedures supported by widespread prejudice, to stay locked in the ghetto-like areas which are no longer transitionary areas to a better way of life, but zones of stagnation where legitimate aspirations are thwarted.

This analysis is important for two reasons both deriving from 'the view of society not as a unitary concept but as compounded of groups in a state of conflict with one another about property and about power as well as of groups with differing styles of life arranged in a status hierarchy'.[1]

In the first place, 'once we understand urban society as a structure of social interaction and conflict, prejudiced behaviour may be shown to fit naturally into or even be required by that structure. Prejudice may be a social as well as a psychological phenomenon.'[2]

Secondly, such a view of the social system requires a modification of the usual vocabulary of race relations which includes such terms as 'assimilation', 'integration', and 'accommodation'. 'Such vocabularies assume a "host–immigrant" framework in which the culture and values of the host society are taken to be non-contradictory and static and in which the migrant is seen as altering his own patterns of behaviour until they finally conform to those of the host society.'[3] Instead it needs to be recognized that the adaptation of the immigrant occurs at a number of places within this total system of conflicts and the kind of group or community adaptation the immigrant adopts is to be interpreted as a means of achieving 'some sort of social and cultural bearings in the new society'[4] appropriate to the group position within the housing class system.

Both these aspects are important for a study of the police. The first is important for an understanding of individual policemen's attitudes to coloured immigrants. Policemen as members of British society may be expected to be no more or less prejudiced than their neighbours and equals: but their profession brings them in contact with coloured immigrants to a degree more marked than that of their neighbours and equals. Likewise, the Police Force as a whole can be seen as operating within a society where prejudice and discrimination exist, to which it can contribute or which it can oppose depending on the way it interprets its task.

[1] Rex and Moore, op. cit., p. 14.   [2] Ibid., p. 13.
[3] Ibid.   [4] Ibid., p. 14.

14

The second aspect is important if the Police Force is to understand the needs of immigrant communities and, along with other social agencies, reach an operationally meaningful definition of integration and multiracialism. As was made clear it is a fundamental requirement of good policing to establish good relations between the police and the communities they serve. Only if the police identify the needs of immigrant communities correctly by understanding something of the complex situation in which they are found can such a relationship be achieved.

Both aspects must be the subject of further discussion.

3. *Police Attitudes and Public Attitudes*

It is usual to stress that prejudice is a psychological phenomenon while discrimination is essentially sociological: 'Extreme prejudice is a means of resolving under conflicts and of handling anxieties the origins of which are largely unconscious. . . . Discrimination is concerned with maintaining and enforcing status relationships between individuals and groups.'[1] Rex and Moore seek to modify this view somewhat.

Many students . . . have argued that the prejudiced belief [about racial groups] is to be explained in terms of the contribution which it makes to maintain the dynamic equilibrium of the personality. Prejudice is thus held to be one aspect of the working of a disturbed authoritarian personality. . . . This approach seems to us to be inadequate because we were concerned to explain the behaviour, not of a minority, but of the majority of the host community. . . . We therefore thought it necessary to explain his prejudice not in terms of the personality system but in terms of the social system, that is, in terms of a structure of social relations. When we speak of two people united by a social relation we mean that in the course of planning their action they have expectations of each other and are influenced in the course of their action by their expectations.[2]

As was noted, Rex and Moore seek to explain the widespread presence of prejudice in terms of that aspect of the social system which is the housing market.

---

[1] Anthony Richmond, *The Colour Problem* (Harmondsworth, Penguin Books, 1961), pp. 20–1.
[2] Rex and Moore, op. cit., p. 12.

It is tempting for the researcher investigating police attitudes to ignore this 'social' aspect of prejudice and to conduct an inquiry along the lines suggested by the researches of T. W. Adorno and his associates into 'the authoritarian personality'.[1] Whether a particular personality type is attracted to the police role has not been explored by researchers and such an approach would seem to be unhelpful in the present context when the social situation in which policemen operate reflects, as Rex and Moore suggest, a widespread presence of prejudice. If this 'social' prejudice is an attitude of citizens at large, policemen as citizens may be expected to share that attitude. The question raised is how such prejudice affects the professional role of policemen. It can be hypothesized in this situation, not a frequency of overt discriminatory actions, but some conflict of citizen and professional attitudes that may prevent or mediate against the establishment of the needed police–community relations. The analysis of crime events indicates that such relations are an essential of effective police work in immigrant areas of the city. Because of social segregation policemen have little or no opportunity to meet coloured citizens except in the context of professional contact. Policemen as citizens aspire to a generally middle-class orientation and life style. Their value system, particularly in terms of housing standards and areas of residence, will lead them to hold in low esteem the areas where their professional duties are most intense. Their contact with residents of those areas invites that they treat them as an out-group. For this kind of prejudice to persist requires the maintenance and reinforcement of an unfavourable stereotype of the coloured immigrant. Stereotyped expectations of an adverse nature are possible so long as there is a limited context in which the contact can occur. The social system which promotes widespread prejudice, because it involves policemen as citizens in a set of attitudes which cannot but affect their attitudes as policemen, also promotes barriers to effective policing.

Stereotype is of very great importance for normal police duties: policing is largely an ever changing series of contacts demanding an individually directed response. A policeman must be able to sum up a person very quickly and determine a suitable manner with which to treat him. He will learn this on the street, from his basic common sense abilities, and from his admired older

[1] T. W. Adorno, *et al.*, *The Authoritarian Personality* (New York, Harper, 1950).

colleagues. The policeman who knows it all by the book, is quick at course learning, but does not know how to handle people is severely criticized by his colleagues. 'Handling people' means having some expectations of their response and moulding the manner of approach to attain some end. At its simplest this means that the good policeman does not treat everyone the same; depending on his perception of class, status, occupation, education, bearing, and so on, and with the situation providing a more independent variable defining the context for action, the policeman discriminates in his behaviour.

In this stereotype of the coloured immigrant the social context provides an unfavourable starting-point. For the general population the modern folk-lore figure of the coloured man seems to be someone flashily dressed and out of work, who makes a flamboyant weekly visit in his garishly multi-coloured car to the 'assistance' to collect his money for himself, his white woman, and his several children. For the policeman instances are more particularized; many betoken the real problem of policing a coloured and immigrant community. Some of these are extremely florid and unusual, and the memory lasts several years: together they reinforce the idea of a strangeness and prevent closer approaches. Within the social context discussed earlier in this section, these prejudiced attitudes can be seen to be in some way necessary. *They* must be kept in their place—controlled and contained, not allowed to infect the whole of society. They are different, they show little desire for change, therefore they want to remain different and stay apart—so the argument goes. Ignorance and fear and resentment of the coloured immigrant place him in an unfavourable light. This stereotype when tested by experience is reinforced rather than modified for the policeman, who, in the main, will have contact with only those sectors of the population in only those situations where his suspicions are confirmed. He is unlikely to have the kind of contact which might break through the ignorance barrier to a more complete idea of the immigrant community. Instead, the idea of the immigrant as worthless or dangerous can grow unchecked.

The nature of the professional contact underlines these tendencies. The crime survey demonstrates the very limited extent of coloured involvement. But where there is contact it is in the potentially more threatening sounding criminal contexts: domestic violence, vice, and drug trafficking. With other minority groups and with white society in general, the operations of a minority do not affect the over-all picture of the majority. Denied contact with the law-abiding majority, policemen are tempted to think of the whole immigrant community in these derogatory terms.

These attitudinal factors are of equal significance for police organizations, which are involved in the general debate of race relations, as for policemen as individuals. Two particular factors in the general debate are of importance: the failure to provide an adequate definition of integration, and the tendency to treat the coloured immigrant as one homogeneous class. The loose definition of integration which implies 'change' on the part of the immigrant, none on the part of the host community, invites a colonialist–paternalist response by white authorities which stresses teaching the immigrant to conform and his learning to change. This fails to grasp the complex nature of the society to which the immigrant has to relate. This has meant that ideas like multi-racialism and pluralism have remained merely notional, while the public has been allowed to welcome and articulate ideas whose logical outcome is separation, apartness, if not apartheid. For the police, as for all, this has meant the stressing of dissimilarities and distinctiveness as things to be modified and as things deviant, rather than as things to be incorporated within society's structure. The police, as for many in contact with immigrants, find among them no great alacrity or ability to conform to middle-class English mores with the cultural castration that process implies. The not unpredictable response of some white people has been to say that as 'they' want to be different and separatist, let them— in separate areas. In some ways this attitude is helped by the shallow definition of integration cited above.

A senior police officer I spoke with, and many with actual rather than 'arm-chair' contact with the problem would agree, saw how the need and desirability of immigrant minorities retaining their cultural identity are a denial of full integration (in these terms), and how retained cultural identity may always be a source of resentment and complaint from the host community. The tendency of such an argument is, however, towards the idea of a well-policed non-slum ghetto. This reveals the tendency to treat the immigrant community as a single entity: a *them* to be treated alike (but apart). Separation or apartheid, it can be argued, might just be tolerable if an accompanying ethic of real equality of opportunity and culture, not oppression, determined the nature of the separation: in a situation where both immigrant and host communities are divided by ethnic, racial, cultural, class, and aspirational distinctions, separation into distinct groups is impossible without a whole gamut of state machinery and legislation of a violent, oppressive, and racist kind. But bolstered by an idea that there is one 'coloured community', the notion of apartness can achieve a spurious plausibility. Again it must be stressed that an imprecise view of the variety of cultures and conditions in the various countries of origin of the immigrant population is not the sole and private possession of the police: it is a general ignorance in which the police partake but which has more immediate relevance to the police who operate among the immigrant communities. Again one finds in expressed attitudes a stress on the primitive, backward, and strange elements in the immigrants' background rather than a concern for the effect of language, culture, and aspirations on immigrant behaviour. Experience, no doubt, is the great educator and gradually one hopes more precise remarks will increase and generalizations about innate tendencies will diminish.

Degrees of ignorance, fear, and resentment affect the attitudes of individual policemen and the operations of the police as an organization. An attitude of disdain is no help to a policeman advising at a dispute in a family or between a landlord and tenant. An official attitude that violence in immigrant families is expected and tolerable so long as it does not get out of hand begs many questions about the role of the police: a tendency to 'excuse' immigrant violence because it does not involve 'whites' is a danger facing police here as in America. An attitude which actively prosecutes a minority of coloured immigrants involved in vice and drugs without reckoning on how such a crusade might seem to be aimed at the whole immigrant population is as dangerous as an attitude which imputes to all immigrants a propensity to tolerate, sympathize with, if not actually condone, the operations of the minority.

What I am concerned to show is how the police share commonly and widely held views about coloured immigrants and the colour problem which are detrimental to good policing and which augur badly for an improvement in the general tenor of race relations. The requirements of good policing are the requirements of good race relations: neither, it might be supposed, will be attained with ease.

4. *The Police and the Irish*

By way of comparison it is interesting to consider the position of the Irish as an immigrant group. While comprising approximately 5 per cent of the total population of the city, crude crime statistics for the year 1965 indicate that persons of Irish origin were responsible for 15 per cent of all cleared crimes of violence and 6·5 per cent of all cleared larceny offences. In the crime survey carried out for this study, persons born in Ireland accounted for nearly 20 per cent of those arrested or summonsed for indictable crimes. In addition Irish persons accounted for over half of all those charged for offences of drunkenness, and for more than 40 per cent of those charged with offences of drunken driving. In Chapter 7 it is noted that about 20 per cent of those being supervised by a probation officer and 20 per cent of boys at approved schools were either born in Ireland or are children with one or both parents of Irish birth.

Yet it is plainly true that in society at large the Irish are respected for the positive achievements of their vast majority in all walks of life in every area of the city, rather than ostracized or held in low esteem for the 'troubles' experienced by a problematical minority. Within the Police Force police personnel of Irish origin are fairly numerous and in Birmingham there is something of a tradition of highly successful senior officers who are Irishmen. In a variety of ways the individual policeman is enabled to base his expectations of behaviour among Irish 'clients' on a wide range of contacts, information, and experience so that no generally unfavourable stereotype was discernible. Of course there was occasional and somewhat derogatory reference to the hard-drinking 'Paddy', but as often it was accompanied by reference to his more positive attributes. For the policeman, the Irishman typically causes no 'trouble', he shows 'respect', is generally compliant, and often fairly disarming when questioned; if and when he comes fighting in a drunken brawl and gets a hiding, there is no suggestion of brutality or viciousness; Irish roguery is mild and basically honest. Particular difficulties attach to policing a population who live in lodging-houses, particularly in relation to motoring offences where the administration grinds slowly and finds addresses frequently out-of-date and not subject to retracing. (This complaint applies to coloured immigrants in lodging-houses as well.)

More problematical is the police role with the tinkers. In Sparkbrook, Rex and Moore found that tinker families, some of whom have settled in houses in the area and give welcome to their more itinerant relations, were the focus of not inconsiderable criticism and resentment by other residents in the area. The real problems are the genuine itinerants who descend on an available open area in an assortment of vehicles and caravans in search of the scrap and lumber from which they make their living. Throughout the period of study there were one or two such groups on or near the development sites near the city centre who required and received busy police attention before they moved on to annoy another area. In the summer of 1967 the tinker 'problem' flared up in another part of the city and led to a number of nasty incidents, petitions from residents to the Lord Mayor and Home Secretary, action by local councillors, and a special debate in the council chamber, before a raid at dawn by the police towed the offending vehicles and their occupants away from the area and out of the city.

I was shown a fairly massive file of complaints and letters and decisions arising from the tinker problem. The senior police officer handling this and his colleagues expressed desperation and exasperation at the utterly negative and fairly hopeless task that befalls them.

Considering the local corporation's attitude to matters concerning coloured immigrants and race relations, the uncompromising negativity of its official attitude to the tinkers need surprise no one. Despite efforts by individual councillors for some positive action, the Conservative majority opposed a special meeting and voted against a regional conference of those councils concerned (although eventually both moves were effected); at the height of the summer troubles the best comment the Conservative leader could manage was: 'It must be made clear that Birmingham will not provide sites as we have not got them. If there are any sites available they will be used for permanent housing. The tinkers must go elsewhere where there are miles of land to pitch caravans; we don't want them.'[1] His likely successor is reported as saying:

[1] *Birmingham Post* (9 September 1967).

'Let us turn them off again and again and if it costs us money to do so, it is money well spent to get rid of these people.'[1]

This situation shows the police being forced into an unenviable position by prevailing opinion. It is the police who have to carry out the city's 'solution', 'to take these unwanted visitors, and particularly their unfortunate children, and dump them over the border [when] either they will come back or they will become a problem for others'.[2] The police find that frequently the vehicles tinkers use are unlicensed and uninsured but before action is possible the offender has moved on; similarly tinkers are not infrequently in court on charges of drunkenness, where invariably they are fined and given time to pay, during which time they depart. Imprisonment is no solution for it may merely leave a wife and children immobile and neglected until release: and mobility is the only aim at which action is directed.

Yet this minority does not seem to be held to reflect badly on the larger majority of settled and successful Irish immigrants. A true minority problem can be identified—a problem attaching to particular aspects of the life style in a sub-community. Most markedly this is seen in relation to the true itinerant, but to a lesser extent applies to a lodging-house population.

It is perhaps too readily assumed that the coloured immigrant because he lives in the same kinds of areas shares a life style with his neighbours; it would seem necessary to distinguish the distinctive communities and groups and their differing aspirations and modes. It is impossible to know whether the coloured immigrant lodging-house includes so mobile a population as the other lodging-house or whether the family and group ties make for a much more fixed address.

What is implied in this discussion is that 'colour', not behaviour, is the key factor which promotes an undesirable set of attitudes which militate against effective policing. What might be termed 'technical' problems attach to effecting good policing in certain areas without the criminal activities of a minority promoting markedly adverse attitudes. With coloured communities, these 'technical' problems seem less potent than those of an attitudinal nature.

[1] *Birmingham Post* (13 September 1967).
[2] Leading article, ibid.

5. *The Police and Coloured Immigrants*

This does not mean that there are only attitudinal problems: speaking of the drug problem, the obvious difficulty was touched upon, that of white detectives infiltrating purely coloured circles —in clubs and cafés. Another basic problem relates to language. In Birmingham the need to employ special interpreters has not been felt, although they are available. The presence in the Force of a sergeant with fluent command of a number of dialects has helped the situation: the normal procedure is for the complainant–client to come to the station with a friend or relative who can speak English. Not infrequently the children of an immigrant family are its only or best English-speakers. This need to use interpreters does undoubtedly pose some difficulties and problems, for the opportunities for misunderstanding are multiplied and the demands on police sensitivity, skill, and intelligence not inconsiderable. The language problem seemed most potent in giving the Indian and Pakistani a reputation for deceitfulness and cunning derived from one or two incidents when the barrier of language seemed to have been used to evade questioning or provide inadequate answers. It was sometimes suggested that in his dealings with officials of any kind, it is customary for the Asian immigrant to presume an absolute corruptibility that may be a needed defence and a true analysis of the prevailing situation in the country of origin but can only appear as devious if not dishonest to the fundamentally incorruptible British official. Between police and Asian immigrants mutual suspicion rather than respect or hostility seems most characteristic.

With the West Indians—although language difficulties may well be underestimated—police relations seemed moulded in expectations of excitability and arrogance on the part of the immigrant, and an immigrant expectation of police violence.

Excitability means the tendency to make a scene and do the opposite to 'coming along quietly'; or it is a panic response in a strange situation. Of several instances recounted to me, the following two provide the essentials.

Example 1. On a Saturday morning in a busy shopping centre, a police officer noted that a car was parked in a restricted zone. He waited and approached the driver when he returned. The driver was a West Indian. His answers to the policeman's inquiries, whether from fear, fright, or ignorance, were unintelligible and to the policeman must have seemed defensive. When he was asked for his name and address and for his driving licence, it would seem that the man assumed that he was being arrested or something and got even more incoherent. By this time something of a crowd had gathered, communication was very difficult, and in the policeman's view the man was behaving very oddly and was creating quite a scene. The policeman suggested that the man accompany him to the police station to sort things out—again this was misinterpreted and the man seems clearly to have grown almost pathetically obstreperous. In desperation the policeman formally arrested the man for making a disorderly act and walked him firmly and briskly to the station where he was left to quieten down for a few minutes. A senior officer interviewed him. In the now quieter situation better communication was possible. It could be explained to him why the policeman approached him in the first place and why he wanted to see his driving licence, etc. In the calmer setting the man's English, which was not good, was intelligible and he expressed concern for what had happened and could show all his driving papers to be in order. Accordingly it was felt that no charge should be made following the arrest and that a caution was appropriate for the parking offence.

Example 2. A patrolling policeman tried to stop a car which was being driven without lights. His torch was knocked from his hand but the car did not stop. He radioed for a patrol car and there ensued a chase over the city before the car was cornered. The occupants were four young Jamaicans who by now were quite terrified and refused to get out of the car: amidst the screaming and shouting there was little chance of communication. To try to achieve quiet, the policemen returned to their cars and one officer tried to reason with the driver. Eventually they agreed to get out and come to the station. But something of a panic ensued and there was quite a struggle and battle before the police finally got them all into police cars and to the station. The police were of the opinion that all had been drinking and it was decided to charge the passengers for being drunk and disorderly and the driver for dangerous driving. (A doctor called in to test the level of impairment of driving ability due to drink found insufficient evidence for a charge of drunken driving.)

The following day in court the three passengers pleaded not guilty and complained that they had been wrongfully arrested and subject to racialist insults and brutality by the police. The case was remanded and on return the three expressed satisfaction at having been able to lodge their complaint, altered their pleas to 'guilty', and were fined a small sum each. The case against the driver was dealt with by summons.

In both instances the response was one of panic in the face of fear; a fear due to a misunderstanding in the first case and, it would seem, a fear of police violence in the latter. In the heat of the situation communication was rendered impossible. With English or Irish persons in a similar situation the policeman has a reasonable expectation of behaviour and can assume some shared expectation of his own action. With the coloured immigrant no such expectations exist except those of unpredictability and aggression.

Arrogance is the opposite of respectfulness; it implies no automatic deference to authority but rather a denial of the right to official inquiry in an assertion of rights. In the earlier description of police work it was noted that 'respect' matters very much in motoring offences and in cases of drunkenness and disorder. The importance of respect can be extended further to most situations involving police and members of the public. The police are sensitive—at times I thought ultra-sensitive—to the way people treat them. The manner of the request rather than the request itself takes on major importance; how a person responds to a question rather than the content of his answer may determine police action. The Police Force needs a good relationship with the public; a policeman requires that individual members of the public show personal respect in their dealing with him. Like any servant he is happiest when requested; he resents *demands*. It has been a central part of the description of police work that much of it is individually directed and defies systematization: the policeman needs to feel free to exercise discretion. He wants people to comply with his requests and co-operate so that a number of possible lines for action are kept open. A man who knows and asserts his rights denies the policeman this favoured role situation —it makes the relationship formal, rule-bound, and lacking in discretion: commands not requests apply. As was suggested, for the C.I.D. the criminal who knows his rights is in some way the most tricky customer to handle. For the police in uniform the citizen who asserts his rights is difficult because so often the policeman's work is more to appease, persuade, and guide than to command. With the English middle class, the police can be effective if circumspect through a manner of approach that implies deference; with the lower class a deal is struck by a number of techniques of bombast, *bonhomie*, or an old-fashioned paternalism. Many of these class differentials can apply to dealings with the Irish without modification. But with coloured immigrants there is no traditional manner of dealings and the old ways may be thought irrelevant. If, as Anthony Lester suggests (see p. 177), the previous experience of West Indians within the Caribbean may promote fear and hostility towards the police, this expectation may be seen at the root of the 'arrogance' that policemen unfailingly impute to the West Indian. The police have limited experience of a population who assume police violence and brutality, for their traditional role in English communities is generally respected and valued. In the second instance cited above some of the terror and panic derived from the fear of violence and the complaint suggests that in the rough and tumble of the arrest firm handling and racialist-sounding insults may have confirmed their fears, although, it must be stressed, the complaint was not serious or pursued and there was no suggestion of undue violence. Arrogance as related to an underlying fear of violence was apparent in the following incident.

Example 3. At about 3 a.m. on Friday morning, the area car was summoned to the help of a patrolling officer in Balsall Heath. He had been called to a café in the area to investigate some 'trouble' involving four young West Indian men and a local English girl. When he got there he found the party leaving in a van: he stopped them and questioned them. The girl complained that she was being forced to go with one of the men against her will. As she was clearly very upset, the policeman thought that a kerb-side discussion was inappropriate and suggested that they all go to the station. At the station, the four men were sat down at a table and the girl was asked to explain the situation. The girl's story was that she had previously been going out with one of the men but had broken the relationship. They had met again that evening and he had tried to persuade her against her will to go with him. He had made her get into his van, her protests and complaints had no effect. She was 17 years old and living with her mother in the area.

When she had finished her story, the man concerned suggested quite vehemently that the police should not just listen to her story but only judge after hearing his version. One of the policemen clearly incensed by the man's manner went up to him and almost shouted: 'Who do you think you're talking like that to. You'd better show more respect. Don't talk to a policeman like that.' The West Indian replied with equal fervour: 'You're not going to frighten me like that. Don't think you can beat me up in a police station and get away with it.' There followed an angry and incoherent exchange during which both men spoke at once and which ended abruptly with the West Indian saying: 'Why pick on me for this, you only do so because I'm black.' 'Oh!', replied the policeman, 'thanks for telling me, I hadn't noticed.' Thereafter any reasonable discussion was impossible. Truculently the West Indian asserted: 'I won't say anything except to a solicitor.'

A few more questions were directed at the girl. It seemed very clear that no offences had been committed: this was a dispute in which the girl found herself in an unwelcome situation from which she was unable to extricate herself and so the police were involved. The manner adopted by the parties prevented 'normal' advice and discussion; it swiftly floundered in resentment and recrimination. Names and addresses were taken, the vehicle checked for licence, tax, and insurance, and the parties sent home. Angered by the 'arrogance' of the West Indian, a policeman remarked: 'In a few years time they'll be ordering us about and telling *us* what to do.'

Such incidents reveal the lack of respect that can exist between the police and coloured immigrants. I am not of course saying that the above is typical but the attitudes expressed on both sides show, I think, how police–immigrant contacts can contain the seeds of resentment and aggression which make the desired level of mutual respect and confidence required for good policing difficult to attain.

Quite distinct problems follow from the lack of coloured policemen and the white police 'visibility' in immigrant areas that follows it. It puts special demands on 'informer' systems and on a general level of trust and co-operation. It poses the problem very clearly of how to achieve a relation between police and immigrants which will lead to good policing. How is co-operation to be won, how distant can the police afford to be, how can the police afford to 'identify' with middle class anti-colour views, what role can coloured immigrants play within the Police Service?

How the Police Force as a body relates to immigrant communities can be expected to become increasingly important as the race relations cycle moves into the crucial phase of the integration of the second generation. The police are seen to represent authority —a white authority. How the police establish a relationship with the parent generation and how they conduct themselves in relation to the second generation will affect the kind of interpretation the coloured communities make of white authority in general. What is so striking and depressing about the situation in America is the way police–Negro relations so often present the firm and brutal reality of American race relations. How the police conduct themselves in public may be thought more important than individual contacts.

Example 4. There had been some suspicions that at a pub-discotheque some of the teen-age clientele had been obtaining drinks under age and that at some of the sessions, pills and other drugs had been obtained. A raid was planned for about 9.45 on Friday evening by uniformed and plainclothes officers. A phone call from an observer indicated that there was a considerable crowd present among whom were a number of West Indians. The raiding party comprised an inspector, two sergeants, six uniformed officers (one woman), and six plainclothes officers. On arrival the uniformed men manned the doors and exits of the large room which was thronged with about 200 teen-agers dancing to music provided by a juke-box. The numbers present made any check on who was drinking what quite impossible and anyway it seemed that at this relatively late hour most pocket-money was spent for there were as many empty glasses as there were people. The tactic of the plainclothes men must to many present have seemed discriminatory; they moved swiftly through the crowd and isolated a group of West Indian lads whom they searched thoroughly and only when they were found 'clean' were a selection of the others present searched. Nothing was found and after a few minutes of observing and discussing the situation with the landlord who expressed some thanks for the police 'showing the flag' in this way; the party retired amidst a cheer and a jolly singing send-off by the kids who seemed to find the visit an added spice to their evening's entertainment.

Singling out the West Indian minority was explained as being necessary for the exercise of tracing cannabis. The clientele was young and there were few of them. As years go by, no doubt, the police may be expected to be more circumspect in their approach.

This incident could give rise to much misunderstanding, both among participants and observers. Such incidents as these where the police are in the public view and actively seen to be maintaining order matter much for the reputation the police achieve. In this public, active policing the danger of a frayed temper, a misinterpreted response, or a panic move makes violence a danger. On such occasions the police have only one sanction with a troublemaker—arrest, and if need be, forceful removal.

6. *The Police and Race Relations*

This discussion has tried to demonstrate how general problems which face police operations in those areas of the city where there is much crime and disorganization have a direct bearing on matters of race relations. Apart from problems facing policemen in their professional contact with coloured immigrants, which derive from the way policemen's expectations of immigrant behaviour are subject to the prejudice they share with their white British fellows, there are problems which have to be faced by the Police Force as a whole in what policy to adopt *vis-à-vis* the coloured areas. The inadequacies of the general policy of integration can lead a Police Force to view the immigrant community as an out-group and approve the idea of separateness and apartness: in this the police appear to be acting consistently with the bulk of English middle-class white authority. This, I believe, multiplies the problems faced by the police and may lead to a deterioration of police–immigrant relations which will result in violence and oppression. Throughout the discussion there is implied a need for the police to be aware of the conditions in the areas they police and particularly to notice the distinct status and variations in the immigrant communities. There is implied that the generally prevailing prejudice and its attendant aura of discrimination will prevent the kind of police–immigrant relations that the discussion of police work as a whole found to be so necessary. Police Forces, like so many other institutions, need to find an operationally meaningful definition of integration that does justice to the variety of aspirations, mores, expectations, and customs that are shown by the diverse elements who constitute the 'coloured community'.

Although there is a very considerable amount of change and experiment in Police Forces—most notably in Birmingham where the 'unit' system of policing has been adopted in a city-wide basis —it would seem that the real problems are not to be solved solely by greater use of technical equipment—for example, cars and radios. If the analysis that has been provided here is correct, the real need is to establish good police–public relations and explore ways whereby they may be attained. Although unit policing is an experiment in new ways of policing a community, it is hailed as a new weapon in the war against crime, a better way of doing what the police did previously. Although the system does create a new relation between police and public, there was, to my knowledge, no retraining of men nor any great exploration of what the system entailed. It was presented as a technique, a new tool, like the introduction of personal radios a few months previously, an additional piece of equipment. The risk is that without a real sense of experimentation, individual responses to the system will vary enormously and the old ways will, in time, prove the safest and the best even though they may appear in a somewhat modified garb.

This problem of how to bring *effective* change to police operations cannot be treated in isolation from the recurring and urgent problems of manpower shortage and quality. A measure of public esteem for the police (and therefore a factor in police–public relations) can be found in the low educational attainment of many applicants and in the paucity of graduate entrants. This is not just a question of pay and conditions of service: the issues are far more complex.

By its nature police work is to do with upholding value

15

systems, maintaining a *status quo*, supporting established authority; the police represent *conventional* authority.

For the university graduate this sense of conventionalism, both in individual policemen and in police administration, is probably considerable. Policing cannot at the moment provide a strong appeal to a sense of professionalism. The impression gained was of an institution constitutionally unprepared for self-analysis and criticism, seeking to prove itself in terms of catching criminals and enforcing laws when the majority of its contact required some other justification. The disjunction between the ethos of policing projected by senior officers and the experience of uniformed officers leads to low morale, defensive attitudes, and low individual self-esteem. If there is to be a significant degree of change in policing that will give new entrants, and particularly graduate entrants, a sense of participating in a creative and valuable enterprise, there would seem to be required a managerial revolution that will associate men of all ranks in an analysis and exploration of the tasks actually undertaken. Such an analysis would, I think, have to focus on more sociological interpretations of crime, on the policing needs of different areas, and on a clearer distinction between 'order' policing and 'crime' policing. Thereafter might follow a greater democratization of police administrations and the recognition that different men with different aptitudes can discover several alternatives within the general frame of police work for more specialized functions suiting their skills. The Force would seem to need to adopt as a model for organization more that of an industrial–commercial undertaking with a greater range of posts with differing responsibilities, and less that of an organizational model based on uniformity of relations between a hierarchy of ranks. A more flexible and varied approach allowing the development of varying degrees of expertise would allow for improved managerial control and co-ordination of the various aspects of police enterprise.

If the general analysis of policing that has been provided in the foregoing chapters, which stresses the need to establish close links between police and the communities, is accurate, and if police–community relations are to be achieved, techniques will have to be found to promote those relations. Instead of trying to improve the image of policing by advertising improved techniques of catching criminals and by presenting 'success' through the spurious clear-up rate, actual contact and real relationships between police and the community need to be valued as an essential part of police work. Most important of all, perhaps, this shift in emphasis requires modification in the training of policemen and policewomen. Currently, police training concentrates mainly on police law and procedure. Maureen Cain, noting how '[the] system of training has not been re-examined for ten years', argues that there is a case for supplementing the present courses ('a large mass of information as yet unrelated to experience which must be digested or at least remembered') with subjects from the related social sciences.

A good pocket-size reference book on police law would obviate the need for much of the committing to memory of great chunks of indigestible material, and leave time on the course for the new subjects. . . . Policemen themselves maintain that 80% of the information is no further use to them. At the moment of the recruit's main learning experience is his initial period on the beat with an older constable, who will instruct him in police lore and mythology and indicate to him which opinions are most acceptable about matters relating to police work. . . . Thus, though the senior officers may accept new ideas, the Force as a body has a built-in resistance to them. Senior officers are powerless to counteract this, for the acceptability of their own ideas is assessed by the men in terms of their general conformism to the conventional pattern.[1]

Apart from preliminary training, promotional and refresher courses, conducted at local Force or district training centre level for a selected number of men, continue to stress legal technicalities which only a learned rather than experienced officer can cope with. These are the subject of frequent criticism by some of the men. The 'police duties' examinations required for promotion also require a certain amount of study at night-school which is an unpopular measure for men whose normal hours of work include evenings, nights, and week-ends.

At the moment local courses may include some lectures on items related to police work that are more of a social studies nature—some of them given by non-policemen. In Birmingham a talk is given to all recruits about immigrants. It would seem that it is at a local level that there is considerable opportunity for

[1] Maureen Cain, in Whitaker, op. cit., p. 109.

extending the scope of police training. And the point made by
Miss Cain about the influence of the experienced officer on the
recruit would indicate the need for training and education to be
seen as continuing and an integral part of policing rather than
as something done with once and for all during the first years of
a policeman's career. If the shift in emphasis away from legalistic
training is accepted, there is clearly scope to involve local colleges
of education and further education, as well as universities, in
providing courses for police officers. Such a move would help
to promote what Michael Banton sees as necessary: 'more
informed and independent opinion in the Universities and among
the public at large about the police and their duties'.[1] And
it might further enhance the standing and purpose of the Police
College at Bramshill in the way Miss Cain foresees:

The college itself could help to develop a sound body of theory concerning the policeman's position, role, and function in various types
of community, and far more attention should be paid to the accepted
facts of social psychology so that the policeman can see his own behaviour and that of those with whom he has to deal both within and
outside the force in a consistent theoretical framework.[2]

Only with some such shifts in the emphasis and organization
of police training will there be a significant change in how the
police interpret and adapt their role in relation to the different
areas and communities which collectively constitute the urban
community. If it is recognized that there is a need to modify the
traditional informal means whereby police–community relations
are made in the face of recognized changes in the structure of
the community, one would expect the problems posed by immigrant and coloured immigrant areas to be given priority since
such areas are, as has been shown, also the areas where most
crime occurs. Basic to understanding areas is understanding the
people who live there, and appreciating something of the social
conditions and background from which crime and disorder arise.
When much contact with coloured immigrants arises, not through
crime and related proceedings but at the level of family or other
minor disturbance, it is clearly necessary for policemen to be able

[1] Banton, op. cit., p. 268.
[2] Maureen Cain, in Whitaker, op. cit., p. 112.

to know something about the origins and cultures of the various peoples with whom they work.

But the training of policemen for work in these areas should not be left there. If the preceding analysis is accurate in showing how the police are subject to the general level of prejudice and discrimination that exists in the community at large, and how their own prejudices and the lack of a coherent policy for integration and equality may make policing contribute to the general discriminatory social setting, these matters too must feature in police training and education. Group discussions on the nature of prejudice and its effects, the airing of attitudes and opinions about coloured people and policies for immigration, must feature prominently in any training schedule. Undoubtedly such an approach will produce great difficulties and set up severe tensions; but increasingly the key factor in promoting a proper kind of race relations will be seen to be, not the behaviour of certain groups, but our white English attitude to those groups. Only by providing an opportunity to express fears, articulate prejudices, and discuss discrimination, can the training of police officers allow their nature and effects to be discovered and acted upon. A third aspect of training police for a proper role in relationship with coloured people would be to provide scope, opportunity, and time for members of the Force to establish relations with schools, clubs, associations, and societies whose members include a number of coloured immigrants. In this way, it might be hoped, policemen will gain from a wider range of contacts with immigrants than is permitted by the area segregation that operates in cities.

It is apparent that these three ways—learning, discussion, and association—could provide the basis for the police to establish a new kind of depth relationship with different communities. It might be supposed that the needed police response to problems of a racial nature may promote not only better race relations but a better general level of policing.

Some of the developments outlined above are already being essayed in the work of special liaison officers who have been appointed by some Forces to take special note of police–immigrant relations. One instance of success by such an officer was cited at the outset of this chapter.

It is of very great significance that such appointments have been made. In the first place they would seem to have arisen because of misunderstandings which affect the policing of immigrant communities. It seems likely that at the outset the problem was seen as one of public relations and the response given was more in terms of the police spokesman making contact with immigrant organizations and communities to help them and instruct them. Clearly there is value in this response. Whether this first contact will reveal the need that I have discussed here for the police to examine their own difficulties and problems remains to be seen. Certainly some Forces through their liaison officers are exploring ways of extending police knowledge about the communities they serve. Conferences have been arranged where outside speakers representing the various immigrant groups have sought to explain and describe aspects of the lives and customs of their peoples. It was most revealing to attend one such conference where the situation allowed the speakers to shift the emphasis from the customs and origins of the immigrant group to their complaints against the police. While being informed the police were also criticized which promoted a lively and prolonged discussion in which the nature and extent of prejudice and discrimination featured largely. Many of the responses were negative and defensive but attitudes and opinions were being expressed which were of great significance for good policing. It was possible for the group to admit their prejudice—a first step, it might be thought, towards its neutralization and control. The danger is that only a first step will be taken and the explorations go no further. Also it will be important to extend such conferences to take in all ranks of men, not just senior officers.

There would seem to be good reasons for the practice of appointing liaison officers wherever relevant to be extended and facilities provided to advise and direct their operations. This can be done if such officers are seen to have full-time duties in this field wherever possible and their position and status within the Force recognized. In Birmingham there was no such officer appointed at the time of this study.[1] In part, this might be attributable to Birmingham's over-all inability to respond with any constructive measures in the field of race relations. On the other hand, it reflects an organizational dilemma related to the numbers

---

[1] In the autumn of 1967 a superintendent of one of the division's was appointed as the city's liaison officer, not as a full-time role, but in addition to his duties as a divisional second-in-command.

of immigrants involved, distributed fairly evenly between the five divisions which radiate from the city centre. A solution will no doubt depend on how the tasks of a liaison officer are interpreted. If the need is for improved public relations between police and immigrant communities, there are required locally-based divisional officers entrusted with the task. If, on the other hand, as might be hoped, the concern of the liaison officer is with aspects of training and re-education within the Force, a senior officer appointment for the city might be thought desirable. His task might be seen as acting as convenor of conferences and adviser of police training schedules as well as having liaison functions with local immigrant organizations and local co-ordinating committees. The tasks certainly require a considerable amount of skill and imagination, for the way the liaison officer uses local resources—colleges, universities, and associations—will determine the success of his enterprise. This puts the Police Force in a new and interesting relationship with such bodies and is as much a challenge to them in handling a new and real situation as for the police. No doubt at the moment there is much variety in practice and there is clear scope for liaison between liaison officers. Their success in this field could hasten the onset of some of the more general changes in police training that were outlined earlier. By appointing liaison officers, the Police Force has created a structure through which some of the kinds of problems discussed here can be solved. If the exact nature and extent of their task was not recognized at the outset, from the beginnings made a worthwhile and constructive contribution to race relations can develop.

The improvement in police–immigrant relations like the improvement in the general level of race relations may be expected to be gradual through education and experience and determined action by governments, legislatures, corporations, and borough councils through the means at their disposal to eradicate and outlaw the more obvious (and some of the more subtle) forms of social discrimination. There is, of course, an issue here which faces Police Forces directly. No great change in police–immigrant relations is likely to occur unless the current doubts over the employment of coloured policemen are resolved. Two reasons may be put forward for the low rate of coloured recruitment. First, few applicants present themselves who are sufficiently well qualified. Secondly, the general public is not yet ready to accept being policed by coloured officers. A third reason, perhaps more potent, is that there would undoubtedly be tensions and conflicts within the Police Force itself if any numbers of coloured recruits were admitted. One officer expressed this very bluntly: 'The police are not yet ready to employ coloured men. . . . Clearly it will have to come . . . but not while I'm here I hope.' Fears about public or police readiness are clearly more potent than the educational barrier. Bearing in mind the generally low educational standard of police recruits, the educational shortcomings of coloured recruits may be exaggerated. Although there may be a good argument for making the first recruits from the coloured communities of exceptional ability, it should not be beyond the scope of the police to arrange for intensive language courses for recruits. If, as I have tried to show, potent barriers of ignorance and attitude impair the establishment of the kind of relationship between police and community necessary for effective policing, the need for police officers who can identify with and understand the needs of the various communities to be served is a first priority. Clearly, the first coloured recruits to the Police Force will have to win acceptance from their white colleagues as a first task (see note, p. 206). Although the recruits will no doubt be familiar with the attitudes and resentment they may experience and capable of dealing with them, this does pose a problem for police managements.

Clearly the long-term value of coloured policemen will be among coloured communities; their immediate value, as well as the source of their problems, will be with their white fellows and with their white public. To place a coloured officer immediately in coloured areas where his duties will be alongside white policemen among the most disorganized and troublesome white areas can only add to the tensions which a coloured policeman will experience. Furthermore, the pattern of immigration in a city like Birmingham has produced areas with racial heterogeneity and to expect a West Indian policeman to be at ease with an Asian immigrant is unrealistic.

In this situation it seems a sensible move to post Birmingham's *single* coloured policeman to a settled white area where the police problems are milder and where the internal resentments can be expected to work themselves out more easily. And it does still allow his value as interpreter where necessary to be used. The danger is that his isolation within a white Force will become a significant factor and to win the respect of his white fellows he will be forced to appear harsher in attitude to his own people and colour than is desirable and he will become even more of a pariah than the white policeman is among a white community. Integration of coloured policemen within the Force will be no easier task than the integration of coloured immigrants with society generally. A single recruit may tend to become something of a guinea-pig *and* showpiece and be used to evidence lack of police discrimination in employment rather than a positive desire to recruit numbers of coloured policemen. It should be self-evident that the recruitment of coloured policemen is an urgent necessity. It should also be self-evident that such a necessity is secondary to the need to ensure that coloured citizens are treated with respect by white policemen.

If the police are to function properly in a multiracial society there will have to be a vigorous commitment to change on the part of the police. Attitudes which resist change and colour will have to be countered by strong leadership. New kinds of training will have to be devised drawing on skills and personnel at present under-represented in police training schools. Methods of recruitment will have to be scrutinized and modified so that the police have manpower of the type, quality, and background sufficient for their many and varied tasks. New projects and programmes which carry information about police and law enforcement and justice to communities who cannot be assumed to be conversant with the intricacies and traditions of British methods will have to be devised. Means must be found whereby the police get a feed-back from communities and peoples to whom they are strangers, whose customs, culture, and needs will be remote from the police officer's experience. These new tasks may require the police to employ persons with a distinct role in community–police relations in an effort to provide a basis for good policing. With the growing civilianization of the Police Force there is added opportunity for Police Forces to make a point of recruiting coloured applicants for a wide variety of tasks, both to broaden the contact and information flow between police and coloured communities and to declare and demonstrate police commitment to removing and barring discriminatory actions in all that they do. The Police Force, as a symbol of authority, as authority in action in a specially visible and vital way, must be prepared to lead public opinion not follow it. The police role in race relations is as complex and varied as the total police role and the interest and needs of good policing interweave at many points with those for good race relations. The ideal to which both are committed and which makes the police interest as participant in race relations so vital is that of making justice in society a reality for all men regardless of race or class or creed or colour.

Note. Ignored here but of great significance is the rejection that a coloured policeman may experience in his own community by 'going over to the other side'. This will also explain why there are so few coloured applicants.

Part III: Children

CHAPTER 7

Families in Need of Care

1. *Delinquency and Immigration: Some Hypotheses*

There is no shortage of studies which have examined certain aspects of juvenile crime among immigrant populations and among American Negroes. Interpretations of comparative rates of delinquents among different groups are very difficult to make because of marked differences within the groups of age, sex ratios, family sizes, and achieved socio-economic position, apart from inherent uncertainties in the nature of the crime statistics upon which such rates are based. But authors have stressed how inconclusive and conflicting much of the data seem and how they require particularly subtle analysis. There is a recognized need to distinguish crimes committed by immigrants whether adult or juvenile, crimes committed by the native-born children of immigrant parents, and crimes committed by children of mixed racial parentage. For each group it is necessary to take into account factors of group social, cultural, and economic integration if true comparisons of like with like are to be effected.

The pattern of delinquency from the numerous American studies would indicate that immigrant children (the first generation) were relatively less delinquent than the native born; but high rates of delinquency were shown by the American-born children of immigrant parents. By the third generation, as the group as a whole became more Americanized, the rate and occurrence of delinquency also became more Americanized, matching that of the economic level the group achieved in American society. Crime and delinquency rates among Negroes have persisted, indicating, in contrast with immigrant minorities who have in time achieved a measure of assimilation and economic integration, that the minority Negro group has remained ostracized, humiliated, and subordinated by discriminatory practices.

Important factors determining levels of first-generation immigrant delinquency will be: (a) the culture of origin: whether the migration is between like societies or from societies distinguished by custom and culture, or whether the migration is from a rural community to urban society; (b) the nature and process of the immigration: whether it was a migration of whole families, or piecemeal immigration involving separation of family members, and, perhaps crucially, whether the immigration pattern involved separation between parents and children; (c) the nature and structure of the family: whether the customs and traditions of family life and child-rearing are supportive and adaptive to the new life, so as to shield a child from the cultural shock or other stressful aspects of immigration, or whether the traditional family is weak or uninfluential in providing the necessary directions and control of children during a period of migration. Clearly these factors are to be seen, not as distinct and all-embracing, but as interrelated and subject to other variables less generally predictable. Overriding all, of course, will be the kind of economic stability provided by the host society.

The key notion in explaining second-generation delinquency is 'culture conflict'. Following Rex and Moore,[1] immigrant minority groups may be considered as groups differentiated by area of residence, culture, custom, and life style existing within the framework of the host society, when the host society is seen not as a unitary concept but as a complex system of class conflict and status. The rejection by Rex and Moore of the usual host–immigrant framework that is the common vocabulary of race relations can be seen to be important in the present context when they say, 'we see the immigrant, not simply as moving from one culture to another, but as being cut off from his native culture and groping for some kind of cultural and social signposts in a colony structure which belongs neither to his homeland nor to the society of his hosts'.[2] The 'culture of the home' with which the children of immigrant parents grow up, then, is not the fixed or stable 'culture of the homeland'; it is to be seen as a hybrid adaptation to the pressing needs of life in Britain. This will be to a lesser or greater extent true of all immigrant families, although clearly the nature of the cultural adaptation and the extent of continuity of the 'culture of the homeland' will depend on the group and

[1] Rex and Moore, op. cit., pp. 13–14.   [2] Ibid., p. 14.

family aspirations and the nature of integration and assimilation permitted by the host society. Older children who have come as immigrants with their parents can be expected to share the vicissitudes and tensions involved in 'groping for some kind of cultural and social signposts'. Younger children, and children born in the host country, may be expected to be involved less directly in this process but to be subject to the family and group systems of norms and values within this culturally distinct setting. In addition, the younger children will be exposed, most crucially at school, to the values and culture of the host society. Furthermore, the immigrant group settles or is only able to settle in areas where the prevailing social conditions are such that there is a cultural gap between the values articulated by the school and teachers and those shown by white children and families in the area. Thus, as is shown in the chapter on 'The Younger Generation' in Rex and Moore's study of Sparkbrook, the children are subject to a double socialization process in which home, school, and peer group may present three sets of role models within which a workable synthesis is impossible. This system of cultures in conflict is seen reflected through American studies in the high rates of second-generation delinquency.

But if culture conflict may be seen to be likely to promote a delinquent response, other forces will affect the actual outcome. On the positive side, within a society where there is no barrier to the social and economic advancement of immigrant youth, the 'escape' from the home and the achievement of independence may be successful. This will be determined by the level of education attained, the development of skills, and the availability of employment. Negatively, failure to provide scope for advancement, satisfaction of legitimate aspirations, and so on, associated with a generally low status achievement for the group socially, may promote a group reaction against the values of the dominant society in the form of delinquency. In America, particularly in areas where there is a stable tradition of crime as a way of life, criminal activities can provide a means of securing economic gain and prestige denied by conventional systems. In less stable areas the demoralization and group degradation may promote violence and disorder, vandalism and thuggery, instead of the cool, orderly, skilled work of crime. Another possible response is retreat or withdrawal to a situation where conventional, criminal, or cultural norms no longer apply, where through drugs or alcohol or other devices the demands of society are neutralized and avoided.

'Failure' as described above is, of course, open for every one, not just immigrants. But where immigrants live—*and* the cultural tensions under which the children live, their being adrift between cultures—places immigrants in a position that is exposed to crime and delinquency. In Britain, the absence, to any great extent, of crime as a way of life, and as a means of obtaining economic gain and prestige, means that crime and delinquency are features of certain areas—the poorest, most deprived, most disorganized neighbourhoods. The typical English delinquent is still the child from the slum-area family. Families, children, and area share a sense of failure. Immigrants in the area will have no such sense of failure although the host society may do its best to associate the coloured population with the inferior status and inadequacy imputed to the area. These discriminative pressures affect the way the parent generation of immigrants adjusts as a group and as individuals: their children may be expected to be less accepting.

The American literature stresses the link between the experience of immigrant minorities and the experience of the Negro by explaining them in shared terms. Recent immigration to Britain is to a great extent an immigration of coloured minority groups and the fact of colour seems likely to be of continuing greater significance than the fact of immigration. Large numbers of Irish immigrants whose general level of assimilation, acceptance, and achievement is high, provide something of a 'control group' whose experience may be compared or contrasted with other immigrant minorities.

Clearly colour may be the most important factor in moulding peoples' attitudes to interracial marriage. Discussions of prejudice often fall into discussion of 'would you allow your daughter [or sister] to marry a coloured man?' Although any foreign-born person is treated with suspicion, particularly as a marriage partner, nowhere is this likely to match up to the hostile feelings towards a coloured marriage partner. The extent of miscegenation will be determined by attitudes to mixed marriages among the members of the host society and the aspirations of the immigrant communities. For the former such attitudes will differ by class grouping. The latter will be affected both by the nature of the immigration as well as by the aims of immigrants: if the migration is largely restricted to working males, the demands for interracial marriage may be great; if the ambition of the migrant is to achieve close identity with the host society and good standing within that society, miscegenation may be seen as a means to that end. Among British society where low status and low esteem attach to coloured minority groups, interracial marriage may be contemplated only by an idealist and educated minority of the middle class or by a deviant and inadequate minority of the lower working class. Thus it is to be expected that racially mixed families will be found at opposite ends of the social spectrum and the situation of the children of such marriage will reflect such distinctions.

To the extent that children of mixed racial origin are associated with low class area and status, the position of themselves and of their families may be thought of as acutely stressful. Such families may occupy a marginal position unincorporated either within an immigrant colony structure or within the British working class. The children may find themselves even more adrift than second-generation immigrant children, having identity neither as a member of an immigrant minority nor with their white peers, and may experience both the discrimination that attaches to coloured status and the deprivation attaching to lower class status. Most potent in determining the stability of such marriages will be the role of the mother. Immigrants may be among the more able and ambitious of their populations. If their adequacy and intelligence are matched by their marriage partners, the family may well enjoy above average stability and success. If, on the other hand, it is only an inadequate and unstable white class of woman with whom marriage is possible, the instability and insecurity of those families will be most marked.[1]

From this discussion it is possible to frame a number of tentative hypotheses which the research reported here has sought to test and explore further. These refer to first-generation immigrant children from the West Indies, from India and Pakistan, and from Ireland; second-generation native-born children of immigrant parents from these countries; and children of mixed racial origins.

1. It can be hypothesized that delinquency rates among first-generation immigrants will be generally lower than a com-

---

[1] See S. Collins, *Coloured Minorities in Britain* (London, Lutterworth, 1957).

16

parable rate per population among native-born non-immigrant children. Within this category the lowest rate will be among Indian and Pakistani families where the strong and continuing sense of culture and family will be such as to preserve the traditional ties and controls.[1]

A somewhat more marked tendency for delinquency will be apparent among West Indian children, reflecting the less secure family structure prevailing in the West Indies, and depending on the extent to which the process of immigration has meant separation between children and parents for any length of time. Also of importance will be the extent to which both parents of such children are wage-earners, thus reducing the kind of supervision the mother can exert on her children (this latter aspect may contrast with the Indian and Pakistani family where the cultural position of the mother within an extended family unit will make it unlikely that she will go out to work).[2]

The rate of delinquency among Irish children will be most like that among native-born children, reflecting the greater ease of assimilation between the groups, but mediated by the socio-economic level that Irish families achieve in the host community.

2. Delinquency rates among second-generation native-born children of immigrant parents will exceed that of first-generation children, and may exceed that of a comparable non-immigrant native-born group.

Differences between second-generation ethnic groups are more problematical to hypothesize: the crucial factors will be educational attainment, employment availability, and levels of discrimination within the general framework of culture conflict described earlier.

Children of Indian and Pakistani parents may be expected to benefit from strong family and cultural influences which may enhance educational achievement, but at the same time be

---

[1] It is interesting to note the findings of Shaw and McKay in their classic study, *Juvenile Delinquency in Urban Areas* (Chicago, University of Chicago Press, 1942). 'In communities occupied by Orientals, even those communities located in the most deteriorated sections of our large cities, the solidarity of Old World cultures and institutions has been preserved to such a marked extent that control of the child is still sufficiently effective to keep at a minimum delinquency and other forms of deviant behavior.' Quoted in Wolfgang *et al.*, (eds.), op. cit., p. 235.

[2] The customary mother role may well change if economic necessity makes demands which require a second wage-earner in the home.

exposed to greater culture conflict than other groups. Thus delinquency may be substantially greater than among first-generation Indian and Pakistani children, but less than other second-generation and native-born children.

Children of West Indian parents may lack the group and family support enjoyed by Indian and Pakistani children and be unable to match their educational achievement. As a group there may be greater exposure to discrimination as their aspirations are more markedly in terms of success within British society: accordingly, the sense of cultural adriftness may be very marked, and delinquency higher than among first-generation West Indians and higher than among other second-generation and native-born groups may result.

Second-generation delinquency among children of Irish parents will reflect the over-all achievement of the Irish within British society and will reflect any unequal class and area distributions of the Irish. The majority of Irish immigrants are from rural areas of Ireland where the traditional close-knit family may provide a pattern of socialization and child-rearing that is inappropriate for life in the more diffuse and impersonal urban centre. Certainly the Irish are over-represented among the working class which determines to a marked degree the economic stability and area distribution of Irish families in Britain.[1] These factors may lead to an over-representation of children of Irish parents among a delinquent population in comparison with other groups.

3. Delinquency rates among children native-born of an inter-racial marriage may be higher than in any other group. It may be assumed that prevailing attitudes oppose such marriages which may mean that at a low class level the white partner's status and capabilities will be limited. This being so a high proportion of such marriages will be unstable unions allowing only a lower class level of assimilation and achievement and a corresponding number will be in the problem family category where delinquency may be a relatively frequent response to family stress. The type and pattern of delinquency among such families may be distinctive from other second-generation delinquency and show many similarities with native-born delinquency much of which derives from similarly placed problem families.

[1] For these aspects, see J. A. Jackson, *The Irish in Britain* (London, Routledge and Kegan Paul, 1963).

2. *Sources of Information and Factual Data*

It was to explore further some of these suggestions that the inquiry among families in need was conducted. The title 'families in need' has been preferred to one referring to delinquency because the research is concerned with a wider age range than is normal or appropriate in studies of delinquency and the family setting is, of course, crucial in understanding the tensions to which delinquency is one response. Also it was recognized that among the coloured immigrant communities there are few second-generation children of the age where a court appearance is the result of behaviour problems and it was hoped that a study of families and younger children might indicate any future trend in this field.

It was hoped to be able to obtain data which might make a confident appraisal of comparative rates of delinquency between first- and second-generation immigrant and native-born groups. It soon became apparent that such a task was impossible without much additional data becoming available. Accordingly the emphasis shifted to an inquiry into the relative proportions of immigrant children and families in contact with certain agencies and, by a consideration of case material, to an assessment of qualitative differences in delinquency and family stress shown by the various groups.

Categorization and nomenclature presented some problem deriving from the uncertainty and growing irrelevance of the 'immigrant' label. In what follows children and families are categorized by nationality of parents: native British refers to the local population, mostly English but including a small number of Welsh and Scottish families; Irish refers to children and families both of whose parents were born in the Irish Republic or in Northern Ireland; West Indian refers to instances where both parents were immigrants from the West Indies, although where possible the numbers from each island were recorded; the somewhat misleading title of Asian refers to Indian or Pakistani families, more for the sake of brevity than anything else; to indicate a family of mixed racial origins the prefix 'mixed' has been used in relation to the above categories depending on the country of origin of the father.[1] The context will make it clear

---

[1] There were no instances of marriages between Englishmen and Asian or West Indian women. There were, however, a small number of cases of children with an Irish mother and an English father; these have been included in the mixed Irish category.

when first- and second-generation children and families are being discussed.

Data were obtained from three sources:

1. The case histories were studied of all boys whose families were resident in the County Borough of Birmingham and who during a three-year period were committed to an Approved School and thereby were sent to Kingswood Classifying Centre. Basic information about nationality of parents was obtained for all boys and some further information for all West Indian, Asian, Irish, and mixed-Asian boys. In addition records were consulted at the local office of the children's department to ascertain the number of Birmingham boys sent to Approved School but who were not sent to classifying school in the same period, and the number of girls so dealt with.

2. During a six-month period information was obtained about the nationality and area of residence of all persons then currently under the supervision of the probation officers working in the division which constituted the study area of other aspects of this research. Additional information was obtained for a sample of native-British cases and all other cases.

3. A survey was made of a sample of all contacts between the population of the division studied and the child care staff of the local children's department; information was taken about the family, the nature of the work involved, and the cause of referral.

It needs to be stressed that data from the above sources cannot provide anything like a complete picture of delinquency and family breakdown in an area. The use of these sources reflects both the limited nature of the resources and the willingness of the agencies and individuals concerned to allow a researcher access to files and case histories and of several probation officers to spend many hours in discussion of their cases. First offenders and adult offenders are excluded from this group. And other agencies are at work in the area to which families in need can refer. It can be argued that the sources provide systematic data and records about the more difficult and problematical families in the area.

3. *Approved School Boys and Girls*
Table 39 provides an estimate of the nationalities of the parents of the 601 boys admitted to Approved Schools from Birmingham

during a three-year period from January 1964 to January 1967.

Table 39 is based on information from 470 case histories examined at classifying school and from an estimate of the nationality of 131 Roman Catholic boys who did not go to classifying school. Only since April 1966 have *all* Approved School boys been first sent to classifying school. Prior to that date Roman Catholic boys were admitted direct to Roman Catholic Approved Schools from their home area. It was possible to assess the number of these boys and make some assessment of nationality by scrutinizing local records of the court section of Birmingham children's department.

The nature of the estimation requires some explanation. The school information was well documented in every case and included information on a number of Roman Catholic boys admitted since the change in the system. But local records immediately available did not indicate the nationality or racial origin of the children and families concerned. From these limited data some assessment of the nationality was made by studying the names, and the proportions compared with those for whom school information was available. As the proportions matched fairly well and as this estimation was amenable to some test on the population for which certain information was available, there are some grounds for confidence that the estimate may be accurate. The proportions of the Irish families, and mixed-Irish families were assessed from the population whose files were available at the classifying school.

The figures relating to girls is even more uncertain because as none of the girls go to a classifying school, there was no check on the estimating procedure. Clearly such procedures are highly unsatisfactory yet unavoidable when there is no systematic recording of such data except in case files. It seemed, on balance, more useful to provide such a table despite these shortcomings for the sake of discussion rather than to exclude it on the grounds of methodological impurity.

Table 39 shows clearly the very small numbers of coloured cases involved. The impression from the table that a somewhat higher proportion of coloured girls present behaviour problems was confirmed in conversation with probation and child care officers. In each case it will be noted that the number of Asian children involved is very small, while there are about equal numbers among boys and girls of West Indian and mixed Asian parentage. It did not seem sensible to risk any assessment for the girls between Irish and mixed Irish but it is interesting to note the larger number and proportion of mixed Irish boys than Irish boys. Although information was not always clear (and of course a high proportion of those about whom a guess was made were Irish), among the cases studied second-generation Irish children outnumbered those who had come as immigrants with their

TABLE 39: ORIGINS OF CHILDREN AT
APPROVED SCHOOLS

Nationality of parents	Boys		Girls	
	No.	%	No.	%
Native British	422	70·3	74	67
Irish	43	7	23	21
Mixed Irish	80	13·3	—	—
West Indian	13	2	5	5
Asian	4	1	2	2
Mixed Asian	14	2·3	4	4
Others/not known*	25	4	1	1
Total	601	—	109	—

* Includes twelve children born of one European parent and one English parent; and thirteen cases where there was insufficient evidence to assess the nationality of either parent.

parents by nearly two to one. Among the mixed Irish group of boys, those with an English mother outnumbered those with an Irish mother by nearly three to one. Table 39 also demonstrates the difficulties of making interpretations in terms of comparative rates. Apart from the fact that information about nationality is collected only incidentally to some other data, there is no way of estimating separate populations or risk for these various groups. This is particularly true of the mixed Asian category which accounts for nearly half of coloured delinquents; and 60 per cent of an over-all immigrant category.

Some figures are obtainable and published about the proportion of immigrant children in schools, but such exclude children of mixed immigrant parentage, children born of parents resident for ten years or more, and, presumably because of these reasons, any information about the Irish. However, such figures do reveal that at January 1966, West Indian boys accounted for 2·5 per cent of all boys aged 11 to 14 years in Birmingham, and Asian boys were 3·5 per cent of that group. As that age category provides most Approved School entrants, it can be seen that Asian children are markedly less delinquent in terms of Approved School referrals than a comparable English age group. The West Indian boys, though more prone to Approved School admission than the Asian boys, are still under-represented in comparison with white children. However, the Approved School figures cited here refer to three years' admissions and include a wider age range than that noted. There is also a slight tendency for West Indian and Asian children to have a higher average age on admission than other groups which makes further qualifications necessary.

About the other groups only speculation is possible: although it might seem that with 5 per cent of the Birmingham population being Irish-born their children are over-represented among Approved School boys, this may not be so. Actual populations of Irish-born and coloured immigrants are numerically similar. It can be supposed that the Irish immigrants have been resident for longer than the coloured immigrant, and being, like the coloured population, one preponderantly of those of child-bearing age, one would guess that there are certainly not less, probably more, children of Irish parents in the city than children of coloured immigrant parentage and there should be a more even age distribution among that population. Currently, coloured immigrant children comprise 6·7 per cent of the school population, the proportion being higher for younger and lower for older children, which might suggest a comparable Irish figure of between 8–9 per cent. Cautiously, then, it seems that Irish boys, who comprise 7 per cent of the Approved School population, are not an over-represented population.

The really unknown quantities are those referring to numbers of racially mixed families and children: it would seem unlikely that there are as many mixed families as unmixed. It seems, therefore, that the hypothesis of a higher rate in this category is confirmed, although the extent of that rate cannot be assessed. These categories will require careful study of qualitative aspects if the figures are to be interpreted properly.

Certain other information about Approved School boys will be presented following that relating to probationers.

4. *Probationers in the Area Studied*

The information that probation officers record on their files is not intended for research purposes; it is rather intended to record the progress of each probationer's period on probation and so tends to be somewhat idiosyncratic to each officer's approach to each individual client. Neither time nor resources were available for a systematic sifting of data from these files. But during a six-month period it was possible to have a series of meetings with a number of officers during which all immigrant cases could be discussed; for some areas it was possible to do the same for English cases. For all areas basic information about the age, nationality, and address of all offenders was available; thus at the end of the limited period during which data could be collected, information was available for all immigrant offenders and for a sample of English offenders. This method did not of course allow for any systematic coverage of attitudinal or psychological factors shown by the offenders: but it did allow those factors which the probation officers themselves felt to be significant to be discussed and thus provide some opportunity to collect, albeit vicariously, some soundly based observational data apposite to the subject.

TABLE 40: NATIONALITY OF PROBATIONERS

Nationality	Males				Females				Total	
	Under 21		Adult		Under 21		Adult			
	No.	%	No.	%	No.	%	No.	%	No.	%
Native British	249	73	56	82	49	60	12	66	366	70
Irish (and mixed Irish)	60	18	12	17	23	30	5	28	100	20
West Indian	11	3	1	1	5	6	—	—	17	3
Asian	4	1	—	—	1	1	—	—	5	1
Mixed Asian	13	4	—	—	2	1	—	—	15	3
Mixed West Indian	3	1	—	—	—	—	—	—	3	1
Other	2	1	—	—	1	1	1	6	4	1
Total	342		69		81		18		510	
Age distribution (%)	83		17		82		18			

Table 40 presents a composite picture of the 510 cases on probation or under other supervision current during a six-month period from November 1966 to April 1967. From this it will be seen that 411 were males and ninety-nine females. Just over 80 per cent of each group were under 21 years of age.

Of the males under 21, 73 per cent were native born British, 18 per cent Irish (including mixed Irish), and a small number were coloured persons, accounting for less than 10 per cent of the population. Of the females under 21, 60 per cent were found to be native British, 30 per cent Irish (including mixed Irish), and again less than 10 per cent coloured persons.

Without exception the West Indian and Asian were first-generation immigrant children, the particular mixed category providing second-generation coloured children. Unfortunately it was not always possible to be certain whether those classed as Irish were immigrants, second generation, or children of mixed origin. From the somewhat limited data it would seem that boys from wholly Irish families outnumbered those from mixed Irish homes by two to one; for girls the proportion was three to one. Within the Irish group there were about equal numbers of immigrant and second-generation children although among the girls more were second generation.

Apart from this Irish distribution, there is a striking similarity in ethnic composition between the population at Approved Schools and on probation. The same interpretative difficulties exist: there is confirmed the relative low involvement of children from Asian and West Indian families. The high number of Irish girls is probably an indicator of an administrative quirk whereby a number of Irish girls from Approved Schools are being supervised on after-care by a probation officer whereas their native British peers may be supervised by a child care officer. Such a shortcoming is unlikely to apply to the tables about male probationers. Considering the age distribution of the various groups, Table 41 sets out the comparative distribution of the male probationers:

TABLE 41: AGE CHARACTERISTICS OF YOUNGER MALE PROBATIONERS IN FOUR NATIONALITY GROUPS

Age	Under 17	17–21
Native British	125	124
Irish and mixed Irish	25	35
West Indian–Asian	8	7
Mixed and other	14	4
Total	172	170

When this information is taken with information about the average number of court appearances for each group it can be seen how those in the 'mixed' group are rather younger but as about experienced in crime as their English peers, which suggests that they are children of problem families who came to the notice of agencies (including the court) sooner than families in other categories.

TABLE 42: COURT APPEARANCES:
MALE PROBATIONERS UNDER 21 MEAN NUMBER OF
COURT APPEARANCES

Nationality	Number
Native British	2·1
Irish	2·5
West Indian–Asian	1·5
Mixed and other	2·0

TABLE 43: COURT APPEARANCES:
APPROVED SCHOOL BOYS MEAN NUMBER OF
COURT APPEARANCES

Nationality	Number
Native British	3·85
Irish	4·2
Mixed Irish	4·2
West Indian	2·3
Asian	2·5
Mixed Asian	3·5

5. *Families in Contact with the Children's Department*

During a six-month period a survey was made of contacts between families resident in the division studied and the local area office of the children's department. It was not possible to survey every case and a random sampling procedure presented certain difficulties as there was to be an on-going collection of data that weighted any sample with immigrant cases. Eventually it was decided to follow a selection of on-going immigrant cases with a random sample of the remainder; in this way 183 case papers were studied which can be considered as a random sample (with variable sampling fractions for each nationality group) of a total of 463 cases.

There are of course many reasons for contact between families and the children's department and by no means all merited serious casework. It was possible to distinguish six kinds of cases in approximate order of seriousness.

1 Cases requiring advice and information rather than action from a child care officer.
2 Cases requiring mild and short-term casework.
3 Cases requiring intensive short-term casework.
4 Cases requiring long-term preventative supervision.
5 Cases requiring short periods in care.
6 Cases where admission of a child to care was to be seen as a probable long-term or recurrent measure.

Table 44 presents the distribution of these categories by nationality of the family.

TABLE 44: DISTRIBUTION OF THE CASES OF CHILD CARE CONTACTS IN EACH NATIONALITY IN SIX CLASSES OF CASEWORK

	Work categories						Est. total numbers	%	Actual cases studied	Sampling fraction
Nationality	1	2	3	4	5	6				
Native British	74	24	6	40	7	14	165	36	47	1/3·6
Irish (and mixed Irish)	30	26	11	7	12	—	86	19	35	1/2·4
West Indian	19	14	22	10	8	3	76	16	43	1/1·8
Asian	1	—	5	—	8	—	14	3	8	1/1·8
Mixed West Indian	2	6	10	—	10	2	30	7	15	1/2
Mixed Asian	2	12	2	2	4	—	22	5	11	1/2
Other*	10	—	4	—	2	1	17	4	9	1/1·8
Not known†	—	—	—	—	—	—	53	11	15	1/3·5
Total	138	82	60	59	51	20	463	100	183	—
%	34	20	15	14	12	5				

* This group consists of mixed European families and a small number of African families.
† For this rather large number the files could not be traced.

If categories 1 and 2 are considered together as those requiring non-intensive casework, it can be seen how a higher proportion of families with coloured children require more intensive work on the part of child care officers (see Table 45).

These tables indicate the extent to which the work of the children's department is with immigrant families and families of mixed racial origin. It is of course difficult to assess a 'normal' rate of referral for the different groups particularly when the needs of the families for the advice and support child care officers can provide are so varied. An attempt was made to explore this variety among cases requiring intensive work, maintaining a distinction between those instances where casework with the

TABLE 45: DISTRIBUTION OF CASES OF EACH NATIONALITY GROUP INTO TWO BROAD CATEGORIES OF NON-INTENSIVE AND INTENSIVE CASEWORK

Nationality	Non-intensive work %	Intensive work %	Estimated no. of cases
Native British	58	42	165
Irish	63	37	86
West Indian	43	57	76
Asian	8	92	14
Mixed West Indian	25	75	30
Mixed Asian	64	36	22
Other	59	41	17

family prevented the need of admission of a child into care and those where admission to care was an unavoidable necessity. Table 44 suggests that although a smaller proportion of native British families requires intensive work, when it is required, it is needed either in the form of long-term casework or long periods in care. For most other categories short-term casework or short periods in care are needed.

Casework, as against 'in care' treatment, was found to be directed at three major aspects of the family situation:

(i) At the relationship between mother and father whose breakdown was threatening the stability of the family as a whole by provoking 'bad' behaviour by children, or by affecting the family economics through the father failing to support adequately.

(ii) At adolescent children presenting behaviour problems so as to put them beyond parental control and guidance but where such behaviour and the parents' response is not such as to require the child leaving home.

(iii) At general relationships with the family when, through absence or desertion, younger children's needs have been neglected: but where the need to support the family through critical phases is clearly indicated.

(iv) Some cases were of a somewhat exceptional nature, falling into none of the above three categories.

Table 46 shows the distribution of these four kinds of casework among the different nationality groups. It seemed sensible to combine the mixed West Indian, and mixed Asian families into one group for this table and also to join the small number of Asian families into the 'Other' category.

TABLE 46: CATEGORIES OF INTENSIVE CASEWORK AMONG FAMILIES OF DIFFERENT NATIONALITIES (EXCLUDING CASES INVOLVING ADMISSION TO CARE)

Category	Native British		Irish		West Indian		Mixed		Other		Total	
	No.	%	No.	%	No.	%	No.	%	No.	%	No.	%
(i) Matrimonial	18	38	7	39	7	22	2	15	3	33	37	31
(ii) Adolescents	18	38	2	11	14	44	—	—	—	—	34	29
(iii) Family	7	15	—	—	9	28	10	70	3	33	29	24
(iv) Other	3	9	9	50	2	6	2	15	3	33	19	16
Total	46	100	18	100	32	100	14	100	9	100	119	100

Although it must be borne in mind that the number of cases in the categories are small, Table 46 suggests that with native British families casework is frequently concerned with matrimonial difficulties and the behaviour problems of teen-age children. The large proportion of the Irish families in the 'other' category is attributable to a number of young, friendless, and homeless young Irishwomen, often unmarried, without anyone to help them through an illness or at time of confinement, a pathetic and lost minority, inadequate as mothers, and living a shiftless life where affection is insufficient by itself to provide for the needs of the children. It is interesting to note how work with West Indian families is not infrequently with teen-age immigrant children 'beyond control' of parent and home; while it is the younger children often with a disturbed family setting who account for much work with families of mixed racial origin.

Turning to those cases where children had to be admitted into care, there were found to be five categories of situations which forced this action.

(i) Cases of 'good' homes where it was yet impossible, at a time of mother being in hospital for illness or a confinement, to find friends or neighbours to help father. In some instances there was a partial success on this front which meant only some (usually the youngest) children of the family being admitted. All these cases are, of course, cases of *short* in-care treatment often only a few days, never more than a few months.

(ii) Cases in many ways similar to the above but where the family itself is unstable or disturbed (i.e. when the union is an unstable cohabitation or a broken marriage or where illegitimate children are not accepted by the stepfather), which makes finding the necessary help of outsiders more difficult, and where the risks of long-term in-care treatment following a severing of already weak family ties are so much the greater.

(iii) Cases where admitting a child to care was necessary following the desertion or inadequacy of one partner (usually the mother), and where the total family situation is so deteriorated that there is no certainty when the child will be able to return.

(iv) Cases of actual neglect where admitting a younger child to care is required for its health and safety.

(v) Cases where older children through neglect, rejection, or some other reason prove to be beyond the control of parents and for whom admission to care has to be seen as a fairly long-term measure.

Table 47 provides the distribution of these five categories among the different nationality groups.

Again remembering the small numbers involved, Table 47 suggests how, not surprisingly, in-care treatment of young children of native British families is an exceptional event, indicating an already stressful family situation, whereas an immigrant family otherwise soundly based may require short-term in care for some of their children at times when mother has to go into hospital.

Mixed families show needs more like those of the native British problem family than those of the immigrant family. Older children requiring admission to care seem to be those from native British or West Indian families.

It will be necessary to refer back to some of the suggestions deriving from this exploration of families in contact with the children's department when in the next chapter some qualitative aspects of juvenile delinquency are discussed. Meanwhile it is interesting to compare the above findings with some information available about the proportion of children of different racial origins in the care of the local authority.

TABLE 47: CATEGORIES OF FAMILIES REQUIRING
PERIODS OF 'IN-CARE' TREATMENT AMONG
FAMILIES OF DIFFERENT NATIONALITIES

Category	Native British		Irish		West Indian		Mixed		Other		Total	
	No.	%	No.	%	No.	%	No.	%	No.	%	No.	%
(i) 'Good' families	—	—	5	42	5	46	2	12.5	7	63	19	26
(ii) 'Weak' families	7	35	5	42	2	18	8	50	2	18	24	35
(iii) 'Broken' families	4	15	2	16	—	—	4	25	—	—	10	14
(iv) Neglect	3	15	—	—	—	—	—	—	2	18	5	7
(v) Children beyond control	7	35	—	—	4	36	2	12·5	—	—	13	18
Total	21	100	12	100	11	100	16	100	11	100	71	100

Between 1959 and 1966 the over-all proportion of coloured children in care in Birmingham rose from 9·7 per cent to 26·3 per cent, and in terms of absolute numbers an increase of about sixty every year to a total of 542 at mid-1966. It must be realized that this is an over-all figure including children of mixed racial origin; and before any assessment of any 'over-representation' of coloured children among those in care can be made, it is necessary to know the proportions of the different categories. Furthermore, it can be expected that for immigrant families in particular, the need for short periods in care may be greater than for native-born families who can be supposed to enjoy greater economic stability, more secure employment, and a wider range of family and kin relations for support at times of need. In fact, breaking down the over-all 1966 figure of 26·3 per cent the following picture emerges:

Category	% of those in care
Native British and Irish	73·7
West Indian	8·7
Asian	0·7
Mixed	16·9

These over-all figures derive from a yearly census at a particular date and include those children in short-term care, hence the discrepancy with the figures and proportions deriving from the survey carried out for this research. But the over-all pattern is confirmed: a very low rate of admission among children of Asian families, rather a high proportion of West Indian children, a higher proportion of children of mixed parentage, and a large majority of white children from British or Irish families.

The basic strength of the Asian family that was suggested by the data about delinquents is again to be noted; while a tendency for the teen-age immigrant West Indian to present behavioural problems is similar to the data on Approved School boys. Among children of school age the proportion of West Indian origin or parentage is slightly less than 5 per cent; among younger children the proportion is certainly higher, so the extent of any numerical over-representation of West Indian children in care is not very marked and perhaps no more than might be expected: discussion of why this might be so will follow. As with the data on delinquency, a major concern must be to examine the situation of families of mixed origin who account for a similarly high proportion of children in court as they do families in need.

CHAPTER 8

Comparative Aspects of Family Need

It was noted earlier that the average age of admission of boys to Approved Schools is slightly older for those of West Indian or Asian origin and younger for those of mixed origins than for the native British boy: it was also shown that coloured immigrant boys, though less inclined to be sent to Approved School, reach such schools after rather fewer court appearances than the English or Irish majority. To attempt to provide some greater depth to comparisons between the five major birth-place and nationality categories, utilizing the data described in the previous section, five aspects of the situation will be discussed. Although some aspects can be illustrated through group factors that are measurable, such as I.Q. or family size, the burden of the description will utilize illustrative case material selected from the files and case histories studied.

Case studies can only hint at the varied and complex home and social backgrounds of delinquent children. The search for the typical is as fruitless as the search for *the* cause of crime. The variety of factors and influences which in conjunction make delinquency likely can be suggested; but it is more difficult to explain why A rather than B has become delinquent. And, as always, it is necessary to bear in mind constantly that we are talking about a tiny minority of families, English or otherwise.

1. *English Case Studies*

Before embarking upon an exploration of certain comparative aspects of delinquency among nationality groups it may be useful to suggest by way of an introduction something of the variety and complexities of native-born delinquency.

Studying the family backgrounds of native British delinquents reveals how many of the families and delinquents experience a variety of adverse pressures through which the normal restraints on delinquent exploits are neutralized. The variety of such exploits is also noticeable; petty larcenies predominate, of course, houses, shops, and parked cars providing plenty of opportunities for theft. Taking and driving away motor-cars or scooters and motor cycles is arguably a less dishonest form of delinquent enjoyment, more nuisance than criminal; while some offences— vandalism at phone kiosks or offences relating to mild drug taking —seem to occur in cult phases and crazes.

The following seven case histories[1] can suggest something of the complexity:

Case 1. The A family has lived in its present home for a great many years—an old terraced house with no bathroom, three bedrooms, an outside w.c., a small backyard, and a front door opening straight on to the street. Soon the house will be demolished in a large slum clearance scheme. Here a family of thirteen has been raised. The two eldest girls have moved away, the eldest boy is at Approved School, so currently the family consists of mother, father, and ten children whose ages range from 15 to 2 years. Despite overcrowding the children are materially well cared for and the house is kept clean and well furnished. Alan, aged 15, was put on probation following his third offence; for an earlier offence he was sent to an attendance centre. On each occasion his offences have been committed by a group of boys and involved breaking into a shop and stealing a small sum of money, sweets, and cigarettes. He is a healthy, outgoing, irrepressible boy of slightly lower than average intelligence, who has frequently truanted from school, and is somewhat retarded educationally. He is an uncomplicated, unsupervised youngster who has escaped his parents' affectionate but strict attempts at discipline and has spent a lot of his free time with other local boys in a similar position to him, getting into mischief and being led and then leading other boys into delinquent escapades. For him and his brother delinquency seems a normal healthy adventurous game unprovoked by severe tensions or stresses in family background. His parents, hard-working honest people, are worried about his behaviour but recognize that they cannot counteract the influence

---

[1] In these cases, and all those that follow, the names are fictional: to prevent any of these cases being identified, some purely factual information, i.e. family size, ages of siblings, has been altered.

of the area; and with so large a family in such overcrowded conditions they have not been able to exert the influence that 'good'
parents in a 'good' area might be expected to exert.

The danger facing boys in Alan's position is that increasing
delinquency may become the only available outlet for them as
they become singled out as special cases for social action and
ostracism. Deprived of other opportunities, and discriminated
against in employment because of their record, a criminal career
may open up for them as the most attractive way to a success that
can discount widespread social approval. Fortunately most
become aware of the isolation and jeopardy such would bring and
are able to adjust to a non-delinquent way of life when school-
leaving makes demands for employment and girl friends make
demands for a secure future.

The A family lives in a slum area in Zone I of the division
studied and will soon be rehoused. A move to less cramped
conditions in a better area does not necessarily erase delinquency.

Case 2. The B family moved eight years ago to a four-bedroom
council house in Zone III from one of the central areas of the
city. The family consists of mother and father, and eleven
children ranging from 17 to 2 years. The four eldest boys who are
'of age' have been in trouble and three have attended or are
attending Approved Schools. For a number of years the boys have
been active in the area with other boys in a variety of delinquent
episodes. The father, preoccupied with earning enough to maintain home and family, has withdrawn from being an active
parent; the mother, understanding but overburdened, copes with
the needs of the younger family members neglecting the older
ones who in consequence are all plausible liars, always ready to
manipulate the situation so as to deny any responsibility on their
part for what has happened.

These two cases are exceptional only in so far as they show
in an extreme way how delinquency can be normal unsupervised
behaviour for basically healthy and reasonably intelligent
children. More usual, perhaps, is to find some grave disturbance
in the family situation.

Case 3. The C family lives in a block of fairly modern council flats near the city centre. Charles is the youngest in a family of six and the only boy. His mother's legal husband deserted her and the three eldest children many years ago. Charles' father deserted just a few months before Charles was born, leaving his mother to cope with six children. The three eldest children are married and live nearby, visiting their mother frequently. Charles has been in trouble since he was 13 for a variety of offences always committed by a group of boys. His home situation is extremely disorganized; his mother is incapable of elementary budgeting; the girls emulate their mother with a host of marital problems; and, most affected by the anxiety and chaos in a fatherless house, is Charles, who since leaving school has wandered in and out of a variety of jobs, shows little ambition or enthusiasm for anything, and, unable to foresee the consequences of his actions, gets involved in lots of trouble and delinquency in the area.

The problems facing families in such areas are great. In many instances families in the area are among the most deprived and most problematical. Yet a closely-knit and seemingly well cared for family can also create problems.

Case 4. The D family lives in a modern four-bedroom council house in a somewhat more quiet, settled (and expensive) area near the city centre. The family consists of mother, father, and five children of whom the second eldest, David, has been the only one to get into trouble. It is a closely-knit family that has tended to keep apart from neighbours and always acts as a unit. All but David are happy with this situation. He, at 13, is a restless, outgoing boy, fairly intelligent but liable to be bullied at school. Somewhat diminutive, having to wear glasses, and with a skin rash that makes him seem rather unwashed, he is the butt for jokes, and frequently in fights which hurt his feelings more than his physique. Yet he enjoys school and tries hard to prove himself with other boys rather than retire to the security of his home. To overcome his inferiority feelings, he has tended to identify with the mischievous, the disruptive, and, inevitably in his area, the delinquent. His behaviour has only increased his isolation from home where he feels misunderstood and unwanted by parents and brothers and sisters. At school, too, as we have seen, he is treated as something of an outcast: the only group where he finds himself accepted is with delinquent boys.

Such a situation is probably not uncommon among 'good' homes in 'good' areas, though the middle-class delinquent may often not find or seek the group support that was noticeable in David's case.

Case 5. Edward was caught attempting to extract money from the coin box of a phone kiosk. His family lives in a large semi-detached house in Moseley where it runs a thriving family business. None of the other children in this family of six has been in trouble. Edward is in the G.C.E. stream of his local school and should fulfil his ambition to join one of the services following 'A' levels. The offence revealed a period of mounting tension at home with Edward stealing from his mother and generally behaving in an unexpectedly irresponsible manner. Reasons and causes are a mystery to his family: there was no real need, for Edward always had sufficient pocket-money and the family is sufficiently wealthy to provide money when wanted on special occasions. This is one of those cases where it is unusual to find the offender on probation or even in court. Probably as it was a case of telephone kiosk vandalism which had been rife in the area, and provoked dire threats from the local recorder, the police were disinclined to caution the boy or the court merely to fine or conditionally discharge him as might have been usual and normal for one in Edward's position.

Among Approved School boys can be found many instances like those in the first four cases outlined above. Sending a boy away from home is rightly looked on as something of a last resort by sentencing authorities and thus Approved School boys tend to have long records and disturbed home backgrounds, although some, as we shall see, are so dealt with on the very first appearance in court if the home situation is felt to be crippling the boys' chances of a normal non-delinquent life. It will be remembered that families A and B both had boys at Approved Schools although there was no gross family disturbances, just family inability to control and direct the boys to a non-delinquent career. It is more usual to find among Approved School boys fairly florid symptoms of acute family stress.

Case 6. Frank is the illegitimate son of a mentally defective mother who married, when Frank was 2, a patient on release from a closed mental institution. The marriage ended after a turbulent six months in separation and the husband's return to hospital. Thereafter commenced the mother's long-standing but not by any means even cohabitation with a Pakistani, which union has produced two children. The family has been in fairly constant contact with a variety of social welfare agencies. The mother is inadequate and unpredictable, sometimes clutchingly affectionate towards her children, at other times aggressive and rejecting. She has effectively prevented the younger children's father from having anything to do with the children. Frank has been under some sort of supervision or other since the age of 5, first of all in an attempt to regularize his school attendance, and later for minor thefts of food or clothes or cycles, all of which were denied him through normal channels. For a time he was in care and was sent to Approved School following his absconding from the children's home and stealing a bottle of milk. Throughout this period schooling has been uneven and ineffectual and at 14 Frank, though of normal intelligence potential, cannot read or write. Emotionally immature, materially deprived, educationally retarded, Frank is overwhelmed in the presence of other children from whom he withdraws frightenedly. He misses his mother acutely, has nightmares which reveal his terrible insecurity, and cannot understand why he is blamed for 'offences'. Frank's situation contains in extreme form elements common among Approved School boys: a history of a disturbed home, insecurity in relation to his mother's affections, lack of identification with a father, poor schooling due to emotional stresses at home as much as actual poor attendance, and periods out of control of home when delinquency occurs. In Frank's case the offences were of the mildest: other boys in response to similar anxieties and uncertainties may show their latent abilities in more sustained, more utilitarian, and sophisticated delinquent acts.

Approved Schools are intended for those who are not so criminally inclined as to be thought to merit Borstal training. Many Approved School boys do, of course, go on to Borstal. But some, coming late to a delinquency career, finding dangers not in the home, but after leaving school, in the adult world, go straight to Borstal.

Case 7. Gerald's first offence was committed at the age of 19 and he is the only member of his family to have been in trouble. He is one of a family of five, living in an old terraced house in Sparkbrook. Everything went all right for Gerald until a bout of unemployment made for tension at home and he moved out into lodgings. He obtained casual employment at a small, local garage run by two older men who were quite sophisticated criminals. They involved Gerald in a couple of warehouse-breaking jobs: they received four years and six years, respectively, when Gerald got Borstal. Gerald is not very bright, rather gullible, and was easily persuaded by the two men to whom, anyway, he owed his only legitimate means of earning money at that time. His period in Borstal was short and enjoyed; he earned a quick release and did work at the plumbing and decorating course that Borstal provided. On release he returned to live at home, quickly obtained a job, and looks confidently forward with no bitterness or resentment about his past.

These seven cases are intended to suggest something of the variety of English delinquency. Individual cases are never typical but they can reveal significant tendencies. Some Borstal boys, unlike Gerald, are much more sophisticated; many Approved School boys less disturbed than Frank, and so on. What is to be stressed is that delinquency cannot be explained by disturbed family backgrounds, delinquent opportunities in an area, poor parent relationships, or other factors. The problems, stresses, anxieties, temptations, dangers, and opportunities which can meet with a delinquent response are available to all but taken by a few; and the situations when a delinquent opportunity is taken rather than rejected can be as varied as the above selection of cases suggests.

This variety is intended as a necessary setting in which to describe the delinquent response of a minority of adolescents from immigrant families.

2. *Case Studies of Delinquency among Immigrant Families*
The five aspects upon which this comparative inquiry will concentrate relate:

(a) to educational ability and attainment;
(b) to factors arising from migration to an urban area from a rural area;
(c) to factors of culture conflict;
(d) to factors present in the neighbourhoods where immigrants have settled; and
(e) to general factors in the family situations of immigrants.

(a) EDUCATION

Table 48 sets out the average I.Q. scores obtained by the boys committed to Approved School and tested at the classifying centre. These have been calculated from a 10 per cent sample of native British boys, from a 50 per cent sample of mixed Irish boys, and from the whole population of boys in the other categories. Also provided is a measure of the standard deviations of these average scores.

TABLE 48: MEAN I.Q.: APPROVED SCHOOL BOYS

Nationality	I.Q.	Standard deviation
Native British	93·5	41·5
Irish	90	45·5
Mixed Irish	92	39·9
West Indian	78·4	45·0
Asian	103	47·5
Mixed Asian	95	34·8

This suggests that all groups, except the West Indian delinquent boys, are not on the whole markedly less intelligent than their non-delinquent peers. Much more important than the over-all average is the tremendous variation in most groups from boys of border-line subnormal intelligence to extremely high. This shows how complex is any relationship between intelligence and delinquency. Without information about tests on non-delinquent groups, the meaning of the low average shown by West Indian boys is difficult to interpret and the tests may be rendered ineffective for this group due to cultural and schooling differences which unrealistically depress attained scores. The average for the Asian boys is calculated only from a very small population of four cases.

More instructive is to consider the extent of educational retardation. This is shown in Table 49, calculated from the differences between the boy's actual age and his 'reading age' measured by testing at the classifying school.

TABLE 49: MEAN RETARDATION OF EDUCATIONAL
POTENTIAL: APPROVED SCHOOL BOYS

Nationality	Years retarded	Standard deviation
Native British	4	1·98
Irish	3·4	2·86
Mixed Irish	3·9	2·27
West Indian	5·5	2·42
Asian	3·4	2·68
Mixed Asian	3·4	2·36

Again, perhaps more remarkable than the extent is the variation in educational attainment shown by delinquents. Again it is noted that the West Indian boys show a higher than average retardation and compare unfavourably with Asian or mixed Asian boys.

Any relationship between educational ability and attainment and delinquency is likely to be complex. Among delinquents' backgrounds there are frequently reasons enough for the low attainment below potential that so many display. As more precise information is forthcoming about the meaning and significance of intelligence tests in relation to the effects of home culture, education, and linguistic stimulus in early childhood on later educational attainment, it may be seen that I.Q. is less and less a measure of innate educational potentiality than a measure of cultural variation in the home. Measured West Indian inferiority may relate to environmental aspects of West Indian family and social structure and contrast unfavourably with that of Asian children and families. Certainly it can be seen how lack of abilities can promote and aggravate acute stress in the home from which delinquency may arise.

Case 8. Thomas came to England from the West Indies when he was 15 years old. His parents had divorced when Thomas was 10 and his father had come to England. Thomas stayed with his mother until 1964 when she was admitted to hospital and there was no one to look after him. He came to join his father in England and had a succession of factory jobs following his arrival which he lost, being unable to carry out even the most basic skills. While unemployed he stole from home and then ran away fearing his father's severity. He was found and brought back and placed on probation. Two months later, he ran away again with a group of West Indian lads, ostensibly because having once stayed out late they would be severely treated by their fathers. On this occasion they stole money and food from houses to keep them going; and were caught. Thomas was sent to Approved School. He is a boy overwhelmed by his own sense of failure. He has a recorded I.Q. of 57 and a reading age of 7 years which probably indicates more about his emotional deprivation and cultural adriftness than being a true measure of potential. Certainly he is preoccupied with his own educational and occupational short-comings, is barely capable of completing a written sentence, and is incapable of making conversation or relationship with any adult. He is strongly orientated to life in England and concerned to overcome his deficiencies; and he is strongly dependent on his older, more intelligent girl friend. He suffers not only from the lack of abilities necessary for success in an industrial society, but also from parental neglect and deprivation which bar him emotionally from attaining those abilities and skills.

But an intelligent boy, working up to potential, can be beset by problems at home which disrupt school attendance and endanger the fulfilment of educational promise.

Case 9. Niall is 11 years old, the third of a family of seven children. His father was born and bred in Dublin before emigrating to England as a young man. His mother was born in Ireland and educated in England. The marriage has not been happy. His father has been unemployed, and on more than one occasion has been in court for being drunk and disorderly. He has served a short prison sentence for a housebreaking offence. During Niall's early childhood there was constant violence and discord in the home and severe physical punishment for any wrongdoing by the children. Niall's two older brothers have been at Approved Schools and Niall has been in trouble for truanting from school and stealing since the age of 7. He is a disturbed and anxious little boy, very worried about his parents and his brothers, all of whom he misses desperately. He is of above average intelligence and despite irregular attendance is in no way educationally retarded. Initially suspicious of adults, his behaviour shows him seeking the support and guidance which his inconsistent and disturbed home has denied him.

(b) THE MOVE FROM RURAL TO URBAN SOCIETY

Educational attainment and intelligence may be thought to measure an individual's ability or potential to perceive the needs and demands made by his social situation. If that situation undergoes change and presents new and puzzling problems, educational ability may determine the likely response. For many immigrants the move may be from a fairly close-knit rural community to a complex, urban, industrialized society which may make telling demands on the traditional manners, mores, and customs of the immigrant group. This may be thought to apply to Irish as well as coloured immigrants, both coming from predominantly rural areas. Different groups may adapt in different ways and show different degrees of making new communities within the host society to provide continuity with the past and a bridge to the future. For adults greater continuity with the past may be possible, though it may lead to acute difficulties for younger immigrants and the children of immigrants if their parents lack the insight to recognize the new demands made by their new society on skills and abilities.

Case 10. Michael, at 15, is the oldest of ten children. His father was born in County Mayo where the family still farm, and his mother was born and educated in Dublin. Both emigrated when in their late teens. Their first homes were as squatters in derelict houses before obtaining an old terraced house near the city centre that will soon be demolished. The mother is capable, vivacious, and intelligent; the father a carefree, jovial, hard-drinking, hard-working labourer. Michael is his father's favourite, and his father has delightedly encouraged him to avoid and ignore his mother's attempts at supervision and control and takes him off to work the allotment and wait outside the pub. Like his father, the area is prone to domestic fighting following fairly hard and plentiful drinking. Michael, too, is aggressive, quick-tempered, and eager to fight. But if for an adult such an area can still harbour a robust, cheerfully irresponsible way of life, for a child it means bewilderment and insecurity. Michael has run away from home many times, is egocentric, attention-seeking, and emotionally immature as well as badly schooled. He succeeded in some sixty shop- and housebreaking offences in the area over a period of a few months before being caught and committed to Approved School.

Case 11. Stanley came to England when he was 13 from St. Kitts. His parents had separated when he was 6. His father came to England with two other children. His mother remained with Stanley, her youngest, at her mother's home, remarried, and eventually left to go to America with her husband and the three children of that marriage. Stanley remained with his grandmother. He remembers attending school and learning to write with slate and chalk; more vividly he remembers being free to play and go where he pleased, staying out and about until nightfall called him back to his grandmother's house. At 13 he finished school and went to cut sugar on the local plantation and continued very much as he had before. But when his grandmother died, he came to live with his father who had remarried and had a family of young children. His entry into an English school provoked alarm among the women staff and girls due to his precocity and cheerful indecency. Children delighted in encouraging his naughtiness. Schooling at home had had but little effect and he had to start learning to read and write all over again. Disruptive at school and unresponsive to his father's attempts to control him at home, he continued to run wild rather as he had done in St. Kitts and was soon in trouble. His father quickly despaired of any hope to influence him and seems to have welcomed the idea of an Approved School. Stanley is irrepressible, outgoing, cheerful, unworried, basically happy, and not disturbed. He has not been helped by home and upbringing, education, or parental guidance to learn what life in a city means. At its clearest, Stanley shows us the extent of the conflict of cultures between rural St. Kitts and urban Birmingham. Added to that is the inadequacy of his preparation and ability to adapt from one to the other, due to the long separation from home and the lack of any significant advice, control, and guidance either at home or when in England. Yet

Stanley is not disturbed or anxious, and provided with the right surroundings and opportunities, his very uncomplicatedness and cheerful extroversion may yet enable him to achieve a measure of success and accomplishment in the new unfamiliar setting of Birmingham.

Both these cases show in extreme form the way an upbringing and education appropriate for a rural setting are deficient in providing the necessary guidance and controls in an urban society. For Stanley the suddenness of the move from St. Kitts and life on a plantation to that of a secondary school in a Birmingham suburb showed him unprepared and unsupported in effecting the change. For Michael, a second-generation child, the effects of the conflict were more subtle for they can be seen as central to the family situation in which, although his mother seems aware of the demands of the new society, his father shows no awareness that his own unsubtle adaptation is inappropriate for his child.

Some interesting research on this front has been conducted in Israel where it has been noted that recent immigrants and second-generation children show a higher rate of crime and delinquency than old-established immigrants. Eisenstadt[1] has suggested that a more important factor in explaining this is not so much an inner and unconscious clash of culture but the level of identification or conflict shown by the group or family towards the new society. He found among groups formed by immigrant youth a high rate of delinquency among those whose families were antagonistic towards the new country. He notes how the adaptation of immigrants requires a re-orientation of needs and of the modes of their satisfaction. 'The lack of integration of needs . . . may affect, in various degrees, the ability of the family to orientate children and adolescents towards their future social roles and to give them the wider social perspective and values that are essential.'[2] Life in the new society may demand that parents readjust their ideas of status and tradition and permit the children to respond to different ideas of authority and custom than exist in the country of origin. Tensions may be set up between families and the new community if and when the group and

[1] S. N. Eisenstadt, 'Delinquent Gang Formation among Immigrant Youth', *British Journal of Delinquency* (Vol. 2, 1951).
[2] Ibid.

family position is undefined *vis-à-vis* the host society, or where there is minimal or only bureaucratic contact between immigrants and host community, or where discrimination prevents full and complete participation in the new system of values. 'Predisposition towards delinquent group formation is minimized where the new immigrants (and especially the children and adolescents) can find or are enabled to acquire new, permanent and recognized social roles and to participate in close personal relations with the old inhabitants.'[1]

This stress on relations between new immigrant families and the values of the new community tests the adequacy of the family to recognize the new demands and to provide means of their attainment. It will clearly be a greater test where the contrasts between the home and culture of the family of origin and the new society are greatest. For immigrants to this country, as the cases outlined above suggest, the particular form of the conflict may be understood in terms of a move from a simple rural life to life in urban society.

(c) CULTURE CONFLICT

The conflict described above is, of course, one kind of culture conflict and reference to the Israeli study focused on the way the demands of the new society may be at odds with the demands of the traditional family unit or group. The two cases cited showed families insufficiently aware of the needs of their children in the new society rather than children being subject to the conflicting demands of home and society. This latter form of conflict is well documented in American (and also in Israeli) literature and is used to explain why the second-generation family is so often more delinquent than other groups. The theory supposes that whereas in the country of origin the family provides certain forms of guidance and instruction to enable the children to participate and succeed according to the norms and values of that society, with immigration the traditional methods may continue to be applied within the family, but they are no longer necessarily apt for enabling the children to participate and succeed according to the norms and values of the new society. Furthermore, in British society where the family is not alone among agencies of socializa-

[1] Eisenstadt, op. cit.

tion and where the school plays a vitally important role in directing children towards social roles and success goals, immigrant children will be exposed to many conflicts in demands. At adolescence an immigrant child may be forced to choose between family and society to a more marked degree than his non-immigrant peers and the nature of that choice is such that children of immigrants may find themselves torn between two sources of influence and support, from which tension delinquency may result.

Case 12. Ranjid is 15, youngest in a family of six, and the only one to react against the family culture in favour of a western way of life. When he was 14 his poor school attendance led to a supervision order to be made. Six months later, when there was no sign of improvement, an Approved School order was made 'in his own interest'. Ranjid was all for appealing against this but was persuaded that it *was* in his own interests. His family are strict followers of the Sikh religion and his father expected Ranjid to continue to observe the practices of that religion as did all his brothers. Father and family find it hard to understand his rejection of their ways. Ranjid's only 'offence', it should be noted, is his freeing himself from his family. It is hoped that by being away from home at Approved School, Ranjid will be able to achieve the break of loyalties without undue stress although the classifying school staff were clearly sensitive lest so abrupt a loss of home and culture should lead to any repercussions, for Ranjid is intelligent, impetuous, and impatient, and probably underestimates the problems facing a 15-year-old without a family in a large city; but they see the need to accept his determination to succeed according to English ways and support his quest for independence.

In Ranjid's case is seen perhaps in its clearest form the clash of cultures that faces an immigrant child. In this case it would seem to have been overcome because Ranjid's own solution was unambiguous; for many children the clash of loyalties may become internalized and for the individual unable to strike a balance, a resort to deviant or delinquent solution may result. Something of this uncertainty is seen in the case that follows.

Case 13. Mohammed's father is a successful small trader who started with an uncle as a street-pedlar and now owns two shops in the city. He is a respected and responsible leader of the community. His home is furnished to a high standard as befits his status; and in his manners and bearing he seeks to reflect the high status he has achieved both in English society (in terms of wealth) and in the immigrant community. His son is the eldest in his family and thus expected by his father to capitalize on his own success. He has been very demanding of Mohammed, particularly in terms of education, in compensation, Mohammed is inclined to suggest, for his own lack of education. Mohammed is of very high I.Q., though his school performance has been very uneven and, though enrolled at a local college for 'A' level studies, he has been a very poor attender. At school and college he was found to be arrogant, domineering, and unable to demonstrate his high claims for his own abilities in any tangible signs of success. He is markedly ambivalent towards the success of his father whose materialism he at times disdains and whose status he does not find useful in his own success goals which require performance on other terms than his father's materialism. His confusion and uncertainty are perhaps best expressed through his offences: he stole from houses, shops, and cars over a number of months whose fruits he then distributed as gifts among acquaintances at his college. Tests at the Approved School to which he was committed for these offences further reveal his fundamental maladjustment: he does not know whether he wants to be 'average and well liked' or 'somebody special', a philanthropist or dictator, doctor or Nazi. It would seem that his father has sought for his son achievement to equal his own but in a different sphere and by different means: in English middle-class society through high educational and professional achievement. But 'culturally' the means Mohammed has tended to utilize in seeking those ends have been a deviant form of his father's materialism (theft and largess) and an assertive form of his father's status (a domineering arrogance). The result is that Mohammed has been hinged away from his father's community and culture and finds himself truly 'cultureless' without the means of gaining legitimate acceptance anywhere.

Mohammed's case is perhaps the most complex and bewildering to be found among all the case papers studied. Apparently endowed with all the ingredients of success—wealth, a secure

18

home, and high educational potential—he yet floundered into insecurity, maladjustment, and delinquency.

Both these cases are of first-generation children; it may be supposed that as more Indian and Pakistani boys grow up in English schools they will experience something of the same tensions and uncertainties. The Asian immigrants as a group show a more marked cohesiveness than other immigrant groups which can be seen to explain an extremely low rate of delinquency and other forms of family breakdown; it may also promote greater strain in the future, depending on the kind of acceptance and mobility they enjoy in British society. For conflict will only occur if identification with one source of influence is seen to disqualify an individual from success in the other. If there is widespread prejudice and discrimination, whereby racial identity permits only a second-class citizenship and low status jobs and housing, immigrant children may be faced with an impossible choice in which bitterness and resentment will occur either way. If, however, a measure of cultural pluralism is tolerated, pride in the culture of the home and a strong sense of family loyalty may not prevent a full achievement of ambitions within the host society through success at school and in employment.

This may become thought of as something particular to Asian immigrants where the cultural differences are most marked. It was not possible to discern any elements of culture conflict on these terms in relation to Irish second-generation immigrants, and indeed the level of Irish assimilation and absorption into English society would seem to have been achieved without a loss of a sense of Irishness. No doubt the proximity to Ireland, the ease of access, the possibility of home visits or visits from relatives, and, of course, the crucial continuing link with Roman Catholicism and the Church, at school and parish levels, can provide a secure base for many Irish immigrants. Irish delinquency seems to occur in much the same way as native British delinquency, as one aspect of depressed economic status and among socially deprived problem families.

Among West Indians it can be expected that the effects of discrimination and prejudice may operate in the way outlined above. It is perhaps unwise to assume that as, by and large, West Indian immigrants have strong ambitions to succeed in English middle-class terms, there are no subtle cultural factors operating in terms of the family. It was noticeable that among the families of West Indian delinquents were many atypical in relation to native British delinquents through achieved economic status: many were families where the parents were buying a house, where both parents worked to sustain a high standard of material well-being for their children, and where the parents were strongly orientated to success on English terms. Sometimes there was a suggestion that the demands made on West Indian children by their parents to match their own success were excessive and unrealistic in terms of the child's abilities or were made at the expense of providing more basic needs. In this way the two West Indian cases cited so far were not atypical of the group as a whole; and these pressures can be seen to operate in the following.

Case 14. Victor, who is 15 years old, came to England when he was 11, following his mother and father who had come five years earlier. He is a boy of very high I.Q., working well below potential. Material conditions in the home are excellent, his mother and father are highly aspiring, hard-working people, very concerned to succeed in this country and impress their ambitions on their children, and are somewhat puzzled and disappointed by their poor attainment. Victor has continually been in trouble at school for pilfering and poor attendances. He has also stolen from home and stayed away for quite long periods. He is particularly hostile to his father who on occasions has treated him severely for his bad behaviour. But he and his brother are really no more than lodgers in the home for both parents work long hours to provide the standards of material comfort which match their aspirations. They see Victor as something of a threat to their status ambitions in his delinquent reaction to what, for the boy, is parental neglect.

Case 15. Barry has been in England for six years, during which time he has lived with his father in a house his father is buying in Anderton Park. Father is a skilled workman earning a large wage which goes on the house and his wife and family (from whom he is separated) in Jamaica. In the past he spent fairly considerable sums on providing Barry with education at a nearby private school. He has (or had) high hopes for his son and kept him on at school for an extra year in an attempt to enable him to obtain a good job. Such hopes have not been fulfilled. At remand home following his only offence, Barry's I.Q. was found to be of a low average level. His excellent spoken English and mature manner (having spent most of his childhood among intelligent and articulate older males) conceal poor educational potential and attainment. His father has reacted to this failure (and 'waste' of money) with no little resentment. Barry's disappointment is shown in a rather restless and shifting existence, frequently staying away from home and ignoring his father and father's friends. Barry works as a kitchen porter in a hotel but somewhat unrealistically expresses an ambition to become a fashion photographer. His only offence was the theft of some gramophone records from a neighbour's house: he was alone in committing the offence. He spends his spare time haunting the night-clubs in the city and associating with a crowd older in years than himself. It remains to be seen whether this will lead to further offences for he would seem to have acquired a taste for a fairly expensive life style which his low employment status may not support, and frustrated ambition may lead to a delinquent response rather than a realistic scaling down of his aspirations.

Another aspect of culture conflict is revealed through studying the children of mixed racial origin. For such children the elements of conflict and uncertainty that are fundamental to culture conflict may be felt to be present in their very make-up. If for the second-generation child there is a choice to be made, no such choice is possible for the half-caste child for whom, maybe, identification is impossible both with the immigrant group and with the host society, and colour consciousness and any discrimination will be felt to a more marked intensity than with children of pure racial origin. It often seemed to be the case that the white mother lacked basic abilities to provide for her children. The lack of identity and the feeling of being an outcast were also continual features in many of these case histories.

Case 16. Ibrahaim Khan is an illegitimate boy whose father's identity has never been established and whose mother at the time was married to a Pakistani. There are four children of this marriage. All the children have been in and out of care since an early age; both parents have served sentences of imprisonment for assaulting the children. At the age of 11 Ibrahaim was committed to Approved School for non-attendance at school. His mother had deserted the home at the time, to return a few months later. Ibrahaim spent four years away and on his return presented intense behavioural problems, refused to be at home, and was again committed to care. Here his behaviour started off very well; and he tried to make a fundamental break with his past by making a conversion to Christianity and asking to be called Michael Evans. But soon his behaviour deteriorated; he tended to experiment in transvestism; he stole from his sister's home (she herself has shown signs of imitating her mother's sexual delinquency); and was eventually recommitted to Approved School after running away from the children's home. He is neurotic, stammers badly, and is thoroughly disturbed. He is of above average educational potential, but slightly retarded. At school an attempt will be made to provide the support, control, and affection that the boy has never had so as to give reality to his half-articulated need: to escape from the uncertainty of his birth and childhood and become 'Michael Evans'.

(d) DELINQUENT NEIGHBOURHOODS

In an earlier section the extent to which immigrant areas are also those where crime is more prevalent was shown; and by considering the areas of residence of those arrested during the period of the survey of crime events it was possible to explore the extent to which the crime areas were also criminal areas.

Likewise, it was interesting to see how boys at Approved School came from certain areas of the city: over 60 per cent came from a ring of ten inner city wards[1]; 10 per cent lived in a ring of ten wards midway between the city centre and the city boundary; while more than a quarter came from eighteen outer wards, and 50 per cent of this latter group came from four distinct housing estates near the city boundary.[2] A similar pattern was observable in those cases of probationers studied, the majority living in Zone I of the study area and a third living in Zone III.

To make further exploration of the area characteristics of delinquency, those Approved School boys resident in the division studied and the under-21 age group of male probationers were considered as a group of 450 cases. Table 50 shows the areas of residence of these cases.

[1] The ten wards are: Deritend, Sparkbrook, Small Heath, Saltely, Duddeston, Aston, New Town, All Saints, Ladywood, and Edgbaston (see Map 1, page 9).
[2] Kingstanding, Erdington, Sheldon, and Fox Hollies.

TABLE 50: 450 DELINQUENTS BY AREA OF RESIDENCE AND NATIONALITY

Area	Native British			Irish			West Indian			Asian			Mixed			Total		
	No.	% within zone	% of area total	No.	%	%	No.	%	%	No.	%	%	No.	%	%	No.	%	%
1. Deritend	30		65	10		21	—		—	—		—	6		13	46		100
2. Calthorpe	12		63	4		21	—		—	3		15	—		—	19		100
3. Balsall Heath	50		55	28		31	1		(1)	1		(1)	10		10	90		100
4. Sparkbrook	66		67	24		25	1		(1)	—		—	4		4	95		100
Sub-total Zone I	158	(48)	62	66	(78)	26	2	(20)	(1)	4	(57)	2	20	(100)	9	250	(56)	100
5. Sparkhill	9		60	3		20	3		20	—		—	—		—	15		100
6. Anderton Park	14		67	—		—	5		24	2		9	—		—	21		100
7. Moseley	10		77	2		15	0		—	1		7	—		—	13		100
Sub-total Zone II	33	(10)	69	5	(6)	10	8	(80)	16	3	(43)	6	—		—	49	(10·5)	100
8. Brandwood	37		90	4		10	—		—	—		—	—		—	41		100
9a. Billesley	35		94	2		6	—		—	—		—	—		—	37		100
9b. Fox Hollies	62		88·5	8		11·5	—		—	—		—	—		—	70		100
10. Hall Green	3		100	—		—	—		—	—		—	—		—	3		100
Sub-total Zone III	137	(42)	90·7	14	(16)	9·3	—		—	—		—	—		—	151	(33·5)	100
Total	328	(100)	72	85	(100)	19	10	(100)	2	7	(100)	1	20	(100)	4	450	(100)	100

From this it will be seen that 48 per cent of the native British, 78 per cent of the Irish, and all those of mixed origin lived in Zone I. Eighty per cent of the small number of West Indians lived in Zone II where they comprised 16 per cent of all delinquents, while the Asian delinquents, of whom there were seven, were equally placed in Zones I and II. Forty-two per cent of the native British delinquents lived in Zone III.

Table 50 shows how although the over-all majority of delinquents lived in Zone I, and many in the associated slum conditions there; quite considerable numbers came from the areas associated with the housing estates to which the former slum families have been moved. It also shows how delinquent children of Irish families and children of mixed families came from the decaying central areas, suggesting that delinquency for these groups is associated with the achieved socio-economic levels of these families. It is of course impossible to estimate how far the Irish families are over-represented in this population due to a large number of the families being mixed Irish.

What is particularly significant is the way West Indian delinquency is associated with Zone II, when the major areas of coloured settlement are Sparkbrook, Balsall Heath, and Calthorpe Park in Zone I, in all of which areas coloured delinquency is very low. Over-all, it will be noted that both West Indian and Asian groups show a very low rate, far lower than might be expected in relation to their numbers 'at risk'.

It is possible to treat these data in another way, whereby the effects of the over-all variation in population size of the ten areas are taken into account. Table 51 provides a delinquency rate calculated from the number of delinquents in Table 50, expressed as a proportion of 1,000 males in the 11 to 19 age category in each of the areas.

Table 51 shows how the rate of delinquency between the areas varies enormously. It must be borne in mind that this is partly due to the way the map was drawn and the way the areas were so designated. Anderton Park, it will be noticed, is ranked second over all, and is the one area associated with the small number of West Indian delinquents. It is interesting to note that even if the immigrants are excluded, Anderton Park compares with Fox Hollies among the areas with a high delinquency rate.

Table 51 allows rather greater precision in designating and

describing delinquent neighbourhoods. The highest rate is associated with Balsall Heath, an area of slum property awaiting redevelopment, where the rate is twice that for other areas with a relatively high rate; these latter are areas like Deritend and Fox Hollies, associated with large council estates, or lodging-house areas like Calthorpe Park, Sparkbrook, and Anderton Park. Low rates are associated with 'better' council areas of Billesley and Brandwood and the settled 'good' working-class area of Sparkhill.

TABLE 51: VARIATIONS OF DELINQUENCY RATE
IN THE AREAS STUDIED

Area	Estimate of young male population	Delinquents	Rate	Rank order
1. Deritend	1,080	46	42·5	3
2. Calthorpe Park	550	19	34·5	6
3. Balsall Heath	1,200	90	75	1
4. Sparkbrook	2,600	95	36·5	5
5. Sparkhill	1,050	15	14·2	9
6. Anderton Park	440	21	47·5	2
7. Moseley	1,500	13	8·7	10
8. Brandwood	1,920	41	21·5	7
9a. Billesley	2,200	37	16·8	8
9b. Fox Hollies	1,900	70	37	4
10. Hall Green	750	3	4	11

Lowest rates occur in the predominantly middle-class areas of Hall Green and Moseley.[1]

Area factors are significant in two ways: as an indicator of achieved socio-economic status and as a contributing factor to persistent delinquency through opportunities existing for delinquent exploits. The first two native British cases cited earlier showed boys of average intelligence from basically sound but large families participating with others in what seemed fairly normal behaviour: in neither case did the parents' efforts overcome the influences of the area. Delinquency in these cases could not be attributed to gross family disturbances or other causes, but to weak family controls operating in a seductive environment.

[1] See also pp. 115–18, and Table 37.

This same process can be seen operating in some of the Irish and mixed origin cases.

Case 17. The H family live in a small terraced house in Balsall Heath that is soon to be demolished. Mr. H deserted the home seven years ago and his wife, who came to this country from Ireland many years ago, now lives with another man whom Henry and his four brothers and sisters accept as stepfather. Relationships within the home are said to be very good. Henry has always helped at home with the younger children and since leaving school has always contributed part of his wages to the family budget. Both his offences have been committed with a group of boys going joy-riding in stolen cars; for his second offence he spent one month at a detention centre. Perhaps no complicated reason for his offences need be sought. Henry seems typical of a bored and directionless youth, with poor employment prospects, for whom the dull world of a slum suburb holds out little that is exciting and attractive. Basically honest, delinquency provides him with a form of entertainment that is more nuisance than criminal but which over-repressive action could turn into resentment and more destructive forms of antisocial behaviour.

Case 18. The Omar family live in an old, large, terraced house in Balsall Heath. The father was born in Aden; the mother was born in a northern town. Since their marriage in 1940 they have lived in Birmingham, mostly in Balsall Heath. They have nine children, aged from 17 to 3 years. The father has been unable to work for the past thirteen years due to a heart condition, but house and children are materially better cared for than many in the area and the marriage has been stable and happy. The two oldest boys were at Approved School, two younger boys are on probation. All are lively, outgoing children of average intelligence who have had to compete for affection and attention in the home, who have driven their sick father to distraction, and who have been at the centre of much delinquency in the area. Uncertainty and inconsistency in the overcrowded home have placed a premium on the boys' peer-group identifications. The oldest boy, who shows some anxiety and disturbance, frequently absconded from Approved School to return home. All the boys are extremely attached to home and parents, resent enforced separations, but are too much for their mother to cope with; and in this area that means trouble.

In such areas the pressures towards delinquency are such that they make great demands on the abilities of the family to counteract those pressures: all too frequently the families in these areas are unable to offer the exceptional controls required, and their children from an early age are released to a host of undesirable influences which operate. What is significant is that children of immigrant families who are numerous in these areas, seem far less inclined to participate in the normal delinquent activities of the area than their non-immigrant peers.

In Sparkbrook and Calthorpe Park delinquency is associated with families among whom delinquency is just one aspect of the 'problem'. Many are in old slum homes, others in less secure lodging-house accommodation, often as a result of family breakdown and insecurity: such is also the case in Anderton Park where much of the population is in lodging-houses. West Indian delinquency, almost entirely restricted to this area derives, it would seem, from homes materially better endowed than the typical Birmingham delinquent family and in which delinquency seems much more a factor of interfamily relationships than deriving from low income, class, status of families in poor areas.

(e) DELINQUENCY AND THE FAMILY

The aspects studied so far all show how the variety of delinquency cannot be explained in simple terms: intelligence and education are no guarantees against insecurity and delinquency; conflicts between the demands of different kinds of social norms and values are minimized or exacerbated by family awareness; the temptations and opportunities of different neighbourhoods can be withstood or otherwise by parental influence. A recurring feature in studies of delinquency is the sometimes mild but frequently chronic breakdown in the families to which delinquency can be seen as one response. A good home provides the balance of affection and authority which brings the security children need if they are to grow to maturity. Through their parents children learn how to relate and respond to other people; children need parents on whom they can model themselves as social beings. Deprivation of affection, authority, and security or poor identification between children and parents can retard the growth of the child's personality or misdirect his potential into antisocial or other deviant behaviour. Conflict and anxiety at home can inhibit proper functioning at school, leisure, or work, and involve children in private acts of delinquency; or, through association with other similarly placed boys, with whom they achieve the group identification impossible in the home, they can engage in group delinquency. If the one necessary cause of delinquency is impossible to find, in many cases sufficient causes are in plenty to explain it.

Among the native British cases cited that of Frank (Case 6) is not untypical of many boys at Approved Schools. Such cases, not all so extreme, can be found among other groups.

Case 19. The I family have lived all their lives in Balsall Heath, in a small terraced house that will soon be demolished. Mr. I, who came from Ireland as a young man, has had a succession of labouring jobs which have increasingly been of a shorter duration, interspersed with lengthening periods of unemployment. He met and settled with an Englishwoman and they have a family of seven. The three oldest boys have all been in trouble, especially Ian, aged 12, who has been in court on four occasions already. The family is well known to various welfare agencies. Most of the father's money is spent on drink, which provokes the mother to a constant battle with him. Amid this the children are largely ignored except when they get into trouble, when 'shout and clout' systems operate or, if it is 'real' trouble, the mother is extravagantly protective, covering up for their numerous misdeeds. Most evenings find two of the boys, aged 12 and 10, haunting the various cafés and shops in the nearby streets, cadging money and sweets and 'fags' from neighbours and friends. An older boy managed to reach school-leaving age having made only one court appearance and seems on the way to a reasonable independence. Neglect and deprivation have most markedly affected Ian who is a skilled thief, dishonest and demanding. Some improvement both in the situation at home and in the boy's behaviour was noticeable when he spent a month at remand home and for him independence may have to be sought through Approved School.

Case 20. Mohjid came with his mother and five brothers and sisters to Sparkbrook in 1955, to join his father who had come two years previously with the eldest son of the family. He was 7 years old at the time. He was first in trouble at the age of 9, and by the time he was 12 had made four court appearances, mostly with other local boys. He was committed to Approved School. In November 1962, while Mohjid was at Approved School where he had settled well, his mother and father and all except the two eldest boys returned home to Pakistan. They had wondered whether Mohjid should go with them but because of his good progress it was decided he should stay. A few months later Mohjid was released to his brothers' home but after three months voluntarily returned to the school. Subsequently, he was constantly in trouble, stole from the school, and continued to thieve when released so that a new Approved School order was made in 1964 when he was 16. Mohjid, though tested to a low I.Q., is quick and skilful in all manual tasks, was speaking English very well within one year of being in England, and has always done well at school. His troubles lay at home where he felt outcast and unwanted—a feeling of rejection that was increased by his parents' departure. His brothers show little interest in him and whenever at home he associates with other delinquent boys in the area.

Case 21. Mr. Ali came to England in 1944, a Pakistani seaman who settled first in Glasgow, where he met and married his wife before coming to Birmingham in 1948. They now live in an old terraced house in Balsall Heath. They have four children, the youngest of whom is 13. On numerous occasions in the past, the mother has deserted the home, going off for unpredictable and varying lengths of time to Glasgow where other members of her family live. She is a suspected alcoholic. The father is a proud man, who has regularly worked in a semi-skilled capacity at a local foundry. He has tried to keep the family together but recognizes his inability to cope with his children, all of whom are very dependent on their mother. The youngest child, Sharma, has presented most problems, he has continually truanted from school to be near his mother and during one of her absences engaged in a series of larcenies for which he was placed on probation. This absence actually followed his mother obtaining a legal separation, giving custody of the children to the father. Her plan was to go and live permanently in Glasgow. As Sharma's behaviour deteriorated, and particularly when he was due in court, the father persuaded his wife to return. She did so for a while, before taking the child with her to Glasgow. Thereupon, the elder boy, Sheriff, began to stay away from school and was made the subject of a supervision order. Again the father persuaded his wife to return home to try to calm the children, and something of an uneasy truce now prevails. Mr. Ali himself is unwell, should long ago have attended hospital for a serious operation, but refuses to leave work and neglect the family. Both boys are of average intelligence but severely retarded due to the emotional stress they have experienced at home. The older girl is living with foster-parents, having previously been in care. Their oldest boy seems to have escaped without 'trouble' and is at work in another town.

Case 20 was interesting in the way it showed how migration can destroy family cohesiveness and deprive children of the support and guidance they need at quite crucial periods. The effects and process of this can be various. It can promote a period of rootlessness and uncertainty as in the following case.

Case 22. The J family have lived in four different places in the last six years. The mother came from Ireland as a young woman and met and married an Englishman, living first in Birmingham, then in London, then again in Birmingham. When John, the second oldest of their six children, was 9, the family moved to a maternal uncle's farm in Ireland. Three years later they moved to Grimsby. Two years later they moved back to Birmingham. The father is a stern disciplinarian, responding to John's poor behaviour with increasingly severe punishment. On two occasions John has left home, living in lodgings, got into minor trouble, and convinced the authorities that he was an orphan. The second occasion followed his leaving home and going to Ireland to find his aunt. Immediately he got there he borrowed money and came back to Birmingham, where a charge of stealing from home and an Approved School order awaited him. At school and wherever the family has lived, John has been a leading troublemaker, lucky to have so short an official record. He is of above average intelligence, aggressive, articulate, unrepentant, and basically rootless and affectionless. Which has been more potent a cause—the constant moving about or his father's rejection of him—is hard to say. Together they have induced in the opinion of a psychiatrist 'an hysterical personality with strong psychopathic tendencies'.

The vicissitudes of housing or employment can likewise set up severe tensions which may lead to a child escaping his family's influence and becoming involved with delinquents in the area.

Case 23. The K family consists of a mother, father, and five children, the oldest of whom is now 16. The parents married in Ireland before moving to Birmingham where, after a number of years in lodgings and flats, they obtained their present old, council-owned, terraced house in Balsall Heath. The father has a poor work record and has deserted the home on a number of occasions, leaving the family in dire need, which has attracted the attention of a number of welfare agencies. For a time the children's department supervised Kenny, the eldest boy, to ensure proper care and schooling. Since leaving school, Kenny has had a number of jobs and even more unemployment, a pattern not unlike that set by his father. His mother expresses her anxiety by constant nagging. Not surprisingly, Kenny looks outside the home for rewards, interest, and acceptance, and since the age of 13 has made four court appearances for such things as trespassing, shopbreaking, and taking and driving away, always with a group of local boys.

Case 24. Arthur came as a school leaver from Jamaica at the age of 16 to join his mother and father who had been here for five years. He had no difficulty in obtaining work in a factory but low ability and poor time-keeping caused him to lose four such jobs in quick succession, since when he has been unemployed. His parents live in one room in a lodging-house in Anderton Park and are unable to accommodate the boy who lodges not far away in another lodging-house. They do their best to support him but found that while unemployed, his bored wanderings soon got him involved with two other boys (Cases 26 and 28) in a series of shop-lifting offences. His mother is particularly anxious for him, both parents are sympathetic and affectionate, and Arthur is determined to stay out of trouble in future. But the employment market does not help one of his ability and poor record, so he is much in need of the structure of a home to support him through this difficult phase: a need his parents are only too aware they cannot fulfil at the moment.

Case 25. The R family came to Birmingham from Ireland five years ago, when the eldest of eight children was 11 and the youngest 1. The father had come three years previously to get a job and a home, returning only at holiday time. During their first three years in Birmingham, they occupied several lodgings and houses in different parts of the city, only staying a few weeks in one place. For the last two years they have lived in an old back-terraced house without bathroom in a crowded suburb just north of the city centre. Severe overcrowding is increased by the recent arrival of an elderly and demanding grandmother whose relationship with her daughter-in-law is not always of the easiest. Richard, the second eldest, now 14, has been in almost constant trouble, truanting from the various schools to which he was sent and getting involved with a group of boys who steal from houses and cars. His parents reacted to his continuing bad behaviour, first with severe punishment, then with increasing hostility and rejection. Neglected at home and ignored at school, due to his low intelligence, poor attainment, and attendance, Richard only found friends and interests among children equally deprived and probably more disturbed than himself. The many moves made by the family, the overcrowding, and consequent inconsistency in home training have left him incapable of reacting to adults except with suspicion and hostility. Six months after being put on probation during which his officer found him difficult and unco-operative, a further bout of offences led him to being sent to Approved School. Among other boys he was noted to be aggressive, bullying, and domineering; to the staff he was continually seeking attention by rowdy and disturbing behaviour which underlines the neglect and lack of attention provided for this boy at a crucial phase in his development.

A constant feature among West Indian delinquents was found to be the way the process of immigration involved separation between parents and children often for quite long periods. Of eleven Approved School boys—seven from Jamaica, three from St. Kitts, and one from Barbados—only one had come to this country with his parents, the rest had been separated from one or both parents for between one and eight years (average 4.4 years). The boys arrived when most were about 10 years old and thus have had some experience of English schooling; one boy arrived after school-leaving age and went to work immediately.

Of eleven West Indian boys on probation in the area, one

boy was born here, two had moved with their families when 6 and 8 years, respectively. Most had been separated for up to six years from their families and come here when between 7 and 15 years. One boy came at the age of 15 to join an older married sister, leaving parents and younger children in Jamaica. Of this group, seven were from Jamaica, one from St. Kitts, one from Guyana, one was from Barbados, and one was born here of Jamaican parents.

Thus it is to be expected that these West Indian boys show much more of the turmoil, upset, and trauma that immigration involves. Not infrequently it is reported how children have arrived to parents to whom they are literally strangers. Sometimes the intervening period has been marred by divorce, separation, and desertion by one parent and followed by remarriage or secure cohabitation. Thus children arrive to an uncertain welcome by stepparents from an often secure and affectionate home of a grandmother or aunt. For many, of course, England will be their first experience of urban living and their first experience of a temperate climate. The difficulties they face are, then, more intense and different in character from those faced by their brothers and sisters and neighbours born here.

In the instances cited so far the effects of such separation could be seen to affect the over-all situation. Where this is accompanied by marital breakdown or failure, the outcome can be acutely problematical.

Case 26. Wendell is 16 and lives with his father, mother, and a younger brother in a large terraced house in Anderton Park that his father is buying on mortgage. The two boys came from Guyana four years ago. Two younger children are still there and are expected to join the family within a few years. His father has been in this country for over ten years and has succeeded to a staff position with one of the nationalized service industries. His mother followed him to England two years later, works as a nurse, but has regularly visited Guyana to keep in touch with her children. Wendell was four years at the local school, stayed an extra year to improve his attainment in basic subjects, and, though he was no behaviour problem and his I.Q. is slightly above average, showed no marked success in his studies. On leaving school he lost his first job through poor time-keeping and has been unemployed for six months. His parents' marriage has not been a success and his mother obtained a legal separation with custody of the children some eighteen months ago. But due to the financial pressures on the home, both to maintain the mortgage repayments and finance the mother's visits to Guyana, his father still lives in the house and supports the home. Relationships between Wendell and his father are particularly poor and at times, especially when his mother is away, the father has virtually thrown the boy out. Wendell on one occasion stole a radio from home which he then sold, and more recently was involved with an older boy (Case 28 below) of more delinquent intent in a series of shop-lifting offences. For this, and particularly because of the boy's unemployment, Wendell was put on probation. The boy seems to reject all his father's ambitions and achievement, and goes out of his way to oppose him. His father, acutely aware of problems of colour and discrimination, has himself sought (and obtained) success through a good, established employment position. In his son—flashily dressed, languidly disinterested, and unemployed—he sees the antithesis of his own position and a slur on his race. An understandable but wholly unhelpful rejecting attitude is the result which only increases Wendell's hostility. The danger is that Wendell's anti-father feelings, his rejection from home, and his being led into delinquency will make him react against all authority and become increasingly aggressive and delinquent.

In studies of delinquency increasing importance is being given to the idea of a delinquent career whereby the process of arrest and court appearance, and perhaps treatment at an institution, is itself important in determining the future outcome of the delinquent's career. Through being isolated, set apart, and given special treatment, a boy may become identified with and only able to identify with delinquents; once so labelled it is hard for the boy to switch back to normality and he may become increasingly associated with delinquents and near criminals and invited to see himself as a criminal and adopt crime as a way of life. Total exclusion or severance from non-delinquent society may effect total commitment to delinquent society.

Among the English cases cited, Gerald (Case 7) can be seen as a late and unsuccessful recruit through his contact with older

19

criminals, but Borstal and a secure home were able to redirect him. In the following case, although the family can be seen to have 'supported' delinquency, it did nonetheless prevent any *total* identification with crime.

Case 27. The L family consists of six children with ages ranging from 25 to 10. The parents came from Ireland with their own parents as teen-agers and have always lived in Birmingham. Until recently they lived in rooms and small houses near the city centre, but have now been rehoused in a modern council house in Zone III. The family is very close-knit and the older children have contributed to the support of the younger ones. The mother died nearly ten years ago, since when the oldest girl (now 19) has looked after the home. Larry, the second son, now 21, has been through probation, detention centre (twice), Approved School, and Borstal for a number of quite sophisticated and well-planned (but obviously not well enough) factory- and warehouse-breaking jobs. In this he has followed his brother, whose criminal career has seemingly ended after a spell in Borstal, marriage, and the arrival of a first child. Larry expresses the same ambitions and looks likely to succeed. Both boys were probably sustained by the loyalty of the family and thus escaped the effects of excessive social ostracism. They have never had any difficulty earning straight money in labouring jobs, express no ambitions to do better, and are both thoroughly well-adjusted individuals for whom, and for a time, crime brought rewards that made the risk worthwhile. A wife and children demand a more secure, less risky, occupation for which home and schooling were no disqualification, as is so often the case with more disturbed and despairing youths.

The analysis of an area's crime indicated a very low involvement of West Indians in property offences. Domestic violence (rather than robbery) brings a very small number of West Indians before the courts. Where West Indians do become offenders is in the particular offence category of dealing with or possessing cannabis. Conversations with police officers and a scrutiny of some court cases for which Social Enquiry Reports were made (but from which a probation order did not result) suggest that there may be a small number of West Indians engaged in crime as an organized way of life. If this is so it is impossible to measure its extent or assess its degree of organization. And certainly it is no more than one would expect in a large city where there is something of an underworld. The presence of this small group does offer some opportunity to a delinquent youth to become involved. Contact may well be through the places where cannabis is illicitly dealt with. Not infrequently cases involving possessing cannabis concern men who have a record for other offences. This suggests that the supply of the drug, because it is a black market drug and not available legally, is in the hands of a class of near-criminals prepared to run the risks of prosecution and imprisonment. It would seem to be true that the smoking of cannabis is not looked upon as any great crime by a large number of West Indians; but it would also seem true that actual drug taking is restricted to a very small minority of that community in certain fairly well defined situations associated with clubs and parties. And it certainly seems true that among this minority, again only a tiny proportion are actually prepared to run the risk of dealing in the stuff. This is left to an already delinquent fringe whose dealing in cannabis reflects a willingness on their part to more widespread law-breaking. This network may provide something of an opportunity structure for delinquent youth.

Case 28. Calvin came to England when he was 9 years old, from Jamaica to the home of his father and stepmother. He attended local secondary school until he was 15, when in an attempt to increase his educational attainment he spent an extra year at a local private school. When he was 12 he was on probation for stealing from home. After school he worked only irregularly and was again on probation for possessing cannabis; he was among those caught in a raid on premises in Balsall Heath. He still failed to obtain regular employment and for a time went off to another city without informing his probation officer or his parents. He returned home to face two charges. As an originator or leader, he involved two young West Indian boys in a series of shop-lifting offences; more seriously, he was involved with older men in a fairly sophisticated housebreaking charge. For this latter offence he received a sentence of Borstal training. His associates were sent to prison for four years. Calvin was never on good terms with his father, although he seems to have been well received by his stepmother. He does not appear much perturbed by what has happened, is superficially mature and 'cool', and seems in danger of finding a life of crime the only means of obtaining success (if it may be called that). His older stepbrother spent a short time in an open Borstal following a breach of a probation order. For him it was a successful period: his intelligence and sporting ability placed him among the leaders. He came out with a glowing report, still visits some of the staff there, and seems unlikely to be in trouble again. But Calvin has none of his brother's charm and intelligence, is more thoroughly delinquent, and more adrift from the influences of home and family. Though from a different home situation, he is not unlike many English boys sent to Borstal. For him (as for them) it is a last chance to break with criminal associates, and prison is the next step. Once sent to prison—after Borstal—the chances of going again increase rather than diminish.

That total and extreme rejection by home and family can cause a boy to go on the run and end up in something of an underworld is exemplified in the following case.

Case 29. Javra, aged 14, is the youngest of a Sikh family who spent several years in Kenya. His behaviour there was bad—he stole from home and truanted from school, which the frequent beatings his father administered did nothing to diminish. At the age of 12 he was sent to an uncle in Birmingham but ran away and soon after was committed to the care of the local authority following his father (who had just arrived in England with his family) having declared to the court that he no longer wanted anything to do with the boy. Since that time Javra has virtually been on the run, usually with money he takes from restaurants where he obtains work (and by all accounts is a skilled chef). At times he has given false names and absconded before they could be checked. For a few months he was living with a hard core of the London criminal underworld in whose criminal activities he was a skilful participant but about whose violence and hard-drinking he expresses some fears. Since he was last caught, he has been kept under stricter surveillance in a closed unit where, it is hoped, the ambivalence he expresses concerning the criminal life he has experienced and witnessed can be used to bring him to a non-delinquent way of life, independent of the family, unharassed by authority, and supported by his not inconsiderable abilities.

3. *Nationality and Need: Summary and Conclusions*

In this variety of ways situations within families, exacerbated by the stress of immigration, can provoke a variety of delinquent responses. It was in an attempt to gain some picture of the over-all stability of families within the various nationality groupings that the research extended beyond just delinquent families to consider the families in contact with the children's department. In the following sections the data from the various sources used will be brought together and summarized for each of the nationality groupings.

(a) THE NATIVE BRITISH FAMILIES

Seventy per cent of all boys at Approved Schools, 73 per cent of all those currently under the supervision of probation officers, and 36 per cent of all contacts with the children's department, were of families where both parents were native-born. Forty-eight per cent of the delinquent families lived in the inner Zone I of the area studied, where the highest rate of delinquency was found to be in the fairly homogeneous slum area of Balsall Heath which had a rate calculated to be almost twice that for other areas in the zone. Ten per cent of the native British delinquents lived in Zone II and 42 per cent in Zone III. One area in Zone III (Fox Hollies) had a rate substantially in excess of others in the zone, while delinquency was almost non-existent in the settled, predominantly middle-class area of Hall Green. The average size of family was found to be 6·1 in Zone I, 3·6 in Zone II, and 5·5 in Zone III, suggesting that delinquency is most marked in a large slum area or slum clearance families, and of a somewhat distinct kind in the lodging-house or more settled areas of Zone II.

The average age of boys on admission to Approved School was found to be 14·9 years, while among those on probation equal numbers were under 17 and between 17 and 21. The average number of court appearances of those committed to Approved School was found to be 3·85, while of those on probation it was 2.

The average I.Q. score of Approved School boys was found to be 93·5, but more remarkable than this finding is the range of scores achieved. The standard deviation of this over-all mean was found to be 41·5. The average difference between the measured reading age and the actual age (a measure of educational retardation) was found to be four years, although again there was a considerable deviation from this mean (1·98 years).

Among families in contact with the children's department, a smaller proportion of the cases (42 per cent), in comparison with the other groups studied, were such as to require intensive work on the part of the child care officers; but in comparison with other groups long-term supervision or long-term periods in the care of the local authority seemed to be more frequently required. Long-term casework for this group was associated with cases of matrimonial breakdown or of teen-age children proving beyond parental control. Periods of admission to care were associated with cases where the mother had to be admitted to hospital and where the family situation was itself disturbed or unstable; likewise, in a large proportion of cases older children had to be admitted to care through proving beyond parental control.

The familiar stereotype of the delinquent being one of a large, low-income group family, living in a 'poor' area, and experiencing not inconsiderable stress in a disturbed or broken home is confirmed by these data, although it is interesting to note that delinquency is fairly frequent in certain non-slum areas and not unknown among other social groups.

(b) IRISH FAMILIES

A major problem facing a researcher concerns unevenness in the data, whereby wholly Irish families could not be distinguished from those where just one parent was of Irish birth. Furthermore, there are only limited data available about the numbers of Irish families and children (particularly in the 'mixed' category of family) in the population at large.

However, fairly definite information was available for boys at Approved School. Seven per cent were from wholly Irish families and 13 per cent were from mixed Irish families. Among those on probation, where 19 per cent were found to be wholly Irish or with one Irish parent, information was less certain, but in twenty-nine cases studied, nineteen were wholly Irish and ten were of mixed parentage. In similar fashion wholly Irish families outnumbered by two to one those of mixed Irish origins among those in contact with the children's department, where over-all 18 per cent were in the Irish category. Seventy-eight per cent of the Irish delinquent boys lived in Zone I, where they contributed

26 per cent of all delinquents, and most noticeable was the large number living in Balsall Heath, the area with the highest rate of delinquency. Only five Irish delinquents were found in Zone II, while fourteen (16 per cent) of all Irish delinquents lived in Zone III. Of those on probation, the average size of family was found to match that of the native British group: in Zone I it was 5·7, in Zone II it was 3, and in Zone III it was 5·5. Again the over-all picture suggests that delinquency among the Irish reflects the extent to which the families have achieved a low income and low status in delinquent neighbourhoods.

The problem of calculating comparative rates of delinquency between Irish and other groups is great because of the above-mentioned uncertainties. But it can be suggested that wholly Irish families with 7 per cent of the Approved School population are not over-represented, for it seems that Irish boys are more than 7 per cent of the age group at risk.

Of those of wholly Irish families, eight out of thirteen of those whose cases were studied were born in this country and thus properly second-generation children; the other five all moved here when very young. Of the nineteen on probation of wholly Irish families, ten were born in this country, two came as very young children, five came as teen-agers with other members of the family, one came to join his father who was resident here for some years, and one came alone and unsupported by family or relations.

The change in the procedure whereby only since recently have Roman Catholic Approved School boys been sent to classifying school makes it difficult to explore the extent to which the families have retained their native Roman Catholicism. This is further complicated by the fact that it was a frequent comment at the classifying school and in the records to find Irish boys registered as 'Church of England' because Roman Catholic Approved Schools have a reputation for stricter discipline and more uncompromising demands on children than other schools. However, it was noticeable that of the wholly Irish families, ten of the thirteen were Roman Catholic, two were Protestant families from Northern Ireland, and one was recorded as Church of England. Among those of mixed Irish origin, families with an English mother outnumbered those with an Irish mother by twenty to seven, and whereas there were none recorded as Roman Catholic among those with an Irish mother, about half of those with an English mother were Roman Catholic boys. There was not one instance among boys of mixed Irish families of a normal or undisturbed home background. Of six instances where the father was English, death, desertion, suicide, and chronic illness cast their disturbing shadows in four cases; while in the other two there was evidence of extreme parental discord and harsh discipline that amounted to actual assault. Of seven instances where the mother was English, three instances of desertion by the father were cited: in one case the mother had died after a long illness and continued discord involving the father's withdrawal, and there were three instances of extreme family discord and violence attended by drink, unemployment, and illness. In these ways the families of mixed origin compare with those of other mixed origin, whereas the wholly Irish families instanced cases of basically secure homes but where some of the children were provided with poor or weak guidance or extreme rejection. In this way these families are comparable to some native British, but show a pattern most like that of the West Indian families.

The average age of the boys at Approved School was found to be 14·1 years for the Irish and 14·9 for the mixed Irish families. Of those on probation rather more were in the 17 to 21 category than in the younger age group. Irish boys at Approved School and on probation showed a slightly higher number of offences than other groups, at 4·2 and 2·5, respectively.

As a group they showed a slightly lower average I.Q. than native British boys and the mean retardation was measured to average rather higher for the mixed category than for the wholly Irish group and less than among native British cases. But, as with the native born, there were considerable deviations to both sets of scores.

What is perhaps striking about the Irish group in contact with the children's department is the extent to which only a small proportion of the cases were found to need intensive casework (37·2 per cent). Intensive work was required not infrequently for cases of matrimonial breakdown, but more often for particularly difficult cases of young and homeless immigrants, often with young children, existing in rooms in lodging-houses where the needs of the children were overlooked. This sort of case made up a fairly large proportion of those cases where children were admitted to care for a short period, although there was an equal proportion of what seems the most frequent reason for immigrant families to need care, namely a fairly secure family where a period in hospital for the mother leaves the father unable to cope on his own.

It is of course impossible to judge what would be a 'normal' rate of referral from a group in a city to an agency like the children's department which is designed to support the needy family, among which category the immigrant group is more likely to fall because the immigrant family may often lack the support of friends and neighbours or relatives that is available to established families.

(c) WEST INDIAN FAMILIES

The survey of boys at Approved School found thirteen of West Indian parentage who comprised 2 per cent of the population; among those on probation, eleven (3 per cent) were of West Indian parentage.

Among those in contact with the children's department, 16 per cent were from families in this group; and from figures obtained from the children's department it was found that 8·7 per cent of all children in care as in July 1966 were from wholly West Indian families.

Among younger delinquents in the area, West Indians as a group comprised 2 per cent: eight of the ten lived in one area. Equal numbers were aged under 17 and 17 to 21. The average family size (2·5) was found to be smaller than for other groups and less than the average for native British and Irish in the area.

It is possible to show that West Indian boys are committed to Approved School at about half the rate for the native British and Irish group combined; and that this same under-representation is apparent among cases of probationers, confirming the generally low rate of West Indian involvement in crime shown in the crime survey.

It has been shown how all the delinquents in the group studied experienced quite long periods of separation from one or both parents. This makes these delinquents quite a distinctive group, not displaying anything of the chronic disturbances so frequently met with in other groups nor showing any tendency for being assimilated to the standards of behaviour of a delinquent neighbourhood: rather each case showed intense problems within a basically good family unit, whereby the delinquent member, through a variety of reasons, was unable to become incorporated within the family which in all other respects showed signs of material success. This aspect was frequently felt to be important, contrasting with parents of 'typical' delinquents; the West Indian parents in the cases studied seemed highly aspiring and highly capable people. The economic pressures in each family seemed great: frequently houses were being purchased on mortgage and loans were being repaid for fares from the West Indies; in some cases there were families back home receiving regular financial support. These pressures led to both parents working long hours. Moreover, it is probably true that the need for financial security and status is greater as other kinds of status are denied them by a generally discriminating host society. Sometimes it seemed that these overriding economic concerns led to neglect of, or insensitivity towards, a child's needs. With high ambitions for success for themselves and their children, 'failure' on the part of the children to match up to expectancy led to severe rejection, underlined by the traditionally stern, somewhat puritanical discipline of the West Indian parent.

The aspect of 'failure' is further suggested by the extremely low average I.Q. shown by West Indian Approved School boys and a high level of retardation (5·5 years). West Indian boys tended to be committed to Approved School at an older average age (15·2 years) than any other group and after fewer court appearances (an average of 2·3). This again suggests how it is rejection from home, rather than degree of criminal sophistication, which leads to Approved School committal.

The difficulties of incorporating unruly children within a family are also the reason for some of the work of the children's department with West Indian families. Within the over-all proportion of 16 per cent, a relatively high proportion of cases were found to need intensive casework (57 per cent). Casework was associated with requests for admission of children to care while the mother was in hospital or otherwise absent. A great many of the mild cases were also of this kind, and not infrequently the case papers recorded some disinclination of West Indian parents to lose income by taking time off from work to care for the children, preferring the idea of the children being admitted to care. Accordingly, more cases where short-term admission had to be effected were from 'good' homes than from disturbed homes. Long-term care was associated with teen-age children reported as being beyond control and exhibiting similar experiences as those West Indian boys admitted to Approved Schools.

To interpret the high rate of contact between West Indian families and the children's department it is useful to consider here a study of West Indian children in care in London by Katrin FitzHerbert.[1] Her starting-point is an analysis of the cultural background of the West Indian family:

Several aspects of the West Indian cultural background, combined with problems of migration, destine many West Indian children to be in care. For example:

(1) A tradition of unstable families.
(2) Many single mothers.
(3) Victorian child rearing practices.
(4) Break-up of the extended family through migration.
(5) Housing and economic problems for first generation immigrants.

But some additional factors sometimes make West Indian parents eager to have children received into care, regardless of the family's need:

(6) A tradition of fostering and informal adoptions, which attaches no stigma to a mother who lets somebody else raise her children.
(7) Desire for financial security and the belief that providing income is a more responsible kind of motherhood than providing personal care.
(8) Eagerness for education and 'culture' and the impression that a children's home run by white householders is a real opportunity for their children.[2]

From a study of case papers in Birmingham, all those above eight aspects will have been met by the child care officers without them perhaps appreciating the cultural significance. Such factors would certainly explain the high rate of contact that was noted in Birmingham. Mrs. FitzHerbert, discussing the 'curiously high' rate of West Indian children in care in London, argues:

In my opinion these numbers give an exaggerated picture of the size of the problem of deprivation among West Indian children and

---

[1] Katrin FitzHerbert, *West Indian Children in London* (London, Bell, 1967).
[2] Ibid., p. 40.

reflect the reluctance to treat West Indians as a separate cultural group with distinct family patterns and attitudes to child rearing. . . .

As the West Indian family system is characteristically very loosely structured de-emphasising the nuclear family and permitting a wide range of unlegalised relationships, many situations arise, which our English context would justify reception into care, but which in a West Indian context are normal and tolerable.[1]

She also notes the tendency among child care officers through ignorance of cultural factors 'to lump West Indians into the category of inadequate social types, from which the majority of their clients is drawn', and stresses that in so doing 'they are making a serious error, as the West Indians who have the initiative and found the means to migrate to England are by far the most adequate members of their society of origin and on the whole form a very capable group in England'.[2]

Certainly this latter point is one that gains confirmation from the Birmingham data. It was noted how the West Indian delinquent family is quite different from the English delinquent family: in economic and material resources and abilities. The same can be said of many of the families in contact with the children's department. Thus it was that 'good' families of immigrant stock required short-term care facilities, whereas it was the 'weak' or broken English family (or family of mixed origin) that makes demands on such services.

In Birmingham, it would seem that child care officers are perhaps more successful in withstanding requests for admission into care by West Indian parents than in other places, for the figure quoted (8·7 per cent) is not greatly in excess of what might be expected from the West Indian population as a whole whose children now number nearly 5 per cent of children of school age and a somewhat higher proportion of children under school age.

Mrs. FitzHerbert's study in London and the data from the Birmingham survey suggest how many, perhaps a majority, of young coloured children in care for long periods will be those of mixed racial origin.

(d) ASIAN FAMILIES

The striking fact among families in this group is the small number and extremely low proportion involved in any aspects of the data.

[1] FitzHerbert, op. cit., p. 107.   [2] Ibid., p. 108.

Among Approved School boys there were four (less than 1 per cent) whose parents were from India or Pakistan. There were two boys whose families were of recent immigration, one a Muslim from Pakistan, the other a Sikh from the Punjab; there was one boy of a Sikh family who reached England after a period in Kenya; in the fourth case, the father had first come to England when 15 with an uncle and was concerned with establishing a family business in Birmingham, frequently returning home to Pakistan. Only in 1953 did his family, wife, and six children come to settle in Birmingham.

Only three of the boys under probation supervision were from 'pure' Indian or Pakistani families. These included a boy of 15 who came to England with his family ten years ago, but whose immediate relatives have all returned; a Sikh boy of 13 whose family arrived within the last five years; and a Muslim family who arrived five years ago, following a period in Kenya.

Likewise, the proportion of contacts with the children's department from this source is very small and most frequently are cases of 'good' families requiring for some children a brief period in care while the mother had to enter hospital.

The extraordinary diversity of the four Approved School cases which have been outlined earlier mirror the complexity of delinquency as a whole.

Mohjid's delinquency (Case 20) derives from weak home controls in an English delinquency area; Ranjid (Case 12) reveals a non-delinquent moving between two cultures; Mohammed's maladjustment (Case 13) reveals the fundamental clash between two cultures; Javra (Case 29), from an intensely disturbed and rejecting home, reacted against all authority to discover the uncertainty and unsatisfactory nature of a life of crime. All can be seen to have experienced through the fact of immigration a total disorganization in their lives where the only support available to them was provided by delinquency.

Otherwise, reflected in the general infrequency of cases in this group, strong family and culture links and an active concern for their children can be seen to reduce the risks and incidence of family breakdown. Yet too complacent a view must clearly be avoided: the very closeness and retained distinctiveness may create widespread difficulties at school, in employment, and in society at large which may defer rather than remove the kind of tensions and difficulties from which delinquency springs.

(e) THE FAMILIES OF MIXED ASIAN AND MIXED WEST INDIAN ORIGINS

Among Approved School boys the survey found fourteen (2 per cent) whose mother was English and whose father was Asian. Among those on probation there were nine families with children under supervision in this category and one case of a boy with an English mother and West Indian father. Among contacts with the children's department 5 per cent were families of mixed Asian origin and 7 per cent of mixed West Indian origin. Furthermore, of children in care in June 1966, 9·5 per cent were of mixed Asian origin and 6·5 per cent were of mixed West Indian origin. All the delinquents of this group lived in Zone I of the study area, mostly in Balsall Heath. The average family size of those on probation was 5·5, which compares with those of native British and Irish resident in that area. The majority of those on probation were under 17 and the average age of admission to Approved School was found to be 14·1 years, which is slightly younger than for any other group. This confirms the suggestion that the children in this category are often from 'problem' families who are apt to come to the attention of the various agencies (often for poor school attendance, it seemed) earlier than most. The children in this group averaged 3·5 court appearances at admission to Approved School, which is slightly less than for other groups, except the West Indian and Asian delinquents, while those on probation averaged two court appearances which compares with that of the native British.

The average I.Q. at 95 was not markedly different from those native-born delinquents, while their mean retardation of 3·4 years was somewhat less so than that group's.

Of the eleven families in this category with boys at Approved Schools, all but two showed signs of grave family disturbance. In six instances the mother showed signs of mental instability or gross inadequacy that had meant constant attention for the family from supporting agencies and periods in care for some of the children. In five cases the boys did not know their real fathers and experienced the uncertainty of a relation with a stepfather. Of nine families with boys on probation, three were intact families, both mother and father being present throughout the child's early life;

the other six families were marred by a history of marriage break-downs, involving divorce, separation, or, what is perhaps more damaging, constant desertions by one or other party. One boy was the son of a prostitute who had lived with four different men in fairly secure cohabitation during the child's fifteen years.

The majority of marriages involved Indian or Pakistani seamen who arrived in England in the early 1940s and who had subsequently moved to Birmingham for work. Some had retained contact with home and culture during the intervening period and continued to practise their home religion. For others settling and marriage here would seem to have involved a severance of all ties with the past. Most of the men showed excellent employment records, though a number seem to have experienced ill health. Many would appear to be the stronger partner in the marriage, but either prevented from playing a proper role by the sheer inadequacy of the mother or unable to respond to somewhat unruly stepchildren. For the children, most experienced great insecurity in their early years and show a poor sense of identity, particularly in relation to their fathers. Not only are most unaware of their real fathers, but are unaware of the colour and cultural barriers and distinctions that exist in their make-up and situation.

This pattern seems repeated among families in contact with the children's department. Just over half of all such cases needed intensive action on the part of child care officers and it was the group making the highest proportionate demand on short-term in care facilities. There were no instances in the sample of long-term casework supervision with families in this group, although there was considerable short-term intensive casework concerned with families where the mother was in hospital or had left the home. It was noticeable that in this group the fathers seemed more capable in some ways than the mothers, who showed signs of frequent desertions; a large number of cases requiring short-term care in treatment were from 'weak' or disturbed homes. The study of West Indian children in care in London tends to confirm this story. Mrs. FitzHerbert studied 150 case histories, drawn from two area offices of the children's department. She acknowledges that her sample had little statistical value, being drawn from two very different kinds of areas where, apart from differences in the social characteristics of the families, there were noticeable differences in the interpretation of child care policies on the part of officers working the areas. But sixty-two of the 150 cases were from families of mixed racial origin; and she also noted for this group that, 'As a rule the mothers had severe social handicaps, while the fathers had average or above average social and economic capacity.'[1]

The absence of any figures relating to the number of families and children in this category makes it impossible to calculate comparative rates with the other groups. It would seem clear that there is some, probably considerable, over-representation reflecting the basic insecurity and instability of many such partnerships at the present time. It is as well to treat these figures and data with care in view of the apparent shortcomings of so many of the English mothers of this group. It seems probable that the over-all proportion of such marriages may decline as, it is to be hoped, immigration continues to allow whole families rather than just single working males to come to this country. Currently, the prevailing prejudice and discrimination are nowhere more marked than in attitudes to miscegenation, whereby it is only possible for a cultured, somewhat idealist, middle-class white girl, where professional status may moderate attitudes to colour, or for a near-deviant fringe of the socially inadequate, for whom the outcasting involved in a mixed marriage may be no new experience. By the same token, as immigrant groups get larger and achieve greater stability within British society, miscegenation may be less necessary for the young immigrant or only one taken by the aspiring socially mobile immigrant who will seek a white middle-class partner, fully aware of the social consequences and able to anticipate and tolerate prevailing white attitudes. These small numbers of 'failed' mixed marriages and unstable unions of persons of different races slightly inflate the over-all delinquency rate and contribute no small proportion of children in care. They can be seen as the consequences of familyless migrations in which basic needs remain to be fulfilled, but in whose fulfilling, the security and stability of a home and family remain an elusive paradise.

4. *Conclusions*

This section at its outset outlined a number of broad hypotheses about comparative rates of delinquency among different groups

[1] FitzHerbert, op. cit., p. 61.

of immigrant children, native-born children of immigrant parents, and children of mixed parentage.

The figures and findings revealed above confirm those expectations, though insufficient population data have inhibited accurate measurement of comparative rates. But it is clear that fewer coloured immigrant children are delinquent in proportion to the numbers at risk than the native-born children of white parents.

More problematical to assess is the level of Irish delinquency which in many ways seems to follow the pattern and trend of typical English delinquency, being a feature of families in certain low-class slum or near-slum areas. Proportionally fewer wholly Irish families have children at Approved School than English families, although among children on probation those with both parents Irish outnumber those with one parent Irish. The families with one parent Irish and with delinquent children seem to include many with gross disturbances, living in extreme poverty in the poorest areas, like many of the other mixed families among whom, so often, the incapacities of the mother were frequently the most potent factor in family instability and distress. Certainly there is nothing of the over-representation among delinquents of Irish children to compare with the over-representation of the Irish among adult offenders, which suggests that the Irish family provides as secure a base for the children as English families similarly placed in terms of socio-economic class and area.

There are insufficient data to assess anything in the way of comparative rates for the second-generation immigrant, coloured or Irish. The families of mixed racial origins, albeit a small number, would appear to have the highest delinquency rates of all.

Among younger children in contact with the children's department, the over-representation of all categories of immigrant children (except those of Asian parents), though to be expected, points to future dangers. Again it must be noted that a considerable proportion of such cases are of mixed families where unstable relationships, economic insecurity, and poor housing conditions combine to bring many to need support and care of caseworkers or children's homes. To a lesser extent are West Indian and Irish children and families so involved, but the same degrees of insecurity and instability exist, exacerbated by the fact that frequently the living conditions and insecure housing provide no real security for family life. As was remarked in relation to crime, immigrants live in areas where disorganization and disorder are fairly marked and if at this stage the coloured immigrants can be seen to be overcoming those pressures and dangers, the consequences of their continuing to have to live under such conditions can only be an increase in crime and delinquency as the security and stability of family life are threatened by the insecurity and instability which surround them.

Part IV: Conclusion

CHAPTER 9

Crime and Race Relations

I

The least significant statistic, perhaps, to emerge from the survey of crime is that which shows a low rate of crime among coloured immigrants. Equally irrelevant is the suggestion from the figures that the Irish commit more than a fair share of crime. The tendency to use crime statistics to promote an attitude towards groups of people is not unknown. Such an attitude, promoted by emotions of fear and dread which can readily accompany the whole idea of 'crime', will find favour more easily among a population bewildered by the complexity of a society undergoing considerable change; such attitudes are particularly potent when they attach, as they do now, to groups distinguished from the majority by race and colour.

The purpose of the descriptive profile of the area's crime, reported in Chapter 1, was to add precision to our conception of that multifaceted phenomenon we refer to as 'crime'. Although there are, to be sure, highly organized 'professional' criminal gangs at work in our towns and cities (and on our highways) effecting daring attacks and robberies on valuable property; and although there are from time to time crimes of a violent and horrifying nature committed on defenceless people; yet it is important to bear in mind their relative infrequency. The crime that is the concern of law enforcement agencies, and the crime that is of continuing effect among neighbourhoods and communities are typically, as we have seen, petty thefts from shops, cars, and houses. Robbery is extremely rare. And violent crime, far from the terrifying thing of folk-lore and headline, in mundane reality is more likely to consist of a black eye sustained in a family dispute or a broken head following a pub brawl. Most important of all it is to be noted how crime, in all its many forms, is far more prevalent in some areas than in others. The consequences of those variations in the distribution of crime are of the utmost significance for the future of race relations in the city.

It should be noted to what extent, in terms of over-all crime, those suburban areas near the city boundary enjoy calm and security. True, there may be an occasional theft from shop or house; some areas may be more troubled with youngsters thieving from neighbours' houses; from time to time cycles and cars may be taken for joy-riding; but there is not found here the sustained varieties of crime and disorder that occur elsewhere. In contrast, the nearer to the core area of the city one goes, rates of crimes of all kinds increase. There exists greater opportunity for stealing from cars, for taking cars, and for breaking into gas and electricity supply meters; the police are involved in more family arguments whose discords sometimes involve violence; drunkenness is not uncommon; and in some well defined parts of these areas prostitution is a flourishing trade. It is a significant datum that the highest rate of house thefts occur among houses in those areas where the multi-occupation of premises as lodging-houses is a common phenomenon.

The survey also showed that much crime is local in character —that is, committed by persons who are residents in or near the place where the crime occurs. By and large, troublemakers do not go outside their own immediate neighbourhood, although youthful offenders may be attracted to the entertainments and cafés near the city centre, near to which their delinquent escapades take place.

Thus the effects of crime are localized. Crime is part of the pathology of certain areas; it is almost an everyday part of the life style of certain neighbourhoods, part of the 'trouble' residents have to put up with—like noise and overcrowding, careless, disinterested landlords, and related insufficiencies. A rising crime wave indicates not so much a threat to the already secure and well established, as more trouble for the less well placed, less well paid, or otherwise dispossessed people. The effect of crime is to underline a prevailing insecurity; it adds to suspicion and hostility between persons. It is a sign of the failure of 'community' and it further adds to that failure. As the urban centres attract more to work in the city and provide insufficient housing, areas of multi-occupation and overcrowding expand and signs of insecurity, divisiveness, and inequity increase, crime being one of them. The process known as urban decay sets in; those who can, retreat; decay deepens and advances; and crime rises.

The nature of crime and its uneven distribution between discrete areas require that crime statistics and interpretations of rates of crime and criminality be treated with caution. The processes whereby areas of crime are created are not random. Clearly, if crime is a feature of certain areas and is local in character, the status of the population in those areas will be reflected in the statistics. The processes whereby certain groups come to live in certain neighbourhoods are not random. The processes reflect the variations in the wealth, the status, the power of the various groups. Comparative rates of crime between classes and between ethnic groups can only be meaningful in relation to those variations and when crime is related to those processes. Crime can only be understood in relation to the sociology of urban society.

II

Now, the processes which create the complex of neighbourhoods and communities, the diverse styles of life, the 'good' and the 'bad' areas of cities are, of course, also the key to an understanding of race relations in the city at the moment.

In Chapter 3 of this book a series of maps and tables were presented which show how the immigrant population in the sector of the city studied is not evenly distributed throughout. It was possible to describe a crescent-shaped zone, consisting largely of older and larger types of houses, mostly now in multi-occupation. This crescent encloses an area abutting the city centre, made up either of small terraced houses or of blocks of flats or houses of recent build as a result of redevelopment schemes. Within the crescent and in the terraces it encloses live most of the area's immigrants. Within the crescent and area occurred the vast majority of the crimes; there, too, lived the majority of offenders, the majority of whom were not coloured immigrants. In these areas is found a significant measure of overcrowding and poor amenity. The areas were typified by the least secure forms of property tenure. The occupational and class distributions suggest the relative economic and wealth variations in the areas. A high rate of population change in the lodging-house zone further points to the transience and insecurity of life styles in the areas. Crime is an attendant pathology of such conditions. Rex and Moore[1] have ably described the processes whereby areas of high coloured immigrant density are created. A system of *de facto* discrimination exists against all newcomers to the city on the part of the local authority; and most visible but not alone among the newcomers are coloured immigrants who suffer further from other kinds of discriminative acts in the highly competitive struggle that characterizes the housing market. Thus are factors of race and crime thrust into a single milieu.

Opposition to immigration is only infrequently expressed publicly in overtly racist terms; more usually it is in terms of our society's inability to accommodate large numbers who cast intense burdens on our housing, health, education, and other services. Less overtly the racist argument appeals to prejudice: the immigrant, particularly the coloured immigrant, is held to be a less capable species of man. His behaviour is offered as proof: his low-level employment, his poor living conditions, his backwardness in education, his propensity to disease, his high rates of crime, and so on. There is, of course, no proof at all. But what there is, is an attitude, not the sole possession of the racist, that expects poor or problematical behaviour from the immigrant. It is in relation to this attitude that the danger of the milieu described above lies. For that milieu provides the racist and anti-immigrant with an argument that takes on, increasingly, a vicious circularity. Expectations become prophecies; prophecies become self-fulfilling: for the immigrant may be forced to live in certain areas typified by the pathologies the racist describes. Assimilation, in so far as it takes place at all, takes place only at a certain level, to something called a slum culture. And complaints and arguments of an 'I told you so' nature arise.

These kinds of considerations, I believe, make the finding amply demonstrated in the crime profile study of the utmost importance. Immigrant areas *are* areas of high crime; immigrants are not, in the main, responsible for that crime. The danger is that the disorder and crime are a lasting and permanent threat to immigrants and their families. Quite simply, there is a danger of contamination. Conditions not of the immigrants' creating, processes not of the immigrants' controlling, differentially associate

[1] Rex and Moore, op. cit.

immigrants with factors threatening their security as families and stability as communities: one of these is crime. Thus, as a first and most important conclusion of this study, it can be stated, almost as a law, that, so long as immigrant newcomers are forced to live in certain high-crime areas, their rate of crime will in time increase to match that of the over-all population in the area.

A similar finding arises from the data provided about juvenile delinquents and families in need of care. Again it was noted that some areas were more delinquent than others. Case studies hinted at the varieties of causes and influences of delinquency. A continuing theme was the instability so often experienced in delinquent families; sometimes gross, sometimes subtle, unequal stresses place children of 'weak' families in a high risk category for delinquency, particularly in some areas. Delinquency may be an almost normal outlet for children in deprived areas. Immigrant areas, because of the difficulties families experience in obtaining decent living conditions, because of insecurity of tenure, overcrowding, poor amenities, are those where the quality of family life is threatened. To a greater or lesser extent, the quality of schooling available to children in these areas may be impaired: schools may lack their fair share of 'good' children, have greater difficulty in attracting and retaining quality staff, and may not enjoy the facilities of buildings and equipment that schools in better, more recently-built areas possess. Thus the need for support and control from school and family is greatest just where school and family experience greatest difficulty in providing that support and control. Some of the results of this are reflected in the variations of intensity of delinquency in certain areas. As was the case with the data on crime, it must be noticed that currently there is less immigrant delinquency than might be expected in view of the congruence of immigrant with delinquent areas. But, as with the crime data, differential association warns that we enunciate a second law: the longer immigrant families are forced into certain areas, rates of delinquency will rise to match that which is normal for those areas.

III

We have been speaking of immigrant areas and immigrant concerns with particular reference to coloured immigrants, those from Asia and the Caribbean. The situation of the Irish immigrant family provides a significant perspective to these conclusions.

The crime profile found not inconsiderable numbers of persons of Irish birth among those arrested for crimes of various kinds. The social data presented in the opening chapter found the Irish population more widely dispersed throughout the various areas of the division than other immigrants, but still by no means equally distributed in each area. It was also apparent that the Irish offenders were not as widely dispersed as the Irish population as a whole. Offenders tend to come from certain kinds of area.

The Irish immigration to Birmingham is no recent phenomenon. In the past, no doubt, the Irish were faced with a somewhat uneven and unpredictable welcome from their English hosts and only quite recently have moved away from the central areas to the suburbs. Today, it is apparent that the Irish are widely assimilated in the city, and enjoy respect and standing in all walks of life. This has been achieved without there being a total loss of 'Irishness' or a complete severance of ties with the homeland. Indeed Sparkhill, at the heart of the division studied, enjoying the characteristics of a secure and stable working-class suburb, has been known as one of the most densely Irish areas of any English city with many features of a distinctively Irish quality. Sparkhill, it is to be noted, has lower than average rates of crime and delinquency. The crime statistics pick out a particular minority atypical of the Irish population as a whole. It is a small minority, often homeless and without a family, thrust into the unstructured world of the lodging-house, employed in hard and somewhat precarious occupations. One can suppose that some are not recent immigrants but those who have been caught up and trapped in the worst of urban living; others are young men, recent arrivals, yet to find a stake in society, yet to remake the firm ties of home and family in the new country. Clearly the reputation of the Irish in the city is neither made nor marred by this minority, for it is possible to recognize a truly minority problem pertaining to a particular, and atypical, area, situation, and life style.

The figures about delinquency suggest how the Irish family may be more than capable of providing the security and stability for its younger members in an urban society. There was no evidence that children of Irish parents are over-represented among delinquents either at Approved Schools or under supervision from probation officers. What was revealed was a number of children one of whose parents was Irish. Any statistical assessment of the significance of the number was not possible. What is important to note is how frequently the social and economic standing of these families was low; the family setting often appeared intensely disordered. Frequently the inability of the mother—usually the English partner—to cope was most marked. Nationality or cultural factors appeared to pale into insignificance beneath a welter of economic, psychiatric, or health problems, or a combination of all three. Thus again the overriding importance of the socio-economic level at which delinquency is found is stressed. This group has little in common with, and is to be distinguished from, the Irish family, if there is to be any precision in a discussion of factors of ethnicity relating to crime and delinquency.

This is an important point if a correct interpretation is to be given to the evidence which shows small numbers, but a relatively high proportion, of coloured children before the courts who are of mixed parentage. To lump all 'coloured' children into one group and then draw conclusions about the relative abilities of immigrant families to cope with the bringing up of their children in their new country is dangerously misleading. The figures from Birmingham, supported by the study of West Indian children in London,[1] suggest that yet another false stereotype must be discarded, for Asian families, and West Indian families, appear to be shaping up to their intensely difficult tasks with success. What is revealed is a number of families, frequently with a florid set of symptoms deriving, more often than not, from an English mother's sadly pathetic inadequacies, whose breakdown leads to admission into care or to delinquency. These are not immigrant families, but more truly, poor English families. Their significance can be magnified by a tendentious polemicist, but they are a small group with little in common with the typical family. Agencies responsible for support and guidance need to pay particular attention to the complex problems the children experience. What seems to be happening is that courts and agencies are facing problems brought by a distinct group, a highly particularized minority—a near-deviant group of English mothers and immigrant menfolk who provide inadequate and insecure homes. To

[1] FitzHerbert, op. cit.

see these as typical of mixed marriages or as typical of immigrant families is wholly unwarranted. A precise view must recognize here a distinct and small minority.

IV

A major purpose of the research reported here was to bring some precision to a complex and sometimes confused subject matter of considerable public interest and importance. As has been indicated, not only is such precision needed to correct false stereotypes and misconceived expectations which can have potent social significance; but such precision is also needed, I believe, by those public agencies entrusted with important tasks of service, guidance, and support, and in daily touch with immigrants and their families. Attitudes and beliefs about reality are often more powerful forces than facts of that reality; this is certainly true in the field of race relations. What is needed is factual description of a wide variety of behaviour if attitudes and beliefs are to be modified.

Studied here was the work of the Police Force; and data were drawn from probation and child care services. It is to be hoped that this research in so far as it suggests fruitful pointers to further and continuing studies will be of interest and help for those agencies.

Probation and child care officers share a style of work that is based on individual casework. Staff of both services currently labour with oversize case loads and a wide range of diverse duties. Pressures deriving from the systems within which they work must mean that there is seldom time to stand back from the mass of individual cases and look at their clients as a group, and distinguish viable groups and categories. To distinguish characteristics and problems deriving from cultural or, especially, local groups, to develop (and test) strategies valid, say, for families of mixed origins, and others for Asian as distinct from West Indian families; these are luxuries the system infrequently allows. That the data necessary for such explorations and developments exist within the departments is not to be doubted, although a clearer rationale of what data and information are valuable would be a help. If problems of race and colour are to be taken seriously, such agencies will have to grasp the nettle of racially distinguishable records and statistics and not conceal from themselves the size and scope of the problems they deal with. It is by no means easy to research with the records of either department and it is to be hoped that both will acquire a research consciousness that sees ongoing studies as an integral part of their operations and not the sole concern of interested outsiders.

The police problem is somewhat different, although here too there exists a need for an awareness of the ways statistics and figures and studies can serve to improve police operations. The police occupy a particularly important position in the community as they are a visible representation of authority and justice. Whatever advances are made by legislation to achieve justice in race relations will depend on how policemen perform their every-day tasks in public, in relation to minority group citizens. In the chapters devoted to policing I have attempted to describe the nature of the police task as it bears on contemporary problems of a race relations nature. The task is a complex one. It seems neither desirable nor indeed possible to reduce police activities to a set of strict rules and procedures. Discretion is at the heart of the police role. But discretion brings dangers: of arbitrariness, insensitivity, and plain illegality. It calls for high quality management, leadership, and training. Discretion is less concerned with a measure of toleration of some criminal practices in some areas than with the recognition that to serve and protect diverse communities in urban society—particularly in those areas where poverty is apparent and crime of all kinds is frequent—requires a variety of police practices, and a sensitive awareness of the different policing needs of various communities. To treat coloured immigrants as poor people in poor areas is a mistaken tolerance and a dangerous condescension. To fail to explore how persons from different lands with different police systems have different expectations of police behaviour is to ignore an important reality. To be disinclined to adapt traditional systems and institutions to the needs of an untraditional social system is a subtle form of discrimination, no less dangerous for being subtle or unintended. The police are not alone in being challenged by the changing demands of a multiracial society: the consequences of the police not responding to that challenge are uniquely serious.

V

Research of the kind reported here can be seen as a precursor of various, more specific, and in-depth studies of the issues involved. Largely, these may be in terms of law enforcement practice, training programmes appropriate for police and other personnel, and in terms of family and delinquency studies of value to treatment and guidance agencies. But—to return to the considerations with which this concluding chapter opened—attention must also be paid to those fundamental processes and conditions which create the problems law enforcement and other agencies deal with. As an eminent American criminologist has said of the American situation:

It is not likely that we will be successful at controlling crime by seriously changing the organization and administration of criminal justice. The ultimate answer is to see crime and violence not only as problems in law enforcement but as problems in education, family organization, employment opportunity and housing. These are the structures which incubate deviance and hence crime, delinquency and violence. It is a myth that man's behavior can be changed directly. It can be changed only by altering the conditions which underlie his behavior. We must learn to treat the causes, not only the effects, of crime and violence.[1]

In America crime and violence are at their most extreme in the ghettos and are, thus, a racial phenomena. The depth and extremity of the American urban crisis are revealed in the succession of riots associated with 'long hot summers'. Over-rapid comparisons between Britain and the United States are to be avoided. Yet it would be complacent not to acknowledge some parallels. As *The Economist* reported of the July 1965 riot at Watts, a suburban 'ghetto' of Los Angeles:

What happened in Los Angeles is pretty certainly going to happen in many other countries. . . This was an American phenomenon only in the sense that the United States is half a generation ahead of the rest of the world in the development of an industrial society with the special problems that brings.[2]

[1] Joseph Lohman, 'Violence in the Streets: Its Context and Meaning', *Notre Dame Lawyer* (Washington, Vol. 40, No. 5, 1965).
[2] *The Economist* (25 July 1965).

I have suggested that the most revealing datum to emerge from this study is that which shows the congruence of immigrant areas with areas of high crime as well as with other indices of social disorganization. The configuration of immigrant areas within the division of the city that was the focus of the study requires careful scrutiny: to what extent are there developing in our cities areas where coloured families are forced to live with the worst conditions our society offers? What processes create this pattern, and how, and how much, can they be dealt with by social policy?

To thwart further ghettoization and reverse the trend is to tackle the conditions which cause crime and delinquency, as well as to serve justice in race relations in our society. The main focus has to be on housing and the urgent need to implement 'fair housing' schemes and legislation and to outlaw discrimination by landlords, their agents, and by mortgage companies. But laws against discrimination, though essential, may be thought irrelevant unless their equivalents apply to local authority housing and its allocation, for it is in the public sector of housing supply that most can be done to alter the shape of city neighbourhoods and areas. By redevelopment schemes, by urban renewal and renovation, by subsidies and controls, and by allocation, the city authorities can strike at the roots of a complex sickness that is endemic to urban societies.

That discrimination, overt and covert, subtle and blatant, is a reality, and not only in the field of housing, emerges from a number of studies. Its ugly truth and the prejudices from which it stems are unlikely to decrease unaided. The opportunities offered to the next generation of coloured citizens and their experience of race relations will be decisive. The effects of subtly various discriminatory processes are, I think, amply shown in the data and maps presented in this book. The consequences of those effects, albeit in the relatively narrow field of crime and delinquency, have been the topic of the preceding pages.

Index